GLOBAL F

GLOBAL FINTECH

Financial Innovation in the
Connected World

edited by David L. Shrier and Alex Pentland

MIT Connection Science & Engineering
connection.mit.edu

The MIT Press
Cambridge, Massachusetts
London, England

The MIT Press would like to thank the anonymous peer reviewers who provided comments on drafts of this book. The generous work of academic experts is essential for establishing the authority and quality of our publications. We acknowledge with gratitude the contributions of these otherwise uncredited readers.

This book was set in Stone Serif by Westchester Publishing Services, Danbury, CT. Printed and bound in the United States of America.

Library of Congress Cataloging-in-Publication Data

Names: Shrier, David L., editor. | Pentland, Alex, 1952– editor.
Title: Global fintech : financial innovation in the connected world / edited by David L. Shrier and Alex Pentland.
Description: Cambridge, Massachusetts : The MIT Press, [2022] | Includes bibliographical references and index.
Identifiers: LCCN 2021030642 | ISBN 9780262543668 (paperback)
Subjects: LCSH: Financial services industry—Technological innovations. | Finance—Data processing.
Classification: LCC HG173 .G636 2022 | DDC 332.1—dc23
LC record available at https://lccn.loc.gov/2021030642

10 9 8 7 6 5 4 3 2 1

To the tired, the poor, the huddled masses yearning to breathe free, the wretched refuse of teeming shores, the homeless, tempest-tossed. May the wizards of Cambridge, Massachusetts, and London, and New York, and Zurich, and Shanghai, and Singapore, and San Francisco, and São Paolo, and other fiery stars of innovation, bring forth the lamp beside the golden door.

—Adapted from Emma Lazarus

CONTENTS

INTRODUCTION   1

I   FOUNDATIONS

1 FINTECH FOUNDATIONS: CONVERGENCE, BLOCKCHAIN, BIG DATA, AND AI   7
David L. Shrier and Alex Pentland

II   TRANSITIONING TO THE DIGITAL ERA

2 EDGE EFFECTS: BRIDGING FROM OLD TO NEW   35
Boris Khentov

3 OPEN BANKING: HOW PLATFORMS AND THE API ECONOMY CHANGE COMPETITION IN FINANCIAL SERVICES   57
Markos Zachariadis and Pinar Ozcan

4 DIGITAL FINANCIAL SERVICES   73
David L. Shrier

5 POLICY AND FINTECH, PART I: FRAMEWORKS   91
Oliver R. Goodenough, Mark Flood, Matthew Reed, David L. Shrier, Thomas Hardjono, and Alex Pentland

6 POLICY AND FINTECH, PART II: USE CASES   137
Oliver R. Goodenough, Mark Flood, Matthew Reed, David L. Shrier, Thomas Hardjono, and Alex Pentland

7 DIGITAL BANKING MANIFESTO 2.0   173

Alex Lipton, David L. Shrier, and Alex Pentland

 FINTECH POSSIBILITIES

8 REGULATORY SANDBOXES   203

Oliver R. Goodenough and David L. Shrier

9 LEAPFROGGING WITH NEXTGEN FINTECHS AND EMERGING TECH FOR THE GROWTH OF AFRICA   219

Michelle Chivunga

10 THE RISE OF REGTECH AND THE DIVERGENCE OF COMPLIANCE AND RISK   251

Amias Moore Gerety and Lev Menand

11 ON GOVERNANCE AND (TECHNICAL) COMPLEXITY   267

John D'Agostino (with contributions from Sharmila Kassam)

12 RESPONSIBLE TECHNOLOGY: ADVANCING TRUST AND SECURING THE ECOSYSTEM   283

Ajay Bhalla

CONCLUSION   293

CONTRIBUTORS   295

INDEX   299

INTRODUCTION

Fintech is without question beginning to permeate every aspect of our daily existence, and it is reshaping how we live our lives. More than 200 million WeChat users are now conducting banking-like activities from their mobile phones, demonstrating that we already have technology that could bring the 3.5 billion underbanked and unbanked people in the world into the global financial system. However, when Facebook announced a desire to help 2.4 billion users obtain financial services through Libra (now renamed Diem, presumably in an effort to distance the effort from the bad name it acquired), it unleashed a firestorm of backlash to this corporatization of a government monopoly—the issuance of currency and control of monetary policy. This reaction was in large part because of the realization that if you combine mobility data and financial data and put them in the unfettered hands of the private sector, you create meaningful risk to society at large. How are we to bring banking services to everyone yet avoid creating this sort of "Big Brother" danger?

When we began our journey to understand how fintech will go global, we had no idea that our online entrepreneurship classes would spread to over 150 countries. It was a chance to grow a philosophy twenty years in the making. Professor Alex Pentland and "venture catalyst" Joost Bonsen created an entrepreneurship program at MIT that, before going online, taught over three thousand students through a philosophy of "solving problems for a billion people." It is this "dreaming big solutions" orientation that we have brought to our digital efforts that has now helped fifteen thousand additional innovators (and counting) build new businesses.

As part of creating our online fintech program, we wanted a good textbook to augment the videos, interactive games, and written materials we created for the class, but at the time we couldn't find a suitable text. Our 2016 book *Frontiers of Financial Technology* was the result, a brief but informative voyage across blockchain, artificial intelligence (AI), new models for financial services, and a policy framework to demystify regulation in a regulated industry. It was widely applauded when it was written and still has relevance and applicability nearly five years later because we looked far enough ahead. However, the future is catching up with us, so once again we need to peer beyond the horizon.

Times have changed. Nearly $500 billion has been invested by venture capitalists in fintech since we started writing *Frontiers*. And we missed some important elements regarding the forces reshaping the financial system in every country on the planet. We talked about high-minded ideas like breakthroughs in applying collective intelligence to prediction markets and skipped over the fact that to deliver AI and blockchain innovation, banks such as HSBC have to digitize over 100 *million* paper documents. While we mentioned blockchain and alluded to the broader context, we didn't truly deliver a book that recognized the global nature of the fintech revolution. It was a surprising oversight because our on-campus activities have been working in the emerging markets and seeding country-level change for decades.

So in your hands you have version 2.0 of our thinking: What if we recognize the current state of the market and extend ideas more tightly from theory to practice? What if we highlight not only online innovation in the wealthiest country on the planet, such as how Boris Khentov describes Betterment's in-the-trenches grappling with bringing the old analog world into the new digital one (chapter 2), but also the "leapfrog" opportunities presented in developing countries, such as in sub-Saharan Africa (chapter 9)? What if we remind people that with the hyperspeed adoption of fintech and other new technologies, we also create ethical and societal risk and need to take steps to address this, as Ajay Bhalla shares with us in his responsible innovation framework (chapter 12)?

Fintech is global. Grab your carry-on bag and let's go collect passport stamps.

David L. Shrier and Alex Pentland
Cambridge, MA, November 2020

FOUNDATIONS

1 FINTECH FOUNDATIONS: CONVERGENCE, BLOCKCHAIN, BIG DATA, AND AI

David L. Shrier and Alex Pentland

1.1 INTRODUCTION: THE CONVERGENCE REVOLUTION

Technology supercycles are accelerating. The digital transformation in financial services has attracted more than $500 billion in investment since 2015.[1] Fueling a disruption of the financial services industry, the transformation is in turn propelled not by one technology trend but rather by several that are converging contemporaneously and often in concert with each other.

The pace of technology-driven change is undergoing an increase of an order of magnitude or greater. It took nearly fifty years for landline telephony to achieve 60 percent market adoption. Social media usage and tablet computing reached that same level of penetration within seven years.[2] As networked communications promotes faster and faster adoption of new technologies, incumbent organizations such as conventional banks and asset management firms find themselves under threat from technology-enabled competitors. During the COVID-19 pandemic, certain segments of financial services digitized at an even greater rate—for example, in 2020, use of digital payments in lieu of cash doubled that of spring 2019.[3]

In this chapter we discuss the impacts of the maturation of an array of technologies within a few years of each other, which is creating a seismic shift in a traditional industry.

1.2 DISRUPTIVE TECHNOLOGIES

A cluster of technologies have been achieving new levels of utility and market adoption in recent years, creating new capabilities that had not been possible with only one or two of the technologies used by themselves. Mobile communications, artificial intelligence, big data analytics, and distributed ledgers are among the most prominent that are driving structural change in the financial services industry, in turn creating dynamic and widespread shifts in how consumers and businesses are served globally.

Mobile communications   Mobile communications technology, developed in the late 1800s by Nikola Tesla and Guglielmo Marconi,[4] has become an economic engine that has enabled the developing world to catch up with, and in some cases overtake, developed economies—particularly with respect to financial services. World Bank research shows—and the University of California, Berkeley, confirms—that for every 10 percent of increased digital penetration in a given economy, there is more than a 1 percent increase in GDP.[5] This digital connectivity has been accelerated by the widespread deployment of mobile communications systems because it is no longer necessary to lay down terrestrial cable through remote, inaccessible, or underdeveloped regions, "leapfrogging" a generation of technology. In Africa, for example, nearly two hundred thousand Kenyans were shown to escape extreme poverty in only eight years through use of mobile money provider M-Pesa.[6] Popular Chinese mobile platform WeChat has more than 1 billion users (including 79 percent of the Chinese market when including all of its apps), and more than 50 percent of these users engage in financial services on the platform.[7]

Artificial intelligence   Artificial intelligence (AI) has been posited for millennia and developed on modern computers for decades. Only recently, however, has it achieved widespread

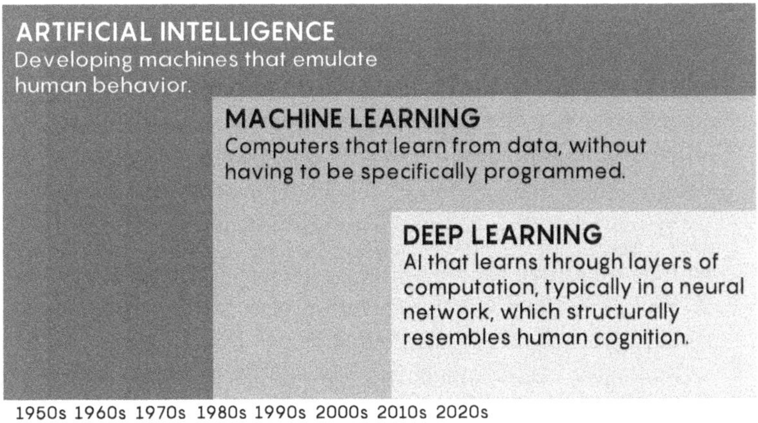

ARTIFICIAL INTELLIGENCE
Developing machines that emulate human behavior.

MACHINE LEARNING
Computers that learn from data, without having to be specifically programmed.

DEEP LEARNING
AI that learns through layers of computation, typically in a neural network, which structurally resembles human cognition.

1950s 1960s 1970s 1980s 1990s 2000s 2010s 2020s

FIGURE 1.1
Different flavors of AI.

and deeply functional adoption. Figure 1.1, adapted from an *Oracle Big Data Blog* posting,[8] illustrates how different flavors of AI have emerged over the past forty years.

Note in the timeline that experiments with AI expert systems have been conducted on digital computers since the 1950s. One famous example is MIT scientist Joseph Weizenbaum's ELIZA digital therapist from the 1960s, which often fooled people into thinking they were interacting with a real human being.[9] More recent work around deep learning enables better speech-to-data translation, such as that found in Apple's Siri system.[10] A seminal event in the evolution of AI adoption was Google's 2015 release of TensorFlow, a software library for machine learning that made computing power and neural networks easily and widely available in an open source library.[11]

Big data analytics With the advent of better AI systems, we have seen the rise of big data analytics, which is now being used across multiple industries and has introduced profound changes in how we work, play, and live. Patterns can be extracted from all sorts of data flows, ranging from intraday trading activity to the physical movement of consumers in and out of retail stores (enabling better predictivity of system-wide sales). Big data analytics can even be used to detect whether company executives are lying or shading the truth on earnings calls. It can also be used to better manage cash liquidity systems, stabilize economies, or reconfigure a workforce.

Distributed ledgers   In our 2016 book *Frontiers of Financial Technology*, we laid out the evolution of network communications, culminating in distributed ledger. Distributed ledger technology, or DLT (popularly known as blockchain), is itself a product of several technologies and methods that had been developed decades earlier, such as Byzantine consensus and distributed computing. As of this writing, nearly $300 billion in value has been created in a nominal market capitalization of the digital tokens that are enabled by DLT.[12]

When we bring together DLT, AI, big data analytics, and better mobile communications networks, we create a perfect storm of efficiency improvements and new capabilities—as well as jobs disruption that PricewaterhouseCoopers estimates could impact millions of financial services workers. Chapter 2 will delve further into blockchain and DLT.

1.3   THE CONVERGENCE REVOLUTION

The convergence revolution opens up the possibility of finally addressing the financial services inclusion gap, whereby 3.5 billion people around the world are underserved or unserved by the banking system. One of the interesting artifacts of this transformation is that it allows new entrants to offer the services. Whereas previously an incumbent bank may have worried about nonbank finance companies, today the threat could equally come from a telecom provider or a digital platform company such as Google, Amazon, Alibaba, or Tencent.

It's not only technology that's driving this change. Over decades of oligopoly, banks grew accustomed to an incumbent mentality and customer service suffered, leaving them vulnerable to the "neobanks."[13] Futurist Benjamin Palmer said, "The only time I talk to a bank is when I've done something wrong or they have."[14]

The new wave of challengers brings a completely different mind-set about customers. We can see this illustrated in the Net Promoter Score (NPS). The NPS is a normalized measure of customer satisfaction developed by Bain & Company and Satmetrix.[15] It measures the likelihood of a customer recommending your product or service to someone else. The scale runs from –100 (everyone hates you) to +100 (everyone loves you). Citi reportedly has an NPS of –41 (yes, that's negative 41).[16] The average for all financial services is about +18. Apple, which recently has been making inroads into consumer credit cards and payments in collaboration with Goldman Sachs, has an NPS of +47. Given these figures, conventional banks should be worried about *platform envelopment*, whereby digital platform companies, already integrated into people's lives and exhibiting warm feelings of trust and dependency, keep extending their services until they encroach on other offerings (such as, in this instance, those offered by incumbent banking institutions).[17]

But let's not count out fintech companies. The low-cost money transfer app Transferwise is reputed to have an NPS of +76.[18] Fee-bearing activities such as money transfer and credit cards are the heart of a bank's profitability—much more profitable than investment banking or other areas, consequently attracting the lion's share of venture capital investment.[19]

We thus see the convergence revolution creating competitors on both left and right flanks of the conventional banking industry, all while they are laying off tens of thousands of employees through the adoption of technologies such as AI.[20] Layoffs might be attributed to global market activity, to Brexit, to poor trading performance, or to some other factor, but they are made possible by digital convergence.

MIT Sloan School of Management professor Erik Brynjolfsson predicts a workforce realignment of 50 percent or more, on par with the Industrial Revolution of the 1800s, owing to digital disruptive technologies such as AI. That said, whereas AI may destroy a large number of jobs, a large number of jobs in new industries will also be created.[21] With the advent of robots comes the advent of robot repairmen. The job title "Interactive UX Designer" didn't exist thirty years ago, and thirty years from now there will undoubtedly be jobs like "Quantum Communications Specialist" and other titles we lack the foresight to envision today.

Convergence is creating financial access and the ability to bring the benefits of robust financial services to nearly half the world's population to enjoy. It is also causing large-scale disruption in the conventional financial services sector. In this book, we will explore an array of topics that explain how, why, and in which direction the industry might evolve.

One of the key technologies that is converging is distributed ledger, colloquially known as blockchain. In the next section we will undertake a high-level examination of this technology.

1.4 BLOCKCHAIN BASICS

Something exciting happened with a sausage.

The story of blockchain, which we discuss in this chapter in terms of both what it is and why it is interesting from a business and societal standpoint, has taken decades to play out. But first we will describe how blockchain is the computer systems equivalent of sausage, a humble bit of food eaten by those who can't afford steak (or Beyond Meat, if vegetarian).

Sausage holds a special place in cuisine. Somewhat grayish, lozenge shaped, made up of little bits of this and that, including what some may believe is fiberglass wall insulation, it becomes palatable with enough ketchup or horseradish or mustard or possibly all three, a dryish conflation of leftovers that begs for seasoning. Not unlike haggis—a Scottish national treasure made out of the parts of the sheep that no one wants to eat, which can be survived only when doused in Scotch whiskey (ideally while reciting the Robert Burns poem "Address to a Haggis")—sausage benefits from a food companion in order to be consumable.

Blockchain is like a technological sausage. It is a kind of database with special features that help it solve certain problems, and in and of itself it doesn't represent new technology. The individual components that go into making blockchain—how it accepts new data, how it secures that data, and how it makes that data visible and available—were around for years before Satoshi Nakomoto's 2008 white paper and the origins of the first large-scale instance, the bitcoin blockchain. Like the scraps of meat that go into making a sausage, these elements were assembled into blockchain, which assumed a new kind of importance by virtue of both composition and timing. And to stretch the metaphor, properly seasoned it makes for an exquisite dish. The financial form of blockchain, cryptocurrencies, had a market capitalization at this writing of about $250 billion; notably during the COVID-19 crisis, as the general equities markets suffered, cryptocurrencies proved resilient. From January 1 to May 31, 2020, the Dow Jones Industrial Average was down 12 percent and the Financial Times Stock Exchange 100 Index was down 20 percent, but traded tokens had a return of 31 percent.[22]

Blockchain has certain features, like immutability, a distributed nature, and a consensus mechanism, that combine to create digital trust that the system is telling you the truth about your data. You don't need to rely on the assurances of governments or of banking institutions, neither of which was particularly trusted after the 2008–2009 global financial crisis. Instead, you can trust in the technology.

1.5   WHAT BLOCKCHAIN IS

Blockchain is simply a database that has interesting features, making it suitable for certain applications that require trust and transparency. These could include financial systems, supply chain management, or even the access and sharing of health data. Also termed "distributed ledger," emphasizing the record-keeping aspect of what distinguishes it from other types of databases, blockchain offers a high degree of assurance that your information hasn't been corrupted by hackers or other bad actors.

As described in more detail in *Basic Blockchain*,[23] parts of blockchain were born out of the distributed computing movement. The concept was that when your computer was at rest, the idle processor cycles would be used for more than running the once-ubiquitous screen saver. Instead, with projects like SETI@home, thousands upon thousands of computers had their downtime applied to the fascinating problem of searching for extraterrestrial intelligence by analyzing radio telescope signals. It was citizen science, and it was empowering the crowd to create new intelligence; but it was also a clever programming hack to take a difficult problem, for which an individual science lab lacked the resources to solve, and make it more manageable. We see many instances of this distributed computing model today aside from blockchain; it could be argued that the edge computing industry, expected to be worth $43 billion by 2027,[24] was born out of a humble hack to find little gray men.

So the first essential element of blockchain is its distributed nature. Thousands of servers all over the world are involved in calculating the math that goes into making blockchain cryptographically secure. For the sake of this discussion, we're going to ignore other variants of distributed ledgers like R3 Corda. (R3 Corda is technically not a pure blockchain but a distributed ledger technology. To understand the distinction, take a look at https://www.r3.com/blockchain-101/.)

Space seems to feature prominently in the history of block-chain. Another critical component of how blockchain works is how it decides to accept new information into the data-base. The concept of Byzantine consensus originated out of SRI International to solve the issue of unreliable computers in space.[25] As Douglas Adams wrote, not only is space "big," it also contains lots of radiation from sources like the sun, which doesn't interact well with computer systems. A fault-tolerant model is required, where even if one computer has its data corrupted by a stray bit of radiation, you can still land your spaceship safely.

As NASA was designing and building America's fleet of space shuttles, it needed to ensure that the computers in the shuttles would be reliable. An elegant solution was generated out of a thought experiment about how to manage trust among a group of rivalrous generals in the ancient Byzantine Empire (called, appropriately, the Byzantine Generals Problem). The solution was the creation of a particular kind of voting mechanism—even if you couldn't necessarily trust one particular general, you could trust the group of them voting together. In NASA's case, four identical computers were built into the space shuttle, and three of them had to agree in order to verify a particular asser-tion. In the case of the original blockchain, 51 percent of the servers in the distributed network needed to agree that some-thing was true in order to accept it as a new piece of informa-tion incorporated into the database.

This construct, a distributed network that has a consen-sus mechanism to accept new data, means that blockchain is *cyber resilient*. Unlike a centralized system, where a hacker who penetrates the computer can modify the data inside of it with impunity, blockchain requires compromise of many different systems in order to inject new data. It is designed to withstand distributed attacks, which consist of large-scale mobilization of computers that seek to overwhelm a system from many points at once. The need for hack-resistant data systems has become exacerbated in recent years, with $6 trillion in cyber breach-related losses estimated for 2021.[26]

As an aside, no one knows who Satoshi Nakamoto, the progenitor of blockchain, actually is. Much like the question "Who wrote Shakespeare's plays?," it is of academic interest, but today it doesn't really matter. Shakespeare, too, stole bits of legend and lore and structure from others in crafting his masterpieces. We have our *Hamlet*, we have our bitcoin, so functionally it's less important which hand authored the creation.

Another critical component of blockchain's resilience is the use of Merkle trees. The basic concept is that as a blockchain grows, each new link in the chain is inexorably (and mathematically) tied to every link behind it. If, for example, your blockchain represents a financial ledger, you can't go change a historical entry (perhaps in an effort to commit fraud) without altering every other entry in the chain.[27]

1.6 WHAT BLOCKCHAIN IS GOOD FOR

The hot topic in the blockchain world is identifying natural use cases that scale. Areas such as digital payments appear to be a natural use case, and others are exploring applications ranging from aerospace to health care.

What limits scale? Blockchain is a complicated database. It typically uses numerous computer cycles in order to cryptographically secure its data payload. While many things could be put onto a blockchain, this does not mean they should be. In many instances, other forms of databases, like a relational database (such as Oracle) or a large-scale unstructured database (like Hadoop), are better suited to managing the data, although some newer iterations of blockchain technology are specifically designed to address historic limitations.

New technology isn't an innovation unless it is applied to a problem at scale. Many hundreds of different use cases for blockchain have been posited. However, not all of them represent a large enough market opportunity or impact to justify the investment in converting technology and process infrastructure to blockchain, and not all of them require the trusted consensus that blockchain delivers. Over the past five years there have been numerous proofs of concept to experiment with blockchain applications. The question now being posed is, aside from the bitcoin blockchain, what are useful applications at scale?

Many believe that core financial systems will be rebuilt using blockchain. Major trading markets such as Nasdaq have active research and prototyping efforts underway in blockchain, and the stock exchange of Suriname has announced its intention to be the first in the world to trade listed equities in blockchain and to serve the broader Latin American and Caribbean region (as opposed to the well-established array of "blockchain exchanges" that allow the trading of cryptocurrencies, Suriname is actually going to trade the stocks of its major companies).[28] International payments and money transfer, traditionally the domain of companies like Western Union or SWIFT, are getting upended by companies like Bitpesa and Ripple.

Notably, government is getting into the act. In the wake of the "Libra backlash," where an overwhelmingly negative reaction arose to Facebook's efforts to create a digital currency outside the reach of government, and the moves by China to corner the digital currency market with the creation of the digital RMB coin, other governments are looking more seriously at national and multinational central bank digital currencies.[29]

Other domains outside of financial services show promise: for example, supply chain management, where a network of interlinked market participants need to trust in the veracity of the data and have perverse incentives. Two and a half percent of aircraft replacement parts are counterfeit, risking flight safety, according to former MIT Future Commerce student Eleanor Mitch, who has created 14bis to solve this problem with distributed ledger.[30] Health care and medical research could be enhanced by management of "granular patient consent" and better secure data management, concepts being developed by companies such as BurstIQ.

The period from 2021 to 2025 should see blockchain applications achieving scale and adoption in mainstream corporate and government environments.

1.7   WHAT BLOCKCHAIN COULD ENABLE

If we step beyond the immediate potential applications of blockchain, it becomes interesting to explore what might be possible with the evolution of blockchain.

Taxes could become automated, relieving the time and expense burdens on people and companies, reducing cost and friction to enable governments to function.

Intellectual property rights for music or video domains could be automatically managed, with payments flowing seamlessly alongside consumption, perhaps enabling better protection of the rights of individual artists.

The distributed, immutable, and transparent characteristics of blockchain could make it possible to better manage elections, with every vote counted (and counted only once). Citizens could have greater confidence in the security and reliability of the mechanisms of governance. We could even make the plebiscite more feasible at scale, allowing direct democracy in a way not seen since the days of ancient Athens (only this time, women and poor people can vote).

Blockchain is still an immature technology. Its final evolution and its greatest use cases are yet to emerge but should become more apparent within the next few years.

At its heart, blockchain is a database. But there is an even bigger revolution around financial services than blockchain, and it is happening in the world of big data and AI. The next section delves into this area.

1.8   BIG DATA AND AI FUNDAMENTALS

What is "big data"? What distinguishes it from other data?

When we speak of big data, we typically think of it as having certain characteristics that distinguish it from other kinds of data that don't need as sophisticated a set of methods and tools in order to process and understand it. The characteristics of big data are commonly called the "three V's" of volume, velocity, and variety:[31]

- **Volume:** Big data is, by definition, "big." The exact definition of "big" is a moving target, as processing power and storage continue to increase in capacity. A few years ago, "big" was terabytes of data. Then, petabytes. Now, we think about exabytes of data, or 10^{18} bytes. One exabyte is equivalent to about 320 billion copies of the King James Bible.[32]

- **Velocity:** Big data is data that is changing rapidly. The locations of every inhabitant of New York City or Shanghai are sets of data that change from minute to minute, as well as being high volume. Individual purchase transactions on credit cards for all of Brazil's day to day are a rapidly moving data set.

- **Variety:** High diversity is another dimension of big data. Instead of simply having repeating text or numbers of uniform size that fit neatly into rows and columns, you might have a mixture of different kinds of unstructured data, such as video or free-form text.

Data provides the feedstock for a particular kind of AI known as *machine learning*. When we talk about AI, there are several different flavors. *Artificial general intelligence* (AGI) is a machine that can think like a human and learn any new idea or skill in an unsupervised manner. We are many years away, at least, from widely applicable AGI—some experts think many decades.[33] Other kinds of AI include *expert systems*, where human knowledge is boiled down to a set of discrete rules (*if A, then B*), and *machine learning*, where probabilistic models iteratively improve themselves. Systems like Google search and voice-enabled software that enables you to call your bank and simply ask it a question (like "What's my account balance?") are built on machine learning algorithms. Machine learning is being applied in numerous areas within institutional and retail financial services, on everything from market forecasting to fraud prevention.

Part of why Google works so well for searching is that its AI has been trained on more than 1.2 trillion searches per year.[34] This massive amount of unstructured data has provided a critical advantage for building a really smart AI, at least for the particular application of internet search (all of those inputs have helped Google with other applications, of course). Financial institutions as well have a significant advantage in building new machine learning applications because they are able to leverage large-scale data sets that are under their control or influence.

1.9 BIG DATA AND FINANCIAL SERVICES

Many exabytes of data (and soon, many zettabytes, 10^{21} bytes) are being generated from people using credit cards, debit cards, and mobile payment platforms like Apple Pay, Amazon Pay, Venmo, and Alipay. These data streams are tagged with rich information, including not only the location of the purchase transaction but also the category of goods and services and the time of day, and, once analyzed in aggregate, can indicate trends of behavior.

The concept of using computers in the banking system has been around for a long time, but it was really the advent of ATMs in the 1960s and 1970s that led to consumer behavior data from electronic devices being used in banking business strategy. For example, after deploying its ATMs, Citi discovered that people withdrew money after work and on weekends, which was antithetical to the conventional banking hours of 9:00 a.m. to 3:00 p.m. Data from ATM network usage led Citi to add branch hours and increase its business through the application of analytics. This, in turn, enabled Citi to engage with its customers around other kinds of financial products, and the business enjoyed rapid growth thanks to extended hours, a practice that rapidly spread across the conventional banking industry.

Mobile communications networks became more prevalent in the 1980s and 1990s. With the advent of high-speed data in the next twenty years, we will see an explosion of information about people and their movements around towns and cities, data that informs financial services. Africa is expected to have 600 million smartphones by 2025,[35] versus 1.2 billion mobile phone lines overall; even the least developed areas on the planet are now getting some form of connectivity. With that connectivity comes the ability to understand human behavior and improve the delivery of financial services. We explore "leapfrog" possibilities from technologies such as mobile financial services in more depth in chapter 4, and around Africa specifically in chapter 9.

Institutional financial services have also enjoyed meaningful innovation through the application of AI and big data. High-frequency trading would not be possible without sophisticated AI systems. Quantitatively driven investment firms like Two Sigma, Renaissance Technologies, and Bridgewater have generated outsize returns for their investors by employing armies of mathematicians and computer programmers to exploit big data analytics for alpha generation.

1.10 DATA QUALITY

When we're trying to build quantitative models that interpret, analyze, or forecast market price movements or an individual consumer's credit behaviors, we are relying on big data streams to power those models. When models are initially created, the baseline assumption is that the data can be relied on, but the reality is often much different.

One big data set we were working with, which involved several terabytes of data, had anonymous location information for mobile phone users. Fair enough as far as it went. However, we found some outliers such as data that suggested an individual was inside the city one minute, was half a mile out to sea fifteen minutes later, then was suddenly back in the city. Such movement is not likely in a real-world setting, at least not until we have commercial teleportation technology. Savvier data science teams will build data assessment engines to automate the evaluation of data quality as it is being ingested and interpolation and extrapolation systems to bridge gaps that may appear in data to facilitate model development.

As AI systems are built and trained using big data, it is incumbent upon technology and business professionals to put into place processes to audit and improve data quality so that the systems in turn can produce better answers.

1.11   SOCIAL PHYSICS AND UNLOCKING POTENTIAL

With the advent of widespread big data / analytics and improved AI systems, we have seen the emergence of new computational social sciences that offer many benefits to financial services. *Social physics* is a dominant example of this new approach to understanding, predicting, and even changing human behavior at scale. The key idea is to use universal regularities in human behavior, such as the "long tails" in distributions of behavioral variables, to explain the data, rather than trying to model the data using general-purpose models like linear regression or neural networks.

For example, conventional lending relies on linear regression models offered through credit bureaus, requiring three years of data and suffering from the "credit trap" that in order to get credit you must have credit, thus excluding 3.5 billion people around the world from meaningful participation in financial services. With social physics, we can in theory improve credit modeling and predictions of credit behaviors by 30–50 percent versus credit bureaus, and we may be able to do this with just one month of data rather than thirty-six (once the model is trained).[36] This holds exciting potential for addressing financial inclusion in the developing world, where most people have thin credit files or no credit file at all.

New methods are emerging to ensure data security while still making data useful. The conventional method of data analytics is to bring all of the data together in a single repository, a *data lake*, and then perform analytics on it. While perhaps convenient for the data analyst, and while data insights can be more profound when data is combined and shared, copying and centralizing data is also highly cyber insecure. The OPAL Project (www.OpalProject.org) says that instead of bringing the data to the code, you bring the code to the data. OPAL is built around the premise that data is left atomized, it is placed in various secure repositories, and carefully vetted algorithms are sent to each data repository. These algorithms can extract insights. So, for example, you could have telecom data, banking data, and health data all sitting in different repositories. *Without* having to copy the data over (which may be illegal in many domiciles, and in all cases creates security risks), a query can instead be sent to each of the databases and the software would merge these insights into coherent information.

The ability to not only predict but actually influence the large-scale behavior of people through the application of big data / analytics creates a set of ethical and moral challenges. The introduction of these kinds of sensing platforms brings with it meaningful ethical and moral risks. The most extreme example is the social credit score in China, where behavioral data from mobile phones and other communications networks is used to determine people's eligibility for loans, housing, travel, and other aspects of participation in society. China has elected to trade individual liberty for social stability. To a lesser degree, these kinds of trade-offs occur across a number of Western democracies as well. For example, the United Kingdom, and particularly London, has opted for a higher degree of surveillance in exchange for greater security, installing a network of closed-circuit TV cameras on streets and in vehicles.[37] Germany, on the other hand, has gone for greater personal liberty and attenuated the ability for the security services to quickly track down bad actors. Each of these societies has made a set of value judgments about data ethics.

1.12 ETHICS OF BIG DATA AND AI

As with many disruptive innovations, there is a gap between what we *could* do with a particular technology and what we *should* do. Splitting the atom led to the ability to annihilate millions of people in an instant, as well as the ability to power an entire country with clean energy and to cure cancer. Commercially viable steam engines enabled military organizations to rapidly deploy troops to conquer territory and to support those troops with appropriate logistics, and they enabled the creation of transcontinental shipping networks to invigorate trade and unify culture. Big data and AI systems likewise have fearsome possibilities that have already been used to the detriment of society, and they have tremendous utopian potential.

The governor in all these decisions is the human ethical framework. When AI programmers are creating a system, what kind of system do they choose to create and what limitations do they place on it? When business or government or individual users apply that AI technology, what do they choose to apply it to?

Professors Luciano Floridi and Joshua Cowls have proposed a rigorous ethical framework for designing and deploying AI.[38]

In it, they map five key concepts derived from meta-analysis of the thinking around this subject across forty-two countries:

1. benevolence (AI should do something good for us)

2. nonmalevolence (AI shouldn't do harm in the process of doing something good for us; having a robust data privacy framework is an example of nonmalevolence)

3. autonomy (humans should be able to make key decisions and regulate how autonomous the AI is)

4. justice and fairness

5. explicability (AI shouldn't be black box; the AI should be able to tell us how it makes decisions)

This work, and other research like it, helps create parameters around which AI systems creators can inculcate *ethics by design* rather than attempt to retroactively assess whether a given AI is falling within certain ethical parameters.

1.13   REGULATION

Concomitant with the discussion of data and AI ethics, new regulations begin to emerge around personal data, such as the General Data Protection Regulation (GDPR) in Europe and the California Consumer Privacy Act in the United States. The European Union is also contemplating specific regulations around AI, and its ethical applications, in addition to the protections enshrined in the GDPR. Regulators are engaging in active consultative processes with the private sector, academia, and public interest advocates in an effort to shape meaningful regulations around the applications of big data and AI to financial services.

The most enlightened companies have proactive regulatory engagement efforts. Rather than waiting for an enforcement letter from a regulator as their first contact with the government, these organizations have teams deployed to share plans with regulators, understanding and addressing concerns proactively and helping to build capacity among government agencies on the implications of new technologies to foster a more informed regulator.

1.14 UNSOLVED PROBLEMS

While big data analytics has performed a number of miracles in the area of financial services, a number of thorny issues remain:

- Large amounts of data are not necessarily good-quality data. For example, credit bureaus are notoriously bad at managing data, securing the data, and providing meaningful insights from it. Correcting errors in an individual personal credit file can be laborious, highlighting poor governance of the data.

- Big data techniques can improve on bureau credit scores by 50 percent or more, but incumbent lobbying efforts and regulatory capture mean that the existing players are difficult to dislodge.

- The introduction of big data techniques for credit raises new questions. For example, Goldman and Apple endured a public relations mess with the launch of Apple Card, as some accused its data evaluation techniques of deliberately discriminating against women. The opacity, the lack of explainability of new algorithmic credit models, is another challenge for the industry.

- It can cost a bank anywhere from $13 to $130 to perform a "Know Your Customer" check on a new client. This legally mandated background check is an effort by the bank to avoid doing business with terrorists or other proscribed individuals. This accelerating cost trend has meant that a number of financial institutions have retrenched from inclusion efforts and have exited certain markets, which is known as *derisking*. The World Bank has identified derisking as harmful to economic progress in developing countries.[39]

• Identity lies at the heart of another unsolved data analytics challenge, that of *ultimate beneficial owner* (UBO). When a business account is opened, the financial organization needs to ascertain not only who has direct signatures on the account but also the upstream individuals who may have financial interest in the account. In a global platform, particularly in the high-growth emerging markets areas, this is a difficult task even for the most well-resourced financial institutions.

The array of challenges presented in this chapter represent only a small part of the areas of potential innovation and entrepreneurial action that can help address the needs of the financial services industry and of consumers and businesses more broadly.

Now that we have established the foundations of financial technology, we can begin to explore use cases, applications, policy, and societal implications.

NOTES

1. I. Pollari and A. Ruddenklau, *Pulse of Fintech H2 2019* (KPMG, February 2020), https://assets.kpmg/content/dam/kpmg/xx/pdf/2020/02/pulse-of-fintech-h2-2019.pdf.

2. H. Ritchie and M. Roser, "Technology Adoption," Our World in Data, 2017, https://ourworldindata.org/technology-adoption.

3. D. Thomas and N. Megaw, "Coronavirus Accelerates Shift Away from Cash," *Financial Times*, May 28, 2020.

4. T. Long, "Aug. 23, 1899: First Ship-to-Shore Signal to a U.S. Station," *Wired*, August 23, 2011, https://www.wired.com/2011/08/0823first-us-ship-to-shore-radio-signal/.

5. C. Qiang, C. Rossotto, and K. Kimura, "Economic Impacts of Broadband," in *Information and Communications for Development* (Washington, DC: World Bank, 2009), https://www.semanticscholar.org/paper

/Economic-Impacts-of-Broadband-Qiang-Rossotto/40e5bf124f1005
6e4b02d7149bf1a0bd1a221b37; C. Scott, "Does Broadband Internet
Access Actually Spur Economic Growth?," December 7, 2012, https://
colin-scott.github.io/personal_website/classes/ictd.pdf.

6. T. Suri and W. Jack, "The Long-Run Poverty and Gender Impacts of
Mobile Money," *Science* 354, no. 6317 (2016): 1288–1292.

7. M. Iqbal, "WeChat Revenue and Usage Statistics (2019)," Business
of Apps, updated March 8, 2021, https://www.businessofapps.com
/data/wechat-statistics/.

8. P. Jeffcock, "What's the Difference between AI, Machine Learning,
and Deep Learning?," *Oracle Big Data Blog*, July 11, 2018, https://blogs
.oracle.com/bigdata/difference-ai-machine-learning-deep-learning.

9. J. Weizenbaum, "ELIZA—a Computer Program for the Study of
Natural Language Communication between Man and Machine," *Communications of the ACM* 9, no. 1 (1966): 36–45.

10. Siri Team, "Deep Learning for Siri's Voice: On-Device Deep Mixture Density Networks for Hybrid Unit Selection Synthesis," *Machine
Learning Research*, August 2017, https://machinelearning.apple.com
/research/siri-voices.

11. C. Metz, "Google Just Open Sourced TensorFlow, Its Artificial
Intelligence Engine," *Wired*, November 9, 2015, https://www.wired
.com/2015/11/google-open-sources-its-artificial-intelligence-engine/.

12. "Top 100 Cryptocurrencies by Market Capitalization," Coin-
MarketCap, accessed February 2020, https://coinmarketcap.com/.

13. I. Vidili, "How Much Time Is Left for Banks? The Lost Battle of
Incumbent Barclays vs Agile 'Neobanks,'" *Medium*, June 4, 2019,
https://medium.com/@thesmartercrew/how-much-time-is-left-for
-banks-the-lost-battle-of-incumbent-barclays-vs-agile-neobanks
-430627a2602f.

14. Personal conversation with the author, August 2016.

15. "The History of the Net Promoter Score," Bain & Company,
accessed February 2020, https://www.netpromotersystem.com/about
/history-of-net-promoter/.

16. "Citibank Net Promoter Score 2021 Benchmarks," Customer Guru, accessed May 2021, https://customer.guru/net-promoter-score/citibank.

17. T. R. Eisenmann, G. Parker, and M. Van Alstyne, "Platform Envelopment," *Strategic Management Journal* 32, no. 12 (December 2011): 1270–1285.

18. M. Gasparello, "What's behind Transferwise Massive +100% YoY Growth?," Strategico.io, 2019, https://strategico.io/transferwise-digital -strategy/.

19. R. Ghose, S. Dave, A. Shirvaikar, K. Horowitz, Y. Tian, J. Levin, and S. Ho, "Digital Disruption: How FinTech Is Forcing Banking to a Tipping Point," *Citi GPS: Global Perspectives & Solutions,* March 2016.

20. A. Cohen, "HSBC Layoffs: 3 Reasons Why the Banking Giant Is Imploded," FastCompany.com, February 18, 2020, https://www .fastcompany.com/90465194/what-went-wrong-at-hsbc; S. Butcher, "Big Job Cuts Coming at UBS after Nasty Quarter," eFinancialCareers .com, October 22, 2019, https://www.efinancialcareers.com/news/2019 /10/ubs-q3-results-2019.

21. "Jobs and the Fourth Industrial Revolution," World Economic Forum, 2016, https://www.weforum.org/about/jobs-and-the-fourth-in dustrial-revolution.

22. Bloomberg.com; Coinmarketcap.com.

23. D. L. Shrier, *Basic Blockchain: What It Is and How It Will Transform the Way We Work and Live* (London: Little, Brown, 2020).

24. Grand View Research, *Edge Computing Market Size, Share & Trends Analysis Report by Component (Hardware, Software, Services, Edge-Managed Platforms), by Industry Vertical (Healthcare, Agriculture), by Region, and Segment Forecasts, 2020–2027,* 2020, https://www.grandviewresearch .com/industry-analysis/edge-computing-market.

25. L. Lamport, S. Shostak, and M. Pease, "The Byzantine Generals Problem," *ACM Transactions on Programming Languages and Systems* 4, no. 3 (July 1982): 382–401.

26. CISOMAG Staff, "Cybercrime Will Cost the World US$6 Trillion by the End of the Year: Study," CISOMAG, March 23, 2020,

https://cisomag.eccouncil.org/cybercrime-will-cost-the-world-us6
-trillion-by-the-end-of-the-year-study/#:~:text=In%20fact%2C%20
the%20damages%20caused,US%243%20trillion%20in%202015.

27. S. Ray, "Merkle Trees," Hackernoon.com, December 14, 2017, https://hackernoon.com/merkle-trees-181cb4bc30b4.

28. N. Ramautarsing, "OuroX Signs LOI with the Suriname Stock Exchange and Takes First Steps to Develop an Innovative Securities Exchange for Latin America and the Caribbean," OuroX, May 2, 2019, https://medium.com/ourox/ourox-signs-loi-with-the-suriname -stock-exchange-and-takes-first-steps-to-develop-an-innovative -46115a5d3015.

29. D. Shrier, "The Future of Money Isn't Libra or Chinacoin, It's Federated," Forkast.News, September 24, 2019, https://forkast.news /opinion-the-future-of-money-isnt-libra-or-chinacoin-its-federated/.

30. M. Wood, "Award-Winning Startup Delivers Blockchain Trace-ability for US Airforce," Ledger Insights, June 11, 2019, https://www .ledgerinsights.com/blockchain-us-airforce-traceability-aircraft-parts -14bis/.

31. D. Gewitz, "Volume, Velocity, and Variety: Understanding the Three V's of Big Data," ZDNet.com, March 21, 2018, https://www .zdnet.com/article/volume-velocity-and-variety-understanding-the -three-vs-of-big-data/.

32. Starry Staff, "How Big Is the Internet?," Starry, July 29, 2019, https://starry.com/blog/inside-the-internet/how-big-is-the-internet.

33. N. Joshi, "How Far Are We from Achieving Artificial General Intelligence?," Forbes, June 10, 2019, https://www.forbes.com/sites/cog nitiveworld/2019/06/10/how-far-are-we-from-achieving-artificial -general-intelligence/?sh=7e205096dc4d.

34. InternetLiveStats.com, accessed March 31, 2020.

35. "2019: The Mobile Economy Sub-Saharan Africa," GSMA, accessed May 28, 2020, https://www.gsma.com/mobileeconomy/sub -saharan-africa/.

36. D. Shrier and V. Raeburn, "Giving Credit, Taking Credit: The Emergence of Predictive Credit Analytics" (unpublished white paper, November 2018).

37. P. Bischoff, "Data Privacy Laws & Government Surveillance by Country: Which Countries Best Protect Their Citizens?," Comparitech, October 15, 2019, https://www.comparitech.com/blog/vpn-privacy /surveillance-states/.

38. L. Floridi and J. Cowls, "A Unified Framework of Five Principles for AI in Society," *Harvard Data Science Review*, July 1, 2019, https:// hdsr.mitpress.mit.edu/pub/l0jsh9d1/release/7.

39. World Bank, "De-risking in the Financial Sector," October 7, 2016, https://www.worldbank.org/en/topic/financialsector/brief/de-risking -in-the-financial-sector.

II
TRANSITIONING TO THE DIGITAL ERA

2 EDGE EFFECTS: BRIDGING FROM OLD TO NEW

Boris Khentov

2.1 INTRODUCTION

Ecologists use the term "edge effects" to describe changes that occur at the boundary between two ecosystems. One type of edge effect is increased biodiversity—connecting a new set of dots opens up more opportunities to secure a resource advantage.

The financial services industry, perhaps more than any other industry, is a gnarled mishmash of ecosystems, and no edge is more jagged than the one between the automated, fully digital world and the manual, paper-based world. Increasingly, however, this edge lies just out of sight. Even the stodgiest century-old institutions have invested in web and mobile interfaces, but from a customer experience perspective, that veneer is often skin-deep.

For retail customers coming of age in a world of one-click shopping, same-day delivery, and ride-hailing apps, doing business with financial services incumbents can feel antiquated to the point of disbelief. Transactions we expect to complete with a couple of swipes suddenly grind to a screeching halt.

When you are asked to print, fill out, and mail a form, you might be forgiven for thinking, "Am I being recorded? Is this a prank?" No, this is merely the twentieth century, oddly resilient two decades into the current one, in an industry that generally attaches little value to nostalgia, at least when it comes to cutting operating costs.

In many corners of retail finance, with no warning, a customer's seemingly routine intent might be whisked into the underworld of legacy back-office workflows, where bits and bytes are inexplicably turned into paper, secured within more paper by a strip of glue, and dispatched across the country (or across the street), only to eventually be revirtualized into disembodied data, roughly five to ten days later.

2.2 WOUNDED WORKFLOWS

Retail finance is riddled with such *wounded workflows*, in which jarring disconnects between different generations of technology—one foot in the old and one in the new—are often bridged by menial human labor. At this edge lies both inefficiency and customer frustration, and therefore opportunity.

Continuing to push the line on automating financial services operations may not have the glamour of pursuing the singularity, but it's where many cutting-edge technologies are having the most immediate impact. Some of the more established applications of artificial intelligence (AI) in the private sector include fraud detection, internal compliance, and cyberthreat detection.

However, as in any dynamic environment, not all "edge effects" are productive, and progress can be nonlinear. The seductive power of "the new" is strong, and it pays to remember that the best tool for the job is the one that best solves the problem at hand.

Through my work of leading operations at Betterment, helping to rebuild the investment management industry, I have spent the better part of a decade on the edge of automation. Founded by Jon Stein in 2010, Betterment is a customer-centric fintech money manager that effectively created an entire category that came to be known as *robo-advice*.

In order to grow, an investment management start-up must gather customer assets held by incumbents and has no choice but to accept certain lowest-common-denominator tech realities imposed by the industry. One minor episode from our scaling of Betterment's technical operations illustrates both the challenges and the opportunities of navigating "the edge" as potentially revolutionary new technologies become real options across every domain.

2.3   WHERE THERE'S FRICTION, THERE'S IRE

Perhaps the most egregious wounded workflow in investment management is the transfer of an individual's retirement savings between two accounts at unaffiliated institutions, known as a *rollover*. Americans primarily invest for retirement in two types of accounts, IRAs and 401(k)s, which by 2018 held $9.2 trillion and $5.3 trillion, respectively.[1]

A technology-enabled newcomer that aims to disrupt this industry, as Betterment did, must not only create a compelling value proposition for potential customers but also be able to logistically process transfers once the assets are in motion. While fully digital transfers are available under certain circumstances, paper checks are inevitable, and with them, the erosion of precision that comes with digital data being expressed in analog form.

There are two primary reasons for this dramatic digital disconnect. The first, not surprisingly, is about incentives. The handful of behemoths that manage custody of the investing public's trillions are not particularly nimble, but mature businesses tend to get *particularly* sluggish when it comes to technology enhancements that make it easier for dissatisfied customers to leave. One need not posit a centralized, inconvenience-loving mastermind at each of these institutions, orchestrating the inertia—work that is likely to decrease revenue in the short term tends to never quite get prioritized.

The second reason is somewhat counterintuitive. Certain financial services processes remain relatively low tech because finance has historically adopted technology eagerly and thoroughly, and even ancient technology can be deemed "good enough" when stability is at a premium. While start-ups have the benefit of starting from scratch, implementing the latest innovations is magnitudes more disruptive to operations when your business is deeply entangled with pervasive legacy technology.

After all, paper checks and the batch systems that print and mail them, and even fiat money itself, were all once a cutting-edge technology, far more efficient at transmitting economic value than, say, taking your chickens to the market and exchanging them for a cow. In a way, this legacy technology remains so entrenched because at some point it was compelling enough to become utterly dominant.

2.4 CHECK TECH

The story of how paper checks came to dominate the US financial system is a fascinating one—the key drivers were not only technological but also legal and political. For instance, legislation passed by Congress during the Civil War suppressed privately issued banknotes, which had the effect of encouraging the use of paper checks.[2]

Usage truly exploded in line with post–World War II prosperity, as the number of US checking accounts nearly doubled between 1939 and 1952, kicking off a multidecade operational crisis for the banks that needed to process this ever-swelling tsunami.[3] Some banks had to close their doors at 2:00 p.m. just to get through the backlogs.[4] The surge created a need for a massive pool of workers, tasked with some of the most tedious, mind-numbing clerical work imaginable.

The quest to leverage technology to mitigate the drudgery of check processing began in earnest in the 1950s, when Bank of

America proposed a collaboration with an arm of Stanford University that would pave the way for a number of game-changing developments: a standardized banking industry font that was printed with special magnetic ink, allowing for magnetic ink character recognition (MICR; an early, rudimentary form of optical character recognition[5] [OCR]), and the first automated check-sorting machine employing these technologies.

Subsequent iterations continued to make progress. In 1977, when Cincinnati's regional Federal Reserve bank adopted the latest and greatest sorting machines, processing throughput reached sixty-five thousand checks an hour. The work still required thirty-seven employees, but just a couple of decades earlier, thousands of employees would have been needed.[6]

And yet, much like adding more lanes to a highway has not been shown to reduce traffic, all this added capacity just strengthened incentives to use more of it. While it was easier for consumers to gradually shift over to credit and debit cards for their personal payments, businesses had invested vast sums in check issuing and processing infrastructure, making checks particularly sticky in the context of business-to-business fund transfers—for instance, IRA rollovers.

2.5 THE PAPER WEIGHT

As Betterment's business took off, customers began rolling over their existing retirement savings into their Betterment IRAs. Paper checks issued by other custodians began to stream in, and we had to ensure that each was invested in the correct account, 100 percent of the time, ideally with zero (or at least minimal) human involvement.

We soon discovered that this process was far more challenging than we'd hoped. While checks issued by different institutions follow some general formatting standards (which began with MICR), these do not rise to the level of a "contract" that is sufficiently precise for rules-based software to process in every instance. The liberties taken by each firm go well beyond font choices.

Our lean operations team was responsible for exponentially more than sorting through this mess, and something had to be done.

2.6   TO BUILD OR NOT TO BUILD? THAT IS THE QUESTION

When an operational challenge calls for a technical solution, managers who have the luxury of access to in-house tech talent should ask themselves some version of the "build vs. buy" question.

Real-world business problems are complex, and the answers are often not binary—solutions may get cobbled together and wind up somewhere on the spectrum. But even if the optimal solution were somehow knowable in advance, many companies tend to have an institutional bias, depending on their profile.

To overgeneralize, *traditional* companies (i.e., the kind that refer to their in-house software development teams as IT) tend to be more inclined toward "buying." When the product calls for substantial customization, that entails some "building," but this is typically accomplished by "buying" the services of outside consultants.

However, building something out of nothing, precisely to the specifications of the problem, is in every start-up's DNA. Plus, the requisite talent is generally at hand—when you have a hammer, everything looks like a nail. Therefore, for a business that identifies first and foremost as a technology company, irrespective of vertical (i.e., the kind where IT means ensuring that software engineers, the stars of the show, have ironclad Wi-Fi), the bias might be toward "building" its way out of any challenge.

Like any rapidly growing tech start-up, a fintech business is constantly asking itself, "We could build this ourselves, but *should* we, even if we could do it better?" (Start-ups may be lacking in resources, but rarely in hubris.) But irrespective of company profile, a good rule of thumb when answering the "build vs. buy" question is to ask yourself two others:

- Is the problem hard? If yes, that's a vote for "buy."
- Is the problem important? If yes, that's a vote for "build."

There are numerous ways for a problem to be hard. Maybe it calls for an inordinate amount of creativity, and one day some engineer will have her eureka moment and solve the problem. But more likely, particularly in financial services operations, "hard" means messy, fragmented, *boring*, death by a thousand paper cuts (literally in this case).

The problem of generating reliably precise metadata from scanned paper checks is universal across the industry. There are countless companies whose core business is to solve this problem. These are both strong signals for the kind of "hard" you may want to "buy" against.

But few ambitious tech companies can resist the temptation to build against any kind of "hard" if the problem is "important"—another ambiguous descriptor. It's clearly important enough to address but likely not "important" if the implementation is not core to *your* business strategically (e.g., not a differentiator that will move the needle on growth, or not a potential moat via patent).

For a business that differentiates on customer experience, even a start-up with an itchy "build" trigger finger, back-office automation can be "hard" and usually isn't "important," so it tends to tilt toward the "buy" side, provided the cost is reasonable.

As long as your solution works, customers don't care how elegant it is—not unless you can tell them you've eradicated the need for checks entirely. So, we contracted with one of the many vendors whose core business is receiving paper checks and shepherding them back into the digital realm.

2.7   FRAGMENTATION ACROSS THE NATION

This so-called lockbox service provided a mailing address and handled physical receipt of rollover checks destined for Betterment. The vendor would open up the envelopes, scan the contents into digital images, and apply some combination of OCR and manual data entry to generate a software-readable metadata attachment. We'd then receive images of the day's checks, along with the metadata, which would include things like the customer's name, the dollar amount of the rollover, and crucially, the destination Betterment account number (since a customer might have several).

There was a "build" component too: internal tooling to ingest this metadata, to allow our operations team to supervise the routing of checks, and to handle exceptions that call for human discretion.

However, the exceptions remained the rule. Because of the maddening fragmentation of the format across different issuers, the metadata from our vendor was nowhere close to 100 percent reliable for full automation, meaning we could not be comfortable with depositing checks with zero human involvement.

Even a customer's name often presented challenges for rules-based automated matching. One custodian might choose to preface the customer's name with "FBO" (for benefit of—an optional legal formality, since retirement accounts are technically trusts). Another might use a customer's nickname, which wouldn't match the full legal name in our database.

Perhaps most frustrating was that each custodian had its own approach for displaying the Betterment destination account number on the check—the single most important data point in determining how to process the rollover. While some have a dedicated field on their checks, many treat it with far less dignity. An exhaustive list of the locations we've seen for account numbers could fill its own (even more boring) chapter:

- Placing it in the "memo" field
- Appending it to the customer's name in the "payable to" field
- Partially truncating it, resulting in a shorter account number that also happens to exist, which wreaks havoc on automated systems and requires extensive cleanup
- Placing it too close to some other number on the check, causing our lockbox service to mistakenly grab a fragment or the wrong number entirely
- Including it in the "supporting documents" rather than placing it on the check itself, resulting in a blank metadata field

2.8 TAXING CONSEQUENCES

At best, a potentially misdirected check would require time-consuming cleanup by our engineering team. At worst, the consequences might be irreversible, depending on how much time had elapsed.

The workings of the US tax code, in all its baroque complexity, call for a particularly high degree of caution. Both IRAs and 401(k) accounts come in two varieties: earnings on which tax is deferred but will be assessed when the funds are withdrawn during retirement (Traditional), and money that is taxed the year it's earned but can be withdrawn tax-free (Roth).

Many customers have both types of accounts and might initiate two or more distinct transfers around the same time. It's critical that rollovers between institutions be processed "apples to apples"—inadvertently depositing funds from a Traditional IRA into a Roth IRA could constitute a taxable event for a customer and may go unnoticed for months. Additionally, a rollover from a 401(k) into an IRA, even if the tax profile matches, needs to be reported to the IRS, whereas a transfer between two IRA accounts doesn't.

None of this important information was printed on various checks in a consistent manner, which called for an approach that is highly intolerant to false-positive matches. Given the operational burden of unwinding an error, you want your automated implementation to err on the side of not making a decision and escalating to a human, rather than risk making the wrong decision. And if you are comfortable automating only about 20 percent of the volume, surely there are more effective uses for your engineering resources.

2.9   AUTOMATION AND MORALE

For a lean tech start-up that is used to building to well-defined specifications on top of predictable application programming interfaces, full contact with the messy, physical world of paper checks ignited a seemingly inextinguishable blaze of demoralizing challenges.

The imperative to be deeply attuned to the morale of employees tasked with the most tedious work does not map directly to a dollar amount on your profit and loss statement, yet it's absolutely critical when navigating a multiyear, marathon high-growth scenario.

Our daily volume of rollover checks went from single digits to flirting with breaking a thousand on a busy day. Betterment's operations team gamely grinded under the yoke of this high-stakes yet largely thoughtless work, which seemed out of place in an otherwise dynamic, tech-forward environment.

Automating non-customer-facing functions is rarely given top priority during a start-up's early stages, but it was clear to even the most junior employees that this workflow simply did not "belong" at a financial services business established in the twenty-first century.

On the flip side, automating human workflows, however menial, is a delicate affair. Depending on their mind-set, employees may need varying degrees of reassurance that, by embracing the process, they will actually enhance their job security—their work will change, but will become more complex and stimulating.

Moreover, managers often have real choices around how to design the scope of the new jobs that emerge after automation. A 2002 MIT study looked at two departments within the same large bank, both of which handled a form of check processing. Both introduced substantial automation improvements around the same time, but the respective managers took different approaches to tasks that were *not* automated.[7]

One department went deeper into specialization, assigning employees to even narrower silos. The other purposefully reshuffled those tasks to create broader-scope roles, designed with the customer in mind, than a single repeatable action.

The latter required a bigger up-front training investment but created higher-paid, more interesting jobs. The findings were consistent with other research, which suggests that such integrative job designs are more commonplace where management attaches importance to increasing the well-being of employees and where customer service is a critical goal.

We were fortunate in being able to attract ambitious, talented people into junior roles and knew they'd have no qualms with solving more customer problems—and solving them faster and with more leverage. The entire team could band together and focus on automating as much of this work as possible.

2.10 MORE DATA, MORE PROBLEMS

Spoiled by the absence of legacy data sets of inconsistent integrity and now forced to absorb the externalities imposed on us by legacy technology outside our control, we stumbled into a classic record linkage (RL) problem (also called "data matching"), studied extensively beginning in the 1950s.[8]

The need to create a link between different representations of the same object across multiple data sources (using one or more "common identifiers") is a typical RL workflow. In our case, the unique object was the customer's rollover transaction. This was represented in three distinct data sources, with a number of "common identifiers" available, but none was reliably sufficient on its own, without reference to others.

Betterment's systems had a representation of this transaction, as did the other custodians. By issuing a paper check, the custodian created a third representation—a particularly troublesome one, when it came to reliably extracting the common identifiers.

While RL problems are as ancient as the IBM mainframes that "nobody ever got fired for buying," machine learning has opened up a new class of solutions for automating RL decision-making in the twenty-first century. Rather than linking on one or two unambiguous common identifiers, overall certainty is achieved by weighting the certainty signals across a potentially wide set of common identifiers. This is called *probabilistic record linkage* or *fuzzy matching*—a seemingly ideal term for the chaotic, unpredictable world of typos, smudges, and formatting shenanigans.

2.11   TO LABEL IS HUMAN, TO STORE, DIVINE

While tech start-ups are perpetually strapped for resources, they offset this by conferring a number of advantages, including the much-touted ability to make decisions rapidly. A more understated advantage is the physical proximity of technical experts to those in nontechnical roles, which leads to spontaneous interactions and serendipitous efficiency gains.

That's precisely what happened when Sam Swift, then Betterment's head of data science, looked over the shoulder of a junior operations associate and was intrigued by what he saw. The associate was using our internal tool, which loaded the metadata that the vendor pulled from the checks, and made a recommendation for which Betterment account each check should be deposited into. The associate was flipping through one scanned image after another, confirming each decision, occasionally pausing to peer at one for longer than the others.

After a few questions, Sam identified a classic machine learning problem, which consists of the following conditions:

1. Well-defined set of inputs (name, dollar amount, source account type, destination account number)
2. Easy to define "success" (check deposited into the right account)
3. Large data store of "human-labeled" outcomes

The third condition is particularly important, and routinely underappreciated.

When considering pricey investments in AI, business leaders readily recognize that their primary data needs to be in digital form and readily accessible. What's less intuitive without a technical background is the need to have been creating a massive record of past decisions *made by humans* based on that primary data, particularly for "matching" problems.

Many of us first experienced the power of a massive human-labeled data set during that disorienting moment when Facebook's "tag your friends" feature suddenly began making eerily precise "recommendations" as to the identity of every person in a photo, trained on untold millions of our own, manual selections.

In many instances, however, an adequate human-labeled data set simply does not exist. This winds up being one of the primary blockers to implementing machine learning solutions, even at large companies with ample budgets, whose leadership is sold on the investment.

2.12 A BOT IS BORN

In our case, by the time Sam's interest was piqued, humans at Betterment had already looked to the same fields to process hundreds of thousands of checks. A machine learning model would train on years' worth of human decisions and "learn" what constitutes a "match" between the occasionally messy metadata pulled from a check and the record of the transaction already in our system.

Mystical terms such as "gradient boosting," "random forests," and "stacked ensembles" began to swirl in a corner of the Betterment office unaccustomed to such wizardry. Incantations of the AI age, they carried hope for lifting the curse of unstructured text fields and fat-fingered typos, and all the frustration they brought.

Thus was conceived the Betterment Rollover Bot, powered by AI. The plan was to run the bot in parallel with the human-supervised process and observe it, before gradually shifting any actual decision-making over to the machine.

In the summer of 2017, the Rollover Bot became sentient, purely in "test mode." Something about this prosaic, unassuming application of machine learning, deep under the hood, where no customer would ever experience it, felt symbolic. While we were patiently waiting for AI to drive our cars and generally "change life as we know it," was it already changing the world in less flashy ways, one healed "wounded workflow" at a time?

A couple of months later, I presented this use case at a fintech industry committee meeting, as an illustration of real-world applications of AI in start-up operations. I ended my talk on a high note, hopeful for additional modest breakthroughs.

2.13   KEEP IT SIMPLE, SOMETIMES

Fast-forward two years, to 2019. David Shrier, who sat on the same committee and had seen the presentation, reached out and asked if Betterment would be interested in contributing a chapter to this book. He suggested that the Rollover Bot story would be a good fit.

My first thought was, "Well, this is awkward," because as much as we appreciated the opportunity, the Rollover Bot had its last test run a few months earlier, having never made the jump to production. Retelling the story today, while leaving that part out, didn't feel right. However, as I mulled it over, it occurred to me that the *whole* story might be an even better fit, so here's what happened next.

Back in 2017, when the Rollover Bot began its daily test runs, our operations team eagerly looked on, anticipating an imminent, joyful handoff of its most thankless work. Yet, something wasn't clicking the way we expected.

The "match rate" was initially promising, but the Rollover Bot never reached a level of confidence in which it could relieve the humans of even half the volume. It's almost as though something was missing—something that humans intuitively know to reference when resolving a variety of edge cases, which wasn't available on the check alone.

A couple of months after the Rollover Bot began its lackluster life, AJ Kramer, Betterment's then-director of operations, had an idea. Comparatively speaking, it was about as high tech as a bag of rocks, but it was in production within a couple of months, and it fully automated nearly 80 percent of Betterment's rollover check volume.

AJ's idea was as simple as it was effective. Rollovers into Betterment are initiated inside our app. When customers express their intent to transfer an IRA to us, they also provide some basic information as part of the flow, which then triggers instructions that are sent to the customer's current custodian. For each rollover *intent* created in the app (customers can initiate several, from and into multiple accounts) we would generate a new, unique alphanumeric ID that began with the three-letter prefix "BMT."

We instructed the transferring institution to put this "rollover intent ID" in the memo field of the paper check (see figure 2.1). We then instructed our lockbox service to look for

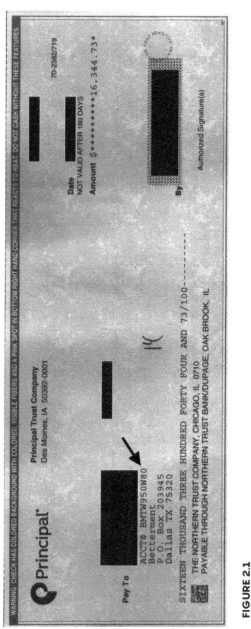

FIGURE 2.1

Rollover intent ID on a paper check.

this ID and to include it as an additional field in the metadata passed on to us. We could then look *solely* at this ID and match the check to our record of the rollover intent (which includes the destination Betterment account number). If this ID was present in the metadata, we could be confident of a perfect match.

2.14 THE MISSING LINK

In RL parlance, AJ had created a new common identifier, which for some reason was dramatically more effective than the existing ones at linking records, on its own, without reference to the others. What advantage did it have over the Betterment destination account number, also a unique ID, which wasn't getting the job done? It turns out there were three factors that, in aggregate, materially reduced error rates:

1. Check issuers know what a destination account number is, and each has its own process for it, driving fragmentation. **Injecting an additional, "unknown" string into the process actually resulted in far more predictable placement on the check.** We asked them to put it in the memo field, and much of the time they did, in the absence of a conflicting internal protocol.

2. Because it was alphanumeric, with a unique BMT prefix, **the new identifier was purposefully designed to "pop" better among a bunch of numbers.** Through whatever mix of OCR and manual data entry our lockbox service employed, it made far fewer mistakes parsing it out.

3. Subtly, but perhaps most importantly, **the new identifier had a one-to-one correlation with the record we were trying to link to** the record of a specific transaction, not the record for the destination account. The account is a good proxy, but it can receive multiple rollovers over the same time frame, from different account types (with

distinct tax implications). A unique identifier, created during the session when the customer expresses the rollover intent, would point to all the data that was available when the transaction record was created (but no superfluous data, which could create ambiguity).

When researchers tag animals before releasing them back into the wild, they are effectively creating *state awareness*, preparing the system to derive meaning when reencountering the same specimen, linking the new impression with the existing record. Similarly, we didn't need more sophisticated pattern recognition across a complex set of signals—just a more reliable, solitary tag to link us back to something we already knew.

As for the Rollover Bot, it continued running in test mode for another year or so. It cost us nothing to do this, and we were either too busy to put it to sleep or morbidly fascinated with observing its now purposeless existence, or a bit of both. But in our minds, it will forever symbolize the somewhat corny but undeniably wise principle of "fall in love with the problem, not the solution."

2.15   WHAT'S YOUR PROBLEM?

So, what happened, exactly? We encountered an easier category of the RL problem masquerading as a harder one, which we might have unmasked sooner, had it not been for our eagerness to deploy the "cool" technology.

Our initial assessment of the problem was informed by the fact that routing a check often requires human judgment because the current process cannot parse checks with accuracy and consistency. Under this framing, reaching for the best technology available that attempts to replicate human "intelligence" seems reasonable. However, there were two implicit assumptions:

- The check contains all the information necessary to make a decision.

- The visual profile of another firm's check is a fixed constraint.

Thanks to his domain expertise, AJ couldn't help but challenge those assumptions.

- Observing his team's wounded workflow, AJ noted that, even after closely studying a "problem check," a human (that paragon of judgment we sought to replicate) would sometimes reach for other data elsewhere in the system to resolve an ambiguity. Something was missing.
- He was also familiar with the check-issuing processes of the big custodians and recognized that we have a limited way to indirectly influence what goes on a check issued by a third party.

He restated his assessment of the problem as: routing a check often requires human judgment because the current process cannot parse checks with accuracy and consistency. *However*:

- Even when parsed perfectly, a check may not contain all the information required to make a decision (though that info is available elsewhere in our system), and
- The visual profile of another firm's check is not entirely immutable.

In this case, the heavy lifting was in assessing the true parameters of the problem. An accurate assessment, made possible through creativity and domain expertise, made the problem "easier."

Though he wouldn't have known the lingo, AJ had turned a "fuzzy matching" RL problem, which calls for fancy AI models to pattern match across multiple identifiers, into the simplest, rules-based RL problem, matching with high confidence on a single common identifier (which he first had to invent).

It was an elegant work-around, which is another way of saying "a better solution."

2.16 THE RIGHT STUFF FOR THE RIGHT KIND OF "NEW"

What made this improvement (and many of our other efficiency gains) possible wasn't the latest and greatest tech.
Incremental breakthroughs are often about new connections
between largely familiar points of reference, which flour-
ish when there's an opportunity to rethink problems from
scratch.

Generating a unique "intent identifier" associated with a
customer-driven user experience flow, solely for the purpose
of solving an RL problem, thereby automating a back-office
workflow, is domain-specific to the point of tears and not
inherently instructive of anything.

What's notable is the set of circumstances under which such
an idea would actually be implemented. In those rare moments
when it becomes viable to rebuild something massive (like a
money manager) from scratch, all kinds of structural assumptions begin to fall, and things just start working better.

The primary challenge facing incumbent financial institutions today isn't technology per se; it's reorienting toward a
holistic customer-centric experience. These giants are throw-
ing huge sums at creating modern interfaces, but the teams
responsible for these experiences, no matter how talented,
simply do not have the scope and agency to control the *entire*
experience, which is also dependent on legacy systems that
have existed for many decades. Matching the experiences
offered by start-ups requires the will and ability to meaning-
fully bridge these two worlds, which can be more of an organizational question than a technological one.

2.17 MEANS, NOT ENDS

No corner of human activity is devoid of parables—not even
a humble fintech back-office operation. Those of us who have

devoted our careers to tech should take great care to remember that technology, in and of itself, isn't the point.

In fact, one of my favorite pastimes when working with technical teams is to ask if we've explored every option to "make the problem go away" without resorting to the tools we're familiar with (or the tools we'd *like* to be more familiar with).

For what it's worth, machine learning has found better (more suitable) applications at Betterment and will surely proliferate to other use cases as well. But I'll always remember the Rollover Bot as a symbol of how hype and desire for "the new" carries with it the risk of distorting judgment and losing sight of what actually matters.

NOTES

1. G. Iacuri, "IRA Assets Will Almost Double Those in 401(k) Plans over Next Five Years," *InvestmentNews*, June 25, 2018, https://www.investmentnews.com/ira-assets-will-almost-double-those-in-401k-plans-over-next-five-years-74724#:~:text=Assets%20in%20individual%20retirement%20accounts,according%20to%20an%20industry%20analyst.

2. S. Quinn and W. Roberds, "The Evolution of the Check as a Means of Payment: A Historical Survey," Federal Reserve Bank of Atlanta *Economic Review* 93, no. 4 (2008), https://www.frbatlanta.org/-/media/documents/research/publications/economic-review/2008/vol93no4_quinn_roberds.pdf.

3. D. Scharfenberg, "Paper Checks Forever?," *Boston Globe*, April 21, 2018, https://www.bostonglobe.com/ideas/2018/04/21/paper-checks-forever/B9KYFwuXGOieb0A35CAEdN/story.html.

4. E. Smith, "Scanning and Sorting," *Tedium*, February 17, 2021, https://tedium.co/2021/02/17/check-processing-history-automation/.

5. E. Smith, "Seek and Spell," *Tedium*, March 22, 2017, https://tedium.co/2017/03/22/ocr-typography-optical-character-recognition-history/.

6. Staff, "At Cincinnati Fed, \$200 Million Is a Normal Night," *Cincinnati Enquirer*, September 11, 1977.

7. D. Autor, F. Levy, and R. J. Murnane, "Upstairs, Downstairs: Computers and Skills on Two Floors of a Large Bank," *Industrial and Labor Relations Review* 55, no. 3 (2002): 432–447.

8. H. L. Dunn, "Record Linkage," *American Journal of Public Health* 36, no. 12 (1946): 1412–1416.

3 OPEN BANKING: HOW PLATFORMS AND THE API ECONOMY CHANGE COMPETITION IN FINANCIAL SERVICES

Markos Zachariadis
and Pinar Ozcan

3.1 INTRODUCTION

In recent years, UK and European regulators have declared that a lack of competition within the retail banking sector has had a negative impact on consumers, and they have deemed the oligopolistic nature of competition in the banking sectors as problematic. In the United Kingdom, acknowledging that unnecessary obstacles deterred retail banking customers from switching providers, the British government's Financial Conduct Authority launched the Current Account Switching Service in 2013 to make it easier and faster to switch providers, including all direct debits and standing orders for consumers and small and medium-sized enterprises (SMEs). However, given the current structure of the industry, comparing relevant products and services remained challenging for customers. Thus, to put more pressure on the older and larger banks (which account for the majority of the retail banking market) to work harder for customers, another regulator, the Competition and Markets Authority (CMA), set out to produce further regulation that would introduce more "openness" in the sector and help "unbundle" or "separate" banking services to create a more level playing field. Open banking regulation was published in 2015 as a framework for the introduction of open application programming interfaces (APIs) in banking in order to drive the implementation of open banking in the United Kingdom. It coincided with the 2015 Revised Payment Services Directive (PSD2) of the European Commission, which has the same purpose. Since then, open banking regulation has been replicated in other parts of the world—Australia, Brazil, Canada, and Singapore, to name a few—to boost innovation in the financial sectors in these countries.

Generally, the key aims of open banking regulation are to further integrate and support a more efficient payments market, as well as promote competition in an environment where new players are emerging. To fulfill this goal, EU and UK regulations enabled third-party payment institutions to access consumer bank accounts, which are held mostly by incumbent banks. To do this, the law required all banks to create interfaces (such as open APIs) through which trusted third parties can automatically connect to customers' bank accounts and access their transaction data as well as initiate payments, upon completion of a three-step process for customer consent.

At its very core, financial services is an information business, and so changing not only the way information is communicated but also the type of data that is being shared between participants in the market could lead to a drastic change in the competitive dynamics and market structure. Fundamentally, open banking does exactly that: it provides a new framework for sharing financial data in a systematic, transparent, and secure way. Such data-sharing activity not only reduces the barriers to entry for new participants but also allows for novel and innovative products to be introduced for the benefit of consumers who gradually gain more control of their data. While this is an attractive proposition, open banking frameworks constitute a challenge for incumbent banking institutions and traditional business models that are based mostly on a vertically integrated arrangement for value creation.

The recent wave of digitalization in the banking industry and the application of new technologies across the broader spectrum of financial services—from payments and accounts to lending and wealth management—have led to the emergence of new entrants (such as *fintechs* and *challenger banks*) that have managed to claim some of the market share from established banks. As competition intensifies, incumbent firms are gradually reconsidering their position in the market and value proposition to customers. In this context, incumbent institutions can either choose to embrace change and be open to collaboration using the opportunities that technology offers by interacting with the greater ecosystem of market participants and other service providers, or defend their position by focusing their efforts on developing competitive solutions for all customer and product segments, limiting access to their systems and platforms.

The introduction of PSD2 in the European Union as well as the Open Banking initiative in the United Kingdom has left little room for traditional banks to follow the defensive route, and thus many have been considering ways to embrace the new regulations and remain competitive. As indicated above, a key technology that has been instrumental in this context (from both a strategic and a regulatory perspective) is APIs. APIs have proved to be one of the safest ways to share financial data securely and in a standardized way. They have been tried and tested in many industries and contexts and thus offer a good way to cross organizational boundaries and develop ecosystems for innovation and value creation. In this chapter we consider how the introduction of APIs and open banking will affect banks' organizational structure and competitive position in the market, how platform business models play a role in this context, and how banks can develop a platform-based strategy to deal with digital transformation in the shifting environment of increased data sharing.

3.2   OPEN APIs IN BANKING

An API is a technology that allows two computer applications to talk to each other over a network using a common language that they both understand.[1] APIs are scalable, secure, and standardized and thus can be reused in different settings with very low development costs. David Berlind, editor in chief of ProgrammableWeb.com, once described them as "electrical sockets that have predictable patterns of openings"[2] into which other applications that match those patterns can "plug in" and consume them in the same way electrical devices consume electricity. This systematic way of sharing data can make it easier for teams across an organization to collaborate and access information when and however they need it, thus helping to interconnect services and business processes, improve employee productivity, and even create better omnichannel experiences for customers.[3] Similarly, APIs can be used to expose business assets such as information, a service, or a product to external audiences, hence reaching beyond the boundaries of the firm. Such *external* APIs can provide further integration with company partners and allow third parties to consume organizational data that can create cross-selling and upselling opportunities down the line.

While APIs in banking are not new, they have been restricted to mostly *internal* or *closed* uses in order to unlock data resources across the organization and to try to break data silos using data in new applications and systems. However, the most innovative and game-changing use of APIs has been their *open* implementation that establishes simplified and standardized connections beyond the boundaries of a single firm. In financial services, such use of APIs is commonly seen in card networks (such as VISA and Mastercard) in order to integrate infrastructures with selected e-commerce partners, leading to more functionality and better customer experiences. The recent emergence of open banking regulatory frameworks around the world—and especially in geographies such as the United Kingdom, the European Union, and Australia—is steering the adoption of open APIs in banking beyond the voluntary phase and toward a requirement. Depending on the jurisdiction and open banking implementation in each country, APIs can be used to communicate account and transactional data but also initiate payments and create accounts. The more "open" the APIs, the higher the potential of radical transformation in the industry.

APIs can be conceptualized in four main ways. First, APIs can be understood as an *integration technology* that allows for interoperability and modularity in systems.[4] Their main benefit is that they "enable interfaces, services, and applications to connect seamlessly with one another, making digital content accessible" between a wide range of independent applications.[5] API technology provides a customary interface (based on a set of agreed-upon standards) and a layer of abstraction that reduces complexity and allows API-consuming systems to "plug-and-play" without the need to know the specifics of the API provider's systems.[6] Second, APIs are *boundary resources* for innovation and become "the software tools and [embedded] regulations that serve as the interface for the arm's-length relationship between the platform owner and the application developer."[7] In this context, organizations can share a core functionality based on a software platform and provide external developers an opportunity to produce modules that interoperate with it,[8] thus adding more value for consumers on the platform. This premise holds important implications for the platform business models discussed below. Third, APIs can moderate and record economic activity (through their documentation of terms and conditions and service-level agreements) and thus act as *contracts* between economic agents in an ecosystem. In economic theory, contracts are a big part of the negotiation costs involved in transactions and have an effect on the organizational structure and production process.[9] Waiving such costs with a simple and scalable technology can be revolutionary for the organization of the firm and its economic activity. Finally, as API usage is distinct and can be logged and managed, APIs can be seen as *products* that can be priced, sold, and developed based on the demands of their users.[10]

Open banking regulatory frameworks, such as PSD2 in the European Union and Open Banking in the United Kingdom, which demand data openness (often through the means of open APIs), offer a unique opportunity to experiment with new business model ideas such as platforms in banking. Using APIs, new banks can enter the market much more easily, as being able to connect to customer data at incumbent banks offers these new entrants an opportunity to switch customers over by showing how much better they can analyze customer data to offer more customized services such as money management tools. Given that these new entrants typically start with a limited number of products—for example, a current and/or a savings account—many have followed a platform business model, letting customers obtain financial services from multiple fintech providers by connecting them on a digital platform, typically in the form of a mobile application. Thus, the first business-to-customer financial platforms, also known as *financial marketplaces*, were born as direct competition to the offerings of traditional banks. This move, which has been coined as "banking as a platform," describes the premises upon which banks can adopt a platform strategy model and change the rules of competition.

Before discussing how platform business models can be used in banking specifically, we discuss what platforms are, how they function, and why they have disrupted more and more industries in the past couple of decades.

3.3   THE ECONOMICS AND STRATEGY OF PLATFORMS

Platform firms such as Google, Amazon, Facebook, and Apple have managed to disrupt their respective industries and outperform their incumbent rivals with their unprecedented growth and economic efficiency. The success of such ventures is driven by a business model that moves away from the traditional vertical integration of the firm (also known as the *pipeline business model*) and introduces a flatter, more inclusive, and innovation-centric approach to economic activity and value creation.[11] Platform businesses often use technology to "connect people, organisations and resources in an interactive ecosystem in which amazing amounts of value can be created and exchanged."[12] This organizational formation can facilitate value-creating interactions among consumers (demand side) and external producers (supply side) and produce a *multisided market*.[13] While the idea of *platform business models* has existed for years, the recently developed *digital platforms* have the advantage of being "editable" and "reprogrammable,"[14] which could make them more agile and responsive to incorporating complementary modules from third-party developers in order to extend functionality. This makes them more scalable and cheaper to run but also allows them to leverage the large amounts of data that are captured while at work.

Successful platforms usually develop a core value proposition or infrastructure in the form of a product, service, or technology on which a large number of firms can build complementary products, services, or technologies, thus creating a loosely assembled business ecosystem for innovation.[15] Two key functions that platform leaders aim to deliver are (1) *bringing together disparate resources* and know-how from different firms, and (2) *matching and connecting users with producers* of products or services (see figure 3.1).

Firms such as Apple, Google, Microsoft, and Linux in the tech sector, but also Airbnb, Uber, eBay, YouTube, Facebook, VISA, and Mastercard in other sectors, have been using these two principles to build successful digital platforms and take advantage of an entire ecosystem of suppliers and users. There are two economic theories at play that give platforms

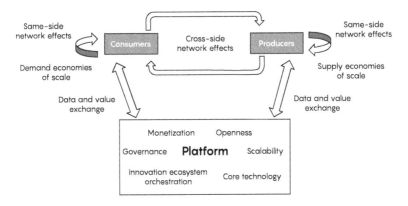

FIGURE 3.1
Platform business model: transaction costs and network externalities.

an advantage over traditional "pipeline" business strategies: *transaction costs theory* and *network effects*. Transaction costs are the search costs, coordination costs, negotiation costs, and information asymmetry costs an organization faces while making choices about its production process. Organizations that struggle to address these costs face the "make or buy" question, in which they must either turn to the market or become more integrated[16] to satisfy their production needs. A platform strategy can potentially be better than a hierarchy or a pure market transaction because it can further reduce the searching, matching, negotiation, and contract costs as well as lower information asymmetries (moral hazard) that are a potential risk to both consumers and suppliers. As a result, a platform business model is mostly about "selling reductions in transaction costs,"[17] as it does not, for example, own any of the cabs or hire any of the drivers.

In addition to the above, *network externalities* or *network effects* describe how the increasing number of network adopters can have an impact on the benefits (or utility) that each user enjoys on a platform.[18] Network effects can be found in almost any platform and can make a real difference in the value that users gain. In financial services, this is mostly apparent in payment systems and financial telecommunication infrastructures such as SWIFT, where the more banks that use the network, the more value everyone gets by being able to transmit payment instructions to an increasing number of counterparts. The presence of such *direct* network effects is well documented in the literature.[19] Similarly, *indirect* network effects can exist when value for one side of the network increases as usage goes up on the other side of the network— for example, you get more value from your VISA card when more merchants accept it as a means of payment. Considering the above, the platform leader will need to moderate platform openness by applying filters and by controlling and limiting the access of users on the platform and potentially even their activities and connections.[20] This process, known as *platform curation,* will safeguard the level of quality of service that platform users enjoy and will uphold the two factors that make a platform valuable: the maintenance of low transaction costs and nurturing of positive network effects. In this context, *data feedback loops*[21] from consumers on the quality and usability of the various offerings will help distinguish between good and bad services and eventually discontinue or discourage those that have mostly negative ratings. Data and the various metrics one can produce around key interactions and performance are used routinely in digital platforms and can have important spillover effects that influence even the pricing of services.

3.4   PLATFORM COMPETITION IN BANKING

The rise of platform business models in banking offered by new entrants (e.g., Atom, Monzo, N26, Starling in the European Union / United Kingdom) forces banks to revisit their role as financial intermediaries and prepare to become re-intermediaries by providing "online automated tools and systems that offer valuable new goods and services to participants on [all] sides of the platform."[22] Platform competition in the sector means that the leanest and most attractive experience for both developers (a new "breed" of client) and wholesale and retail customers will prevail. Therefore, banks will need to cultivate and manage growth on all sides of their platforms while keeping and investing in some core applications central to their value proposition, such as basic account products, national payments, and information enrichment. The formation of such an ecosystem may help keep transaction costs low and maximize the benefits of network effects and data feedback loops.

In order to realize value in this new way, however, banks will need to reconsider several elements of their structures and business models. Their legacy IT infrastructures, built over several decades as new products were added to their portfolios, may stand in the way, requiring massive IT overhauls before a platform infrastructure can be built. Second, their hierarchical organizational structures may hinder the creation of customer-centric bundles of products and services across the organization. Finally, their organizational cultures, which have treated data security and data analysis as mutually exclusive priorities, will need to be adjusted to offer both.

In an environment where open data drives flatter rents and lower prices, the ability to engage customers with better experiences through more valuable applications may act as a counterincentive to move to a different platform. The more opportunities there are to create value for customers on a particular platform, the less inclined customers will be to leave, thus creating a customer "lock-in effect." In this context, openness can be managed in order to maximize positive network externalities and win more customers.[23] For example, banks should be able to match customers' demands with respective services and user experiences that cannot be found in other platforms. Failing to do so will decrease consumer confidence in the particular bank. To avoid such frustration, platform banks need to use customer data more effectively to track preferences and engage their clients with products they are likely to use. This is of particular significance in financial services, where consumers can be price-sensitive and likely to move once a better opportunity appears (e.g., better interest rates for individual savings accounts or deposits and mortgages). While banking customers may often exhibit a degree of "stickiness" and inertia due to information asymmetries, introducing more transparency and openness in the market will encourage movement and eventually change the pace of the competition.

In addition, banks will need to make sure that the quality of external services (e.g., fintech offerings) provided on their platforms is adequate to maintain customers' loyalty. Poor quality or unreliable services will damage the reputation of both the bank and the respective fintech. As platform owners, the banks will need to absorb any transaction costs from the various fintech interactions and take responsibility for the reliability and security of the service. This is similar to the fundamental responsibilities of platform owners who broker transaction costs and charge a premium for the matching between the demand side and the supply side. Banks will thus have a new role of "re-intermediation," which essentially will be to not only facilitate transactions but also provide trust between the two sides of the market—for example, the fintechs and end customers. This is similar to how iTunes can guarantee the quality of products for those who purchase music from its platform and how Uber can guarantee the quality of its transportation services through its app.

Keeping the platform open versus closed is another challenge to tackle. While having an open platform may create difficulties in monetizing the benefits, as it reduces the switching costs and so the possibility of locking customers in, a closed system may stifle innovation and lead to isolation. There are plenty of examples where firms ended up "on the wrong side of history"—Nokia, Myspace, BlackBerry, and Apple's Macintosh computer in the 1990s, to name a few—because they did not let outside innovators add complementary products and tried to do everything in-house with limited resources. A hybrid approach where platform owners invest their resources in a small number of core applications can be a healthier option to provide balance and guide competition. However, platform owners will still need to decide what their core competencies will be and what key features they should invest in before opening up the platform to external competition. In the case of traditional banks, this may lead to the discontinuation of several product lines that are no longer competitive.

3.5 EXTERNAL THREAT: BIG TECH

When considering platform competition within the banking industry, we need to take into account possible challengers that may emerge from different markets. Existing platforms that have "overlapping user bases and employ similar components"[24] can be notable contenders. In such a scenario, "platform envelopment" strategies could be deployed in order to pursue entry into a new market by expanding the functionality of one's own platform to leverage communal user relationships and mutual components.

We currently observe this platform-as-a-bank strategy in the case of big technology platforms—for example, Facebook and Google moving toward the banking domain, taking advantage of their user bases, trusted brands, and existing functionalities to offer banking services. Some of these platforms already function at the fringes of the financial services sector. For example, Amazon already operates a payments service and a lending business to SMEs that sell products on its web page, thus enhancing further cross-side network effects and gaining business. Facebook recently incorporated peer-to-peer payments between Messenger accounts in the United States, then obtained an e-money license in the Republic of Ireland to pave the way for Messenger payments in Europe.

The disruption in banking by big-tech platforms will be exacerbated by fintech start-ups that, frustrated by traditional banks' closed strategies, may view these global technology firms as go-to platforms for distributing their innovative services. Banks will need to compete with these existing firms and learn how to operate on a platform and ecosystem basis in order to remain competitive. It is possible that such competition will lead to a multiplatform bundle where multiple platforms sit on top of each other (vertical stacking) trying to explore inefficiencies in the existing banking system and extract value from customers. While this is expected to bring certain benefits to customers in the midterm, it will also rearrange the banking services' value chain and redistribute market share and profits in the sector. Depending on the market response, this may have an effect on the banks' pricing strategy and customer premiums.

3.6 CONCLUSIONS

Digitalization is changing the competitive landscape in a plethora of industries and for a wide range of firms from local start-ups to global conglomerates. These changes have the potential to make what we know about business strategy and competition obsolete. Open banking and PSD2 are regulatory attempts to transform the banking industry and bring it to the age of digitalization. However, as with other cases of disruption, the effectiveness of these attempts will depend on the response from customers, incumbents, and resourceful market entrants. The tricky issue in regulated markets like banking or health is that the sensitivity of the data to be shared may create cognitive blocks in customers, leading to slow uptake of innovative offerings in the market. In these cases, in addition to regulations to bring down entry barriers, governments should also employ policies and programs to educate customers to leverage the new opportunities created in the market.

NOTES

1. D. Jacobson, G. Brail, and D. Woods, *APIs: A Strategy Guide* (Beijing: O'Reilly, 2012).

2. D. Berlind, "What Is an API, Exactly?," ProgrammableWeb.com, December 3, 2015, https://www.programmableweb.com/news/what-api -exactly/analysis/2015/12/03.

3. S. Nijim and B. Pagano, *APIs for Dummies*, Apigee special edition (Hoboken, NJ: John Wiley & Sons, 2014).

4. R. Bodle, "Regimes of Sharing," *Information, Communication & Society* 14, no. 3 (2011): 320–337, doi:10.1080/1369118X.2010.542825; C. Y. Baldwin and K. B. Clark, *Design Rules: The Power of Modularity* (Cambridge, MA: MIT Press, 2000).

5. Bodle, "Regimes of Sharing," 325.

6. P. F. Cowhey, J. D. Aronson, and D. Abelson, *Transforming Global Information and Communication Markets: The Political Economy of Innovation* (Cambridge, MA: MIT Press, 2009).

7. A. Ghazawneh and O. Henfridsson, "Balancing Platform Control and External Contribution in Third-Party Development: The Boundary Resources Model," *Information Systems Journal* 23, no. 2 (2013): 173–192, quotation at 175.

8. A. Tiwana, B. Konsynski, and A. Bush, "Platform Evolution: Coevolution of Platform Architecture, Governance, and Environmental Dynamics," *Information Systems Research* 21 (2010): 685–687.

9. R. H. Coase, "The Nature of the Firm," *Economica* 4, no. 16 (1937): 386–405; O. Williamson, *Markets and Hierarchies* (New York: Free Press, 1975); S. J. Grossman and O. D. Hart, "The Costs and Benefits of Ownership: A Theory of Vertical and Lateral Integration," *Journal of Political Economy* 94, no. 4 (1986): 691–719.

10. Jacobson, Brail, and Woods, *APIs*.

11. A. Gawer, ed., *Platforms, Markets and Innovation* (Cheltenham, UK: Edward Elgar, 2009).

12. G. Parker, M. Van Alstyne, and S. Choudary, *Platform Revolution: How Networked Markets Are Transforming the Economy and How to Make Them Work for You* (New York: Norton, 2016).

13. J. C. Rochet and J. Tirole, "Two-Sided Markets: A Progress Report," *RAND Journal of Economics* 37, no. 3 (2006): 645–667.

14. M. De Reuver, C. Sørensen, and R. Basole, "The Digital Platform: A Research Agenda," *Journal of Information Technology* 33, no. 2 (2018): 124–135.

15. A. Gawer and M. Cusumano, *Platform Leadership: How Intel, Microsoft and Cisco Drive Industry Innovation* (Boston: Harvard Business School Press, 2002).

16. Williamson, *Markets and Hierarchies*.

17. M. Munger, "Coase and the 'Sharing Economy,'" in *Forever Contemporary: The Economics of Ronald Coase*, ed. Cento Veljanovski (London: Institute for Economic Affairs, 2015), 187–208.

18. C. Shapiro and H. Varian, *Information Rules: A Strategic Guide to the Network Economy* (Boston: Harvard Business School Press, 1999); J. Farrell and G. Saloner, "Standardization, Compatibility, and Innovation," *RAND Journal of Economics* 16, no. 1 (1985): 70–83; S. Scott, J. Van Reenen, and M. Zachariadis, "The Long-Term Effect of Digital Innovation on Bank Performance: An Empirical Study of SWIFT Adoption in Financial Services," *Research Policy* 46, no. 5 (2017): 984–1004; N. Economides, "The Economics of Networks," *International Journal of Industrial Organization* 14, no. 6 (1996): 673–699; M. Zachariadis, "Diffusion and Use of Financial Telecommunication: An Empirical Analysis of SWIFT Adoption" (NET Institute Working Paper No. 11-10, October 2011).

19. Scott, Van Reenen, and Zachariadis, "The Long-Term Effect of Digital Innovation on Bank Performance"; Zachariadis, "Diffusion and Use of Financial Telecommunication."

20. Parker, Van Alstyne, and Choudary, *Platform Revolution*.

21. These data-related effects can be characterized as demand-side economies of scale, which are present when platforms are more valuable to their users (on any side of the network) as they scale their operations. C. Shapiro and H. Varian, *Information Rules: A Strategic Guide to the Network Economy* (Boston: Harvard Business School Press, 1999).

22. Parker, Van Alstyne, and Choudary, *Platform Revolution*, 71.

23. M. Van Alstyne, G. Parker, and S. Choudary, "Pipelines, Platforms, and the New Rules of Strategy," *Harvard Business Review,* April 2016, 54–60.

24. T. Eisenmann, G. Parker, and M. Van Alstyne, "Platform Envelopment," *Strategic Management Journal* 32, no. 12 (2011): 1270–1285, quotation at 1271.

4 DIGITAL FINANCIAL SERVICES

David L. Shrier

4.1 INTRODUCTION

Digital financial services (DFS) offers a vehicle by which the gap can be bridged between the 3.5 billion people who are under-served or unserved by financial services today, and the cost and compliance requirements that international laws and regulation mandate. While many digital financial services are delivered through mobile devices (mobile financial services), the more comprehensive services also capture nonmobile technologies, such as Paytm, which is used in India.

4.2 CONTEXT

In contemplating DFS, it is useful to have a framework of the financial services system. Figure 4.1 was developed by Professors Peter Tufano (Saïd Business School, University of Oxford) and Robert Merton (MIT Sloan School of Management) to provide a functional explanation of how the global financial system works.

Broadening financial access through digital means can unlock productivity and investment, reduce poverty, empower women, and help build stronger institutions with less corruption—all while providing a profitable, sustainable business opportunity for financial services providers. The benefits for individuals,

Paying for goods and services	Moving money from today to tomorrow (saving/investing)	Moving money from tomorrow to today (credit)	Managing risk

Decision support

Infrastructure

Rules of the game (laws, contracts, regulation)

FIGURE 4.1

Framework of the financial services system.

Source: Adapted from D. B. Crane, K. A. Froot, S. P. Mason, A. Perold, R. C. Merton, Z. Bodie, E. R. Sirri, and P. Tufano, *The Global Financial System: A Functional Perspective* (Boston: Harvard Business School Press, 1995).

businesses, and governments can transform the economic prospects of developing economies.[1]

DFS often fills the gap left by banks that have been unable or unwilling to service those at the bottom of the wealth and income scales, and is often driven by nonbank financial institutions that are providing the financially excluded with an alternative to reliance on cash as a means of payment and transfer.[2]

Most people and small businesses in developing economies today do not fully participate in the formal financial system. They transact exclusively in cash, have no safe way to save or invest money, and do not have access to credit beyond informal lenders and personal networks. Even those with financial accounts may have only limited product choices and face high fees.[3] In more developed countries, the banking experience has left many feeling frustrated, and financial institutions often receive negative customer satisfaction ratings (expressed as a Net Promoter Score).

Using digital channels rather than brick-and-mortar branches dramatically reduces costs for providers and increases

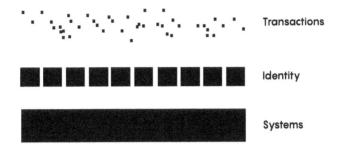

FIGURE 4.2
Three dimensions of DFS.
Source: D. Shrier, "Digital Financial Services" (webinar, University of
Oxford, Women's World Banking, Alliance for Financial Inclusion
"Leadership and Diversity for Regulators," June 13, 2019).

convenience for users, giving people at all income levels and
in far-flung rural areas access to financial services. For businesses, financial services providers, and governments, digital
payments and DFS can erase vast inefficiencies and unlock significant productivity gains.

As we consider the digitization of financial services, it's
useful to add a second, simplified functional model that
examines the layers of the digital realm. The model in figure
4.2 focuses on three specific dimensions of DFS, disaggregat-
ing them from the broader context of the Tufano functional
model.

These foundational layers of DFS provide a ready way for a
central banker to understand where a particular offering fits
into the "stack."

4.3 DESCRIPTION

We will now examine the core elements of DFS using this simplified three-layer model:

• *Transactions*: movement of money from one person to
another, from a person to an organization (such as a bank,

a company, or a government), from an organization to a person, or from one organization to another organization.

- *Identity*: a model of uniquely representing a person or organization. Identities can be derived from government documents, corporate-issued identifiers (such as the DUNS number from Dun & Bradstreet or the Legal Entity Identifier), biometric data, financial data, or other sources.

- *Systems*: the infrastructure that lies underneath other activities. It can include communications networks, hardware, software, and other technologies.

While most instances of DFS at the transaction and identity layers are delivered through mobile platforms, a number of deployments of DFS are delivered digitally but not via mobile devices. Paytm is an example (see below).

Transaction-layer DFS   Payments, remittances, and transfers have been revolutionized by digital technologies. Private companies such as M-Pesa and Bitpesa, both based in sub-Saharan Africa, have introduced lower-cost, higher-throughput transactions. In doing so, they have reduced cross-border remittance rates from 12–15 percent to 1 percent or less by replacing antiquated systems that use layers of manual labor and rent-extracting intermediaries with digital technologies. Bitpesa, for example, replaced Western Union activities with bitcoin technology to manage and account for the movement of money from one account to another. Peer-to-peer payments systems eliminate some conventional functions of the banking system and lower costs. Transactions and payments, which are perhaps the most common financial activity by an individual, have provided the entry point for financial inclusion for millions. Some market providers engage in a hybrid model where a human agent, digitally connected by a smartphone, interacts in person with a consumer. By pairing the technology with a human face, this hybrid model helps overcome some of the mistrust in certain countries toward digital systems.

Identity-layer DFS   Identity is a keystone issue for societal and financial inclusion. Three and a half billion people are under-banked or unbanked,[4] and approximately 1 billion (mostly women and children) lack any legal identity.[5] In addition, small businesses lack adequate corporate identity functions, directly related to the fact that 65 million formal micro, small, and medium-sized enterprises are underbanked or unbanked.[6] Credit, whether for consumers or small businesses, is an identity attribute; it is derived from the actions of the consumer or business and is tied to other identifiers such as a national ID number or business ID number (in other words, it is an enhanced set of data that is attached to that identity). A credit profile is a subset of your identity attributes. Digital data streams, including transaction-layer data, are providing inputs for the new forms of credit modeling, driven by alternative data, and are enabling lending to a broader audience. New data portability (driven by open banking regulations[7]) empowers consumers by giving them control over their personal identity-linked data.[8] Identity is discussed at greater length in the "Digital Identity" section of the "Commonwealth Fintech Toolkit" and in the 2019 book *Trusted Data* (Hardjono, Shrier, and Pentland: MIT Press).[9]

Systems-layer DFS   Digital technologies are helping to modernize systems-level activities in various banking environments as well as enable better security across all dimensions of infrastructure. The gaps across components of the financial system can be quite large; some developing economies lack even basic process flow systems for loans (processing loan applications on paper forms, and doing so poorly). New digital platforms can help with this transition. Blockchain-based systems are enabling interbank transfers at a dramatically reduced cost and increased speed (see the "Blockchain" section of the "Commonwealth Fintech Toolkit").[10]

It is worth mentioning types of DFS that are not mobile. One example is Paytm, a machine similar to an ATM that allows a consumer to transfer money, pay bills, and engage in other financial services activities without having to own a mobile phone, a smartphone, or a computer with telecommunications connectivity. It is a vehicle for financial access for some of the poorest individuals.

The critical building blocks for effective DFS, according to the think tank Consultative Group to Assist the Poor, are illustrated in box 4.1.

Box 4.1
Four Building Blocks for Effective DFS Regulation

Based on its work in 10 countries in Africa and Asia, non-profit think tank CGAP (the Consultative Group to Assist the Poor) has identified four building blocks for creating an enabling and safe DFS regulatory framework. These four building blocks are:

- **E-money issuance by nonbanks**—A basic enabling condition for DFS is a special licensing window for nonbank e-money issuers (EMIs).

- **Use of agents**—Retail agents make inclusive DFS possible and are therefore a key focus of enabling regulation. Providers use agents—third parties such as retail shops—to provide customers easy access to their services close to where they live, thus expanding their outreach at relatively low incremental cost.

- **Risk-based customer due diligence**—DFS operate within regulatory contexts shaped by policies on anti-money laundering and countering the financing of terrorism (AML/CFT). Proportionate AML/CFT frameworks use a risk-based approach to protect the integrity of the system while imposing the least burden on DFS outreach.

- **Consumer protection**—In order to drive financial inclusion, DFS must cultivate trust and reliability, and this in turn depends on effective financial consumer protection (FCP).

Source: Reproduced from Consultative Group to Assist the Poor, "Regulation for Inclusive Digital Finance," accessed July 11, 2021, https://www.cgap.org/topics/collections/regulation-inclusive-digital-finance.

4.3.1 The Role of Central Banks in DFS

Government bodies, and central banks in particular, have a crucial role to play in the success or failure of the implementation of DFS in a country.

Enabling environments The regulatory environment allowing provision of DFS is said to be "enabling" or "nonenabling," terms first used by the mobile communications industry's nonprofit trade association, the GSMA, in relation to the impact of local regulatory regimes on provision of DFS.[11] The "enabling" component refers primarily to whether any and all nonbanks can independently provide DFS without a (mandated, "nonenabling") need to partner with a licensed bank for that purpose.[12]

Central bank In most jurisdictions, the central bank's role as the apex bank in the country establishes it as the lead regulator in DFS. It will, at a minimum, set licensing and authorization criteria for DFS providers and e-money issuance; establish consumer protection mechanisms; set safety and soundness guidelines including schemes for safeguarding of pooled funds and user accounts; set AML/KYC ("anti–money laundering" and "know your customer") policies for use by the financial sector; establish quality of service and risk management guidelines for services; set agent standards; and often also set interoperability standards and policies. In some cases it may also act in a catalytic role of establishing or building a national interoperable platform or switch that integrates a DFS ecosystem with its e-money-based financial services provider and agent networks with "traditional" financial ecosystems such as those involving ATM and card networks.[13]

Businesses and government leaders will need to make a concerted effort to secure the potential benefits of DFS. Three building blocks are required: widespread mobile and digital infrastructure, a dynamic business environment for financial services, and digital finance products that meet the needs of individuals and small businesses in ways that are superior to the informal financial tools they use today.

4.3.2 Examples of DFS Deployments

A number of Commonwealth nations have had significant success in deploying DFS.

Kenya M-Pesa and similar DFS are representative of the mobile banking revolution in Kenya: financial institutions have embraced M-Pesa as a platform to manage microaccounts, build customer deposits, and broaden their customer network. Consequently, Kenya has emerged as a leader in financial inclusion in sub-Saharan Africa. In 2006, just before M-Pesa was launched, only 26.7 percent of Kenyans had access to formal financial services (such as bank accounts and money transfers); this figure now exceeds 80 percent.[14]

Zambia The Zambia National Commercial Bank (Zanaco) invested in a distinctive brand for financial inclusion. Zanaco successfully launched Zambia's first mobile banking service, Xapit, in 2008. The Xapit account, which a customer can open at the bank in only minutes, offers a VISA card and other banking services over a mobile phone. Targeting Zambia's underbanked markets, Xapit now serves more than two hundred thousand customers and conducts more than 1 million transactions per month. Xapit users include other Zanaco customers that have easy access to the product through their "current accounts" (checking or savings accounts).[15]

Malawi Having launched the first mobile money pilot in 2012, Malawi has seen the number of adults using DFS leapfrog from 1,000 to 2.3 million active users as of June 2018, representing 25 percent of the adult population. This tremendous growth was highlighted in the 2017 Global Findex, released by the World Bank in April 2018. The Reserve Bank of Malawi (RBM) has played an important role in creating a regulatory environment that has fostered private-sector-led innovation and growth. RBM permits both banks and nonbank financial institutions to offer DFS. Critical laws passed by parliament in 2016, including the Payment Systems Act, the E-Transactions

Act, and the Communications Act, have provided a guide to further development of the DFS market. Following the Payment Systems Act, RBM issued a directive in September 2017 mandating interoperability of DFS through the National Switch, a central part of the telecommunications infrastructure. Malawi has also achieved what is considered the "dream" of many countries, which is "interoperability" (or seamless communications) between mobile network operators (MNOs).[16]

Nigeria According to the World Bank's 2016 *World Development Report*, the 2012 Growth Enhancement Support Scheme introduced mobile technology to transfer fertilizer subsidies directly to farmers, taking the government out of the business of procuring and distributing fertilizer. The support scheme now helps up to twice as many farmers at one-sixth the cost. The transfer system relies on a database of more than 10.5 million farmers, who, as registered recipients of the subsidies, now have a better chance of gaining access to formal or regulated financial services. This initial success has led to an expansion of the system, aided by a digital identification system and biometric signatures, taking financial services far into Nigeria's rural hinterland.[17]

India Paytm is a digital payments platform that enables online as well as cash deposits via select banks and partners to be transferred into an integrated wallet. Once the Paytm wallet is prepaid, it can be used to pay for a number of goods and services without having to use cash—for example, topping up minutes on a mobile phone, paying utility bills, paying travel fares and booking hotels, buying tickets for movies, and making online purchases.[18] The funds held in the Paytm wallet are protected under an escrow account (a type of account where funds are released once an agreement is fulfilled).[19]

Bahamas In May 2019, the Bahamas Central Bank entered into an agreement to deliver the first national digital currency by 2020 with NZIA as its key collaborator, along with the

Singapore-based software development firm Zynesis. Called the Sand Dollar, the initiative is intended to deliver access, compliance with regulation, and, most importantly, to create climate resilience around the economy after Hurricane Dorian literally blew away the life savings of many residents.[20]

United Kingdom   Monzo is seeking to provide basic financial access for asylum seekers in the United Kingdom, which CEO Tom Blomfield feels would be accelerated by better digital identity. OakNorth, in turn, believes that coordinated access to government data could assist with lending to small and medium-sized enterprises.[21]

4.4   KEY CONSIDERATIONS FOR FUTURE DEVELOPMENT

4.4.1   Critical Issues and Obstacles in DFS

A number of issues have arisen in the past several years as DFS has begun to gain widespread adoption:

- Digital inclusion/exclusion
- Rising usury
- Paradigm limits (KYC)
- Privacy
- Cybersecurity
- Financial literacy

Digital inclusion/exclusion   Financial inclusion is driven by digital inclusion, but digital inclusion remains such a large problem globally that it has been identified as a UN Sustainable Development Goal (SDG 9).[22] It also offers opportunity: for every 10 percent increase in internet penetration, there is an increase of 1.35 percent in GDP.[23] A total of 3.8 billion people still lack fast and reliable internet, making digitally delivered financial services a difficult endeavor.[24] The fact that the world seems mired at about 54.8 percent connectivity, with a slowing growth rate (2.9 percent), inhibits the potential for financial inclusion via DFS.[25] Gender ratios are further exacerbating the problem, with 313 million fewer women than men using mobile internet in low- and middle-income countries, according to the GSMA.[26] To advance policy outcomes around DFS that seeks to drive inclusion, a systems view is needed—for example, Africa is predicted to have more than 700 million smartphones by 2025, up from 302 million in 2018,[27] but access to power and access to bandwidth remain limiting factors, so the entire array of technologies and services needs to be considered and supported.

Rising usury   DFS inclusion platforms have been criticized for high interest rates, forming an effective "poor tax" whereby poorer people have to pay higher rates than wealthier people on a like-for-like basis. The question is being raised, in an era of historically low interest rates in developed nations (in some cases negative interest): Why is it that developing economies and underbanked/unbanked populations remain subject to high-cost loans? At the same time, policy initiatives to try to limit interest rates in some economies have had the unintended consequence of making it uneconomical for companies to compete, and several players have left the market. Economists argue about a variety of solutions; Leora Klapper of the World Bank, among others, argues strongly for policy tools such as fostering competition and reducing cost of funds to lenders rather than interest rate caps.

Paradigm limits (KYC)   An identity-linked challenge is how current KYC regulations are interpreted. KYC currently requires a physical address tied to a customer. This prompts the question of how to perform a KYC check on someone who doesn't have a formal address. New technologies from mobile phones can deliver GPS coordinates and device-acquired biometrics that can provide high-resolution means of identifying customers in a manner that is better and more secure than

current methods. Some domiciles are exploring alternate
methods of identifying individuals along these lines.

Privacy   Alternative data introduces new issues regarding digital privacy, causing citizens to lose the "anonymity of crowds."
Telecommunications and bank data sets can also breach personal privacy in new ways, such as (if misused) enabling targeting of ethnic groups and discrimination against protected
classes. In the past three years, elections have been increasingly
manipulated by the use of personal data. The General Data Protection Regulation provides a model for addressing personal
sovereignty of data, but regulators struggle to apply it.

Cybersecurity   Applying a cyber lens to the simplified three-
layer model of DFS, we see that new vulnerabilities arise at
each layer of the DFS stack. Transactions lead to transaction
fraud; identity experiences identity theft; easily accessed computer systems lead to systems hacks. Figure 4.3 shows how
cybersecurity fits into our DFS model.

The downstream impacts of cybersecurity issues are con-
sequential. Rising fraud and identity theft rates reverse financial inclusion. For example, false decline rates are highest

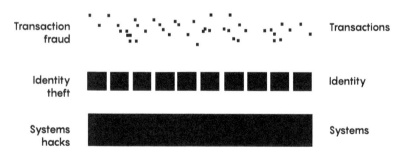

FIGURE 4.3
Cybersecurity in the DFS model.
Source: D. Shrier, "Digital Financial Services" (webinar, University of
Oxford, Women's World Banking, Alliance for Financial Inclusion
"Leadership and Diversity for Regulators," June 13, 2019).

in emerging markets (e.g., Bangladesh, sub-Saharan Africa, Colombia, Mexico) with 50 percent or more of transactions being declined because fraud systems are unable to determine whether the transaction is from a legitimate customer or a hacker. Systems-level hacks undermine confidence in the banking system, decreasing comfort among consumers and businesses to grow deposits.

Financial literacy Modest levels of financial literacy make adoption of DFS difficult at times. In interviews with central banks, it was found that they had experienced consumers questioning new offerings because they didn't understand the need for a savings account or a credit facility, indicating that greater investment in financial literacy is needed.

4.4.2 Future Opportunities

DFS offer a powerful tool for inclusion and improved economic velocity. A systems view of DFS should include efforts around the following:

- Greater financial literacy
- More investment in modern technology infrastructure
- Policy interventions to engage and empower the private sector
- Consumer protections informed by a sophisticated view about the effects of different DFS offerings

A characteristic of digital finance has been the rise of nontraditional providers of financial services such as money transfers, savings, and lending. This raises several concerns, as highlighted in the World Bank's World Development Report,[28] which I summarize below.

One concern is that traditional financial regulation does not always cover these companies or that they are held to a different standard, such as reduced oversight, even though they can scale up quickly. These problems are somewhat similar to the "shadow banking problem" that preceded the global financial crisis, and regulators are exploring ways to shift from regulating entities to regulating activities.

A second concern is that digital finance is bringing large numbers of people into the financial system for the first time. This requires strong consumer education, financial literacy, and consumer protection, including promoting financial literacy and fraud prevention, dispute resolution mechanisms, and data privacy.

A third concern is that financial innovations could pose a systemic risk to a country's banking sector, including credit, liquidity, operational, and consumer risk. Prudential regulation of digital finance reduces this risk, but it may involve high compliance costs that raise barriers to entry, and thus to competition.

Risks to the banking system were raised about bitcoin, but analysis by the Bank of England, for instance, suggested that most digital currencies play too small a role (at present) to threaten financial stability.[29] A greater concern may be that financial innovations create distortions in financial markets that could have larger implications. For example, if automation and big data approaches make it much easier to issue consumer credit but not commercial credit, financial institutions might overallocate to the former, potentially creating a credit bubble and reducing credit availability for investments that increase productivity.

However, despite many countries' general dismissiveness toward the systemic risks presented by bitcoin, new questions have been raised with the advent of Libra, a private consortium of companies led by Facebook that is seeking to deploy a multinational digital currency, on the one hand, and the RMB Coin, issued by the People's Bank of China, on the other. In August 2019, outgoing Bank of England governor Mark Carney called for a digital currency that would be backed by a number of countries and that would address US dollar hegemony as well as rising concerns around Libra and RMB Coin.[30]

Finally, there are concerns about increased fraud in the financial system. With the rise of electronic banking, cyberattacks on financial institutions and on other sectors processing electronic financial transactions have increased. Massive theft of credit card information from retailers has highlighted the stakes involved. Larger financial institutions have the resources and know-how to continuously upgrade online and mobile security through tools such as encryption or strong authentication. In fact, banks have been at the forefront of developing secure transaction processes. But smaller and nonfinancial institutions may be more at risk. Apart from monetary losses, a large risk is also a loss of trust in digital financial systems that may hinder further innovation in the sector.

NOTES

This chapter previously appeared in a substantially similar form as part of the Commonwealth, "Commonwealth Fintech Toolkit," September 2020, https://thecommonwealth.org/our-work/commonwealth-fintech-toolkit.

1. McKinsey & Company, *Digital Finance for All: Powering Inclusive Growth in Emerging Economies*, 2016, https://www.mckinsey.com/~/media/McKinsey/Featured%20Insights/Employment%20and%20Growth/How%20digital%20finance%20could%20boost%20growth%20in%20emerging%20economies/MGI-Digital-Finance-For-All-Executive-summary-September-2016.ashx.

2. L. Perlman and M. Wechsler, "Mobile Coverage and Its Impact on Digital Financial Services," *SSRN Electronic Journal*, 2019, https://dfsobservatory.com/sites/default/files/Mobile%20Coverage%20and%20its%20Impact%20on%20Digital%20Financial%20Services%20-%20PUBLIC.pdf.

3. McKinsey & Company, *Digital Finance for All*, 7.

4. Chamber of Digital Commerce, "Blockchain and Financial Inclusion: The Role Blockchain Technology Can Play in Accelerating Financial Inclusion" (working paper, March 2018), https://digitalchamber .org/assets/blockchain-and-financial-inclusion.pdf.

5. ID4D global data set (web page), World Bank, 2018, https://id4d .worldbank.org/global-dataset.

6. International Finance Corporation, *MSME Finance Gap: Assessment of the Shortfalls and Opportunities in Financing Micro, Small and Medium Enterprises in Emerging Markets*, 2017, https://www.ifc.org/wps /wcm/connect/03522e90-a13d-4a02-87cd-9ee9a297b311/121264-WP -PUBLIC-MSMEReportFINAL.pdf?MOD=AJPERES&CVID=m5SwAQA.

7. M. Zachariadis and P. Ozcan, "The API Economy and Digital Transformation in Financial Services: The Case of Open Banking" (SWIFT Institute Working Paper No. 2016-001, 2017), https://papers.ssrn.com /sol3/papers.cfm?abstract_id=2975199.

8. B. Chakravorti, "Why It's So Hard for Users to Control Their Data," *Harvard Business Review*, January 30, 2020.

9. The Commonwealth, "Commonwealth Fintech Toolkit"; T. Hardjono, D. L. Shrier, and A. Pentland, *Trusted Data: A New Framework for Identity and Data Sharing*, rev. and exp. ed. (Cambridge, MA: MIT Press, 2019).

10. The Commonwealth, "Commonwealth Fintech Toolkit."

11. For the GSMA view, see S. di Castri, "Mobile Money: Enabling Regulatory Solutions," SSRN, 2013, https://bit.ly/2kGPgqX.

12. L. Perlman, "An Introduction to Digital Financial Services (DFS)," November 20, 2018, SSRN, https://ssrn.com/abstract=3370667.

13. Perlman, "An Introduction to Digital Financial Services."

14. N. Ndung'u, "Practitioner's Insight—M-Pesa, a Success Story of Digital Financial Inclusion," Global Economic Governance Programme, University of Oxford, July 2017, https://www.geg.ox.ac .uk/publication/practitioners-insight-m-pesa-success-story-digital -financial-inclusion.

15. Accenture and Care International, *Within Reach: How Banks in Emerging Economies Can Grow Profitably by Being More Inclusive*, 2015, https://insights.careinternational.org.uk/media/k2/attachments /Within-Reach_CARE-Accenture-2015.pdf.

16. F. Mdwazika and N. Harihareswara, "Exciting Changes in Malawi DFS Market," *UN Capital Development Fund (UNCDF)* (blog), December 28, 2018, https://www.uncdf.org/article/4270/exciting-changes-in -malawi-dfs-market.

17. World Bank, *World Development Report 2016: Digital Dividends*, 2016, www.worldbank.org/en/publication/wdr2016.

18. "How to Recharge Your Mobile on Paytm," https://paytm.com /offer/recharge/mobile-recharge-process.

19. R. Sharma, "What Is Paytm, and How to Use Paytm Wallet?," Gadgets 360, December 30, 2016, https://gadgets.ndtv.com/apps/features /what-is-paytm-and-how-to-use-paytm-wallet-1625271.

20. H. Partz, "Bahamas Central Bank Enters Agreement to Deliver First National Digital Currency by 2020," Cointelegraph, May 29, 2019, https://cointelegraph.com/news/bahamas-central-bank-enters-agree ment-to-deliver-first-national-digital-currency-by-2020.

21. H. van Steenis, chair, *Future of Finance: Review on the Outlook for the UK Financial System: What It Means for the Bank of England*, June 2019, https://www.bankofengland.co.uk/-/media/boe/files/report/2019 /future-of-finance-report.

22. "Sustainable Development Goal 9: Build Resilient Infrastructure, Promote Inclusive and Sustainable Industrialization and Foster Innovation," United Nations, 2015, https://sustainabledevelopment.un.org /sdg9.

23. M. Minges, "Exploring the Relationship between Broadband and Economic Growth" (English), World Development Report background papers (Washington, DC: World Bank Group, 2016), https:// documents.worldbank.org/en/publication/documents-reports /documentdetail/178701467988875888/exploring-the-relationship -between-broadband-and-economic-growth.

24. Broadband Commission for Sustainable Development, *The State of Broadband: Broadband Catalyzing Sustainable Development*, September 2017, https://www.itu.int/dms_pub/itu-s/opb/pol/S-POL-BROAD BAND.18-2017-PDF-E.pdf.

25. "Global Internet Growth Stalls and Focus Shifts to 'Meaningful Universal Connectivity' to Drive Global Development," International Telecommunications Union, September 22, 2019, https://www.itu.int /en/mediacentre/Pages/2019-PR16.aspx.

26. GSMA Connected Women, *The Mobile Gender Gap Report 2019*, 2019, https://www.gsma.com/mobilefordevelopment/wp-content/up loads/2019/02/GSMA-The-Mobile-Gender-Gap-Report-2019.pdf.

27. GSMA Intelligence, *The Mobile Economy: Sub-Saharan Africa 2019*, 2019, https://www.gsmaintelligence.com/research/?file=36b5ca07919 3fa82332d09063d3595b5&download.

28. World Bank, "Enabling Digital Development: Digital Finance," in *World Development Report*, 2016, http://documents.worldbank.org /curated/en/896971468194972881/310436360_20160263021313/ad ditional/102725-PUB-Replacement-PUBLIC.pdf.

29. The Canadian Press, "Bank of England's Mark Carney Says Cryptocurrencies Aren't Financial State Risk, but Likely to Be Regulated," *Toronto Star*, April 12, 2018, https://www.thestar.com/business/2018 /04/12/bank-of-englands-mark-carney-says-cryptocurrencies-arent -financial-state-risk-but-likely-to-be-regulated.html.

30. P. Inman, "Mark Carney: Dollar Is Too Dominant and Could Be Replaced by Digital Currency," *The Guardian*, August 23, 2019, https:// www.theguardian.com/business/2019/aug/23/mark-carney-dollar -dominant-replaced-digital-currency.

5 POLICY AND FINTECH, PART I: FRAMEWORKS

Oliver R. Goodenough, Mark Flood,
Matthew Reed, David L. Shrier,
Thomas Hardjono, and
Alex Pentland

5.1 INTRODUCTION: FINANCIAL INNOVATION AND REGULATORY CONCERNS

Technology has driven innovative changes in many areas of human activity over the past half century, and the financial industry has been no exception. Advances such as the SWIFT system, electronic trading systems, and automated settlement were revolutionary a generation or two ago; now they are business as usual. Aside from the movement toward arm's-length trading fueled by advances in derivatives and securitization, however, the overall structure of the financial system hasn't changed that dramatically. In this way, finance is following a pattern of development common in many industries.

We are moving from a model of technology that empowers human players within the current system to one that replaces many of the human players within the current system, to (inevitably) one where technology overturns much of the current system and replaces it with something else.[1] Much of the innovation already digested in the financial system falls into the first two categories. As the chapters in this book suggest, we are facing developments in finance that begin to look like the third category: something with new and not fully anticipatable outcomes. A series of developments such as blockchain, mobile money, smart instruments, big data, predictive markets, and secure identity are part of the possible revolution.

Among the many uncertainties raised by this vision of disruptive change, regulatory concerns have a significant role. As anyone active in the field knows, the financial system operates within a highly developed set of government rules that can be thought of as the *regulatory framework*. Rules apply to the markets and the transactions within them, to the institutions and to their governance, operations, and net worth, to the nature of currencies, and to the use of data. The list goes on and on. Trying to anticipate the shape of regulatory response, whether prohibitive or enabling, is a key factor in trying to formulate strategies for playing in the world that is dawning.

Against this background, we will explore some of the fundamental policy, regulatory, and governance issues confronting blockchain and related innovations in finance.[2] For the purposes of this chapter, we use the term "regulation" and its variations to encompass a broad range of legal rules, including those made by statute and court decisions as well as those made by regulatory agencies.[3]

Although a full discussion of the implications of fintech is beyond the scope of this chapter, some basic definitions will help orient the discussion. We define *fintech* as any new data- or computation-intensive process or activity that delivers a financial service. Necessity is the mother of invention. Fintech is necessary, because finance, like so many other fields, is confronting a big data revolution, in which the rapidly growing scale of data and information resources overwhelms existing processes.[4] Banny Banerjee argues that one can't fix exponential problems with linear solutions.[5] Fintech is the set of nonlinear new technologies emerging to address the exponential big data challenges. Blockchain and cryptocurrencies are emblematic and high-profile cases, but they do not define the scope of fintech. They merely represent a popular recent use case that has attracted a great deal of attention from private-sector as well as public-sector actors.

We argue that fintech, like any sociotechnical system, will require formal governance mechanisms—including laws and regulations—to achieve its full potential. The details of these mechanisms should vary, depending on the specific use case under consideration. For example, a digital currency for retail-scale payments will have different needs than a registration system for land titles. This is especially so where currency, unlike land, must travel across jurisdictional borders.

We suggest that regulation has an important, even helpful, role to play in fostering the adoption of fintech.

It is easy to see, for instance, how laws requiring everyone to drive on the same side of the road can speed travel and improve road safety, how standardized weights and measures can facilitate gains in specialization in manufacturing, or how regulations forbidding Ponzi schemes can reduce overall borrowing costs by attracting investors to the market. In contrast to these established examples of productive intervention to solve coordination problems and market failures, fintech is still in its early days. Predicting where its pain points will be most severe or where its successes will be most transformative is necessarily a speculative enterprise.

Regulators and policy makers have increasingly become aware of the need for more sophisticated efforts and greater focus in the area of fintech. Interviews with Commonwealth governments conducted in 2019 by innovation consultancy Visionary Future[6] revealed an array of approaches and levels of sophistication. Twenty governments (primarily their central banks) out of the forty-six Commonwealth central banks were investigated across a range of geographies, country size, and scale of economic development (ranging from the United Kingdom to Trinidad and Tobago). The interviews revealed the following:

- Sixty-five percent of those interviewed had engaged in formal policy development, specifically regarding fintech policy.
- Fifty-nine percent had a fintech policy specialist.
- Only 29 percent had engaged in any form of specialized capacity building regarding fintech.

This clear discrepancy between practice and preparation highlights the importance of documenting effective interventions regarding fintech policy that benefit from appropriate context. The governors of the Commonwealth Central Banks determined that the need for improved practice and expertise was so important that they specifically tasked the Commonwealth Secretariat with developing a policy toolkit and dissemination vehicle.[7]

The discussion that follows is intentionally illustrative rather than exhaustive. We want to show the diversity of challenges that arise in engineering technologically based innovations in our financial system, as well as provide a frame of reference for thinking about those examples. The catalog of possibilities is meant as a starting point. We hope to inspire critical thinking about the issues and approaches to developing fintech, and to encourage stakeholders (government officials, entrepreneurs, ethicists, community activists, developers, and others) to pursue a reasoned approach to regulation.

5.2 REGULATORY GOALS AND TECHNIQUES

5.2.1 Why Do We Regulate?

This section focuses first on why and how regulation happens, highlighting some key guiding principles. It then explores some of the players in the existing regulatory structure governing the financial system. In later sections we apply these principles to blockchain and other fintech innovations. The topic of regulatory design is not a settled one; there are significant arguments and disagreements over where, what, and how regulatory approaches should be applied.[8] That said, there are also some generally recognized guidelines that cut across the debates.[9]

Maximizing the benefits and minimizing the detriments of fintech is not simply a matter of technology. As the economist Paul Romer notes, "Economic growth is driven by the coevolution of two sets of ideas, technologies and rules. Governments can increase the rate of growth—in ways that benefit all citizens—by creating systems of rules that are both encouraging of and response to innovation; the various goals do not always line up."[10]

To the economist's goal of efficiency we should properly add the lawyer's additional criteria of fairness, justice, predictability, and sustainability.

5.2.2 Jurisdiction

There is a diversity of possible sources of authority in the *making* of rules and also in *applying* them to a particular activity. Who gets to do what is often framed as a question of jurisdiction. What is criminal in one country may be perfectly acceptable in another. Some countries exert *extraterritorial jurisdiction* for some activities, such as the criminal treatment of genocide, but this is relatively rare. More commonly, a country sufficiently concerned about the *effects* of an activity within its borders will assert jurisdiction even if the primary event takes place outside the country. Particularly in the financial markets, where money flows across borders and often to the places of highest yield or safest harbor, countries often affirmatively coordinate common standards of conduct to avoid creating arbitrage opportunities or unfair advantage for one jurisdiction over another. For instance, fraudulent offers are commonly outlawed regardless of the country of origin, and capital adequacy is negotiated to avoid arbitrage.

A further wrinkle on jurisdiction is the ability of the authority in question to get physical control over the person, asset, or other item that is the target of the regulation. This is particularly challenging in the case of cyberactivities, where, for instance, the effects may be felt in the United States but all of the players are in another region of the globe, perhaps one that is antagonistic to US interests. A country may attempt to extend its legal reach, perhaps through extradition, blocking web access, or freezing local accounts, but these measures often have only limited effect and depend on the goodwill of the other jurisdiction.

Blockchain-enabled activities present particularly interesting jurisdictional challenges because of their inherently dispersed and virtual character. The decentralized and sometimes anonymous nature of blockchain-based transactions is unlikely to remove them from the power of governmental oversight, notwithstanding certain libertarian claims. The internet has posed similar questions, and governments have responded by asserting authority in many contexts. Enforcement of government authority over a dispersed worldwide activity may be a challenge, but as the travails of Silk Road demonstrated, a determined government can overwhelm someone it views as a serious criminal.[11]

5.2.3 Regulatory Goals

What are the proper goals for regulation? Some are cast in negative terms: to prevent harm, both intentional and accidental, whether direct or incidental. Preventing outright predation is usually easy to justify. Innovation, on the other hand, typically harms incumbent interests, and judging when to let such harm proceed is more difficult to assess. The Luddites of eighteenth- and nineteenth-century Britain are often mocked for their opposition to progress, but the negative *local* implications of innovation for wealth and job security may be quite severe (e.g., when the plant closes in a company town), even if the innovation is raising productivity in the aggregate.

Some goals are more positive: to provide an institutional framework within which an activity can grow productively. In this view, the failure to innovate can be seen as causing more harm than the innovation itself. Such a debate is present regarding cryptocurrencies, digital payment systems, and access to banking for the underbanked. Others, such as whether to raise revenue or to consolidate power over an activity, are in the selfish interest of government itself. These interests can be perfectly legitimate, even when they impose a drag on the activity in question. Less justifiable are examples of *regulatory capture*, where private interests (sometimes intentionally and sometimes unintentionally, such as where information asymmetry produces reliance by the captured) use the power of government to entrench their position in an economic activity. Further complicating the regulatory response to innovation, the various goals do not always line up. Careful regulatory policy often involves balancing competing goods and competing harms so that both the utopian hopes of the innovator and the catastrophic fears of the traditionalist are seldom fully realized. The Clinton-Magaziner e-Commerce Principles shown in box 5.1 provide a case example of a balanced policy intervention that successfully navigated these diverse factors.

Preventing harm   The easiest case for legal intervention involves rules against intentional predation, such as physical attack, theft, fraud, and deceit. For example, Bernie Madoff was very properly jailed for willfully defrauding his investors. The Securities and Exchange Commission (SEC) investigates these kinds of activities in the financial markets under its jurisdiction and has recently moved against some particularly questionable promoters of initial coin offerings (ICOs).

Also objectionable is reckless behavior, where the harm per se is not intentional but where any consideration for the prevention of harm is lacking. The failure of underwriters to scrutinize poorly documented subprime mortgages adequately at the point of origination could fall into this category. A third category is harm arising through accidents or unintended systemic effects. A classic example is the bank run, in which the infectious panic of nervous depositors can force even a healthy bank into default.

To justify regulation, a harm need not be inherent in an activity itself, if it is frequently a means to carry out some other harmful action. For instance, a concern sometimes voiced

Box 5.1
The Clinton/Magaziner e-Commerce Principles

The Clinton/Magaziner e-commerce principles, which helped
provide a foundation for successful commercial development
of internet e-commerce in the United States without sacrificing
the public good, are instructive for considering how to regulate
other fintech innovations.[12] Briefly, the principles seek to

- maximize the possibility of human freedom because the
  medium holds great potential to support individual liberty;
- expressly allow voluntary communities to form;
- encourage, where possible, rules set by private, nonprofit,
  stakeholder-based groups (such as the Internet Engineering
  Task Force or the W3C Consortium);
- encourage government action that occurs sparingly, transparently, in a targeted manner, and via a common agreement that action is needed;
- respect that internet e-commerce is a decentralized, fast-
  moving medium, and foster policies that are neutral to specific technologies;
- be global, and therefore an international framework is
  needed from the outset (rather than the legacy systems
  where markets evolve locally and then governments coordinate with each other as internationalization occurs).

---

over virtual currencies is that they can be used to facilitate
illicit trafficking in drugs, arms, and people. These secondary
effects may cause us to constrain the primary activity.

Providing an institutional framework for private creativity   Commercial law provides institutional scaffolding for the design
and enforcement of *private* bargains. Contract law is a prime
example. At its best, contract law creates a toolkit for designing the enforceable obligations that make specialization and
exchange possible, and opens up possibilities for mutual gain.

By making bargains enforceable in *law*, they become much more reliable, and a number of strategic pitfalls can be avoided. On the other hand, contracting between parties with too much disparity in experience or power has risks for deception and predation as well. A good contract framework will discourage fraud by stipulating requirements for disclosure and boundaries of unconscionability.[13] Thus, an appropriate legal scaffolding will *promote* the activity it regulates by solving trust problems that might otherwise hinder adoption. Government intervention to encourage *confidence* in a process is a buttress, not a burden. A familiar example is the oversight of our stock exchanges, where private rules receive public scrutiny under the Securities Exchange Act of 1934.

Much of the interest in blockchain technologies, for example, is that they may be able to help solve these sorts of trust dilemmas. The technology, however, involves relatively arcane cryptographic techniques that can be hard for nonprofessionals to understand and therefore put their trust in them. Moreover, early experiences with fraud in ICOs indicate that a blockchain is not a panacea.[14] A legal framework that helps create confidence that a particular blockchain is properly governed and administered could foster adoption. Box 5.2 reviews a selection of examples that illustrate jurisdictional competition and variation.

Raising public revenue Governments often seek revenues from economic activity, typically through fees or taxes, such as property assessments, customs duties, stamp taxes, value-added assessments, or estate and income taxation. Although the blockchain has libertarian appeal, all competent governments assert the power of taxation broadly. For fintech innovations like the blockchain to evade taxation, they would have to do so in ways analogous to how all illegal activities avoid taxation. Because finance is so information intensive, it is difficult for tax evaders to cover all their digital tracks. At the

Box 5.2
Enabling Rules and Jurisdictional Competition

Each of the fintech innovations discussed in this book raises questions about the current and future adequacy of the legal and regulatory framework to allow its adoption, support its utility, govern its conduct, and resolve disputes.

Adoption of fintech will benefit from adaptations in the code and regulation to foster its growth. This has led to some competition over adopting useful legal infrastructure, as a number of different jurisdictions have sought to attract business. Early movers in the United States include Arizona, Vermont, and Wyoming.

Vermont jumped in early, with a 2015 law setting up a study commission[15] that, in turn, led to a 2016 statute giving evidentiary recognition to records maintained on a blockchain.[16] Subsequent actions have included commissioning a further report on fintech opportunities[17] and, as a result, enacting an enabling provision for a blockchain-based limited liability company (BBLLC).[18] These provisions are aimed at broad support of blockchain activity.[19]

Wyoming has been prolific. In 2018 it set up a blockchain task force that helped promote the adoption of a number of provisions, aimed to a large degree at supporting cryptocurrency initiatives.[20] While undoubtedly useful, this focus is hampered by the SEC's more restrictive posture. At least one SEC commissioner has sought to use a regulatory "safe harbor" to allow public offerings of cryptocurrencies so that they can get to critical circulation levels without running afoul of existing securities laws.[21]

Arizona was the first US jurisdiction to enact a regulatory sandbox for fintech innovation (sandbox approaches are dealt with more extensively in chapter 8 of this volume).[22] This 2018 initiative is under the authority of Arizona's attorney general.[23] As of early 2020 eight companies were participating in the program.[24]

Other states have been active in the past year and are seeking to catch up with these early adopters.

Two states stand out as not being successful with blockchain. In 2016, Delaware, seeking to preserve its leadership

Box 5.2
(continued)

position as the premier state of incorporation, set up the Delaware Blockchain Initiative. In 2017 it passed legislation permitting the use of blockchain as a means of keeping corporate records, including those relating to corporate shares. It began a joint project with a private vendor, Symbiont, with the goal of moving its own public records to blockchain. This all came to a halt, however, with the election of a new governor, John Carney, who was wary of the disruptions this could cause.[25] The state has proceeded at a cautious pace.

In New York, which should be on the forefront of financial innovation, the initial reaction to blockchain was suspicion and tough regulation. In 2015, the state set up the "BitLicense" regime, which requires cryptocurrency businesses to come under licensing and regulation in order to conduct many kinds of transactions. The core provision, set out in 23 NYCRR 200.3(a), is that "No Person shall, without a license obtained from the superintendent . . . , engage in any Virtual Currency Business Activity." In 23 NYCRR 200.2(q), "Virtual Currency Business Activity" is defined as

the conduct of any one of the following types of activities involving New York or a New York Resident:
receiving Virtual Currency for Transmission or Transmitting Virtual Currency, except where the transaction is undertaken for nonfinancial purposes and does not involve the transfer of more than a nominal amount of Virtual Currency;
storing, holding, or maintaining custody or control of Virtual Currency on behalf of others;
buying and selling Virtual Currency as a customer business; performing Exchange Services as a customer business; or controlling, administering or issuing a Virtual Currency.[26]

Relatively few businesses have sought these licenses, and many have criticized the process as being too restrictive. In December 2019, New York, citing the need to be more open to innovation, proposed amending the approach to provide both greater flexibility and greater guidance for cryptocurrency businesses.[27]

(continued)

Box 5.2
(continued)

There is also competition for innovation at the international level. A number of different jurisdictions have set out to make themselves welcoming to fintech innovation. The United Kingdom, seeking to protect London's powerhouse status as a financial center (notwithstanding the challenges of Brexit), has created a number of opportunities for experimentation, including the most developed fintech sandbox program in the world. First announced in 2015, this initiative of the Financial Conduct Authority is now (2020) in its fifth cohort.[28] Even without this regulatory flexibility, London has been at the center of a fintech boom, with established companies and dozens, if not hundreds, of start-ups working on innovative projects.

Other established financial centers, from Singapore and Switzerland to smaller havens such as Bermuda, Gibraltar, Malta, and the Cayman Islands, have set up initiatives to attract blockchain and other fintech business.

The failure of a financial center jurisdiction to supply the supporting regulatory or legal framework for fintech innovation could encourage the migration of blockchain-based services away from the traditional financial sector and the purview of existing supervisors. There is a long history of jurisdiction shopping by ambitious entrepreneurs, often matched by a "competition in laxity" among eager regulators.[29] The challenge is to prevent support for innovation from devolving into thoughtless permissiveness. Despite the challenge from eager start-ups, however, as yet there has been only limited uptake in friendly jurisdictions that do not already have a thriving financial sector (such as Singapore and the United Kingdom). That said, island nations such as Barbados and Mauritius; US states such as Vermont, Arizona, and Wyoming; and, more recently, the Commonwealth of Nations[30] as an organization have begun developing frameworks to support fintech innovation.

Facebook's Libra is a prime example of this: its creators have argued that the failure of the public sector to provide for a

Box 5.2

(continued)

> cross-jurisdictional payment system motivated the entry of this
> nonfinancial company into the financial sector. This argument
> is partly self-serving. Cryptocurrencies offer a new avenue for
> competition in the market for payments services, but incum-
> bent service providers indeed exist for both retail and whole-
> sale cross-border payments. Meanwhile, a payments platform
> would allow Facebook to integrate purchase and cash-transfer
> data with its already extensive information on its users.

same time, an open digital ledger facilitates the migration of
financial activities, including payments and messages, across
borders; in the process, the ledger also potentially exposes the
ledger to many legal jurisdictions.

In the United States, the IRS has provided guidance on how
to tax cryptocurrency transactions.[31] The basic starting point
is that "virtual currency transactions are taxable by law just
like transactions in any other property. Taxpayers transacting
in virtual currency may have to report those transactions on
their tax returns." If you fall under US income tax jurisdiction,
there is no legal insulation, because the cryptocurrency asset
is virtual.

That said, novel questions may arise when applying the
general principles of US taxation to the specifics of cryptocurrency transactions. For instance, in the 2019 Revenue Ruling,
the IRS gave guidance on the tax treatment of a "hard fork."
It determined that a hard fork in itself did not create a taxable
event for a crypto holder, but if the fork was accompanied by
an "airdrop" of new tokens, a taxable event would occur.[32]

Protecting existing interests   Governments often use their power
to protect the economic status quo. This is not always bad;
supporting principal providers of goods and services can

benefit both the enterprises and their consumers. In some cases, incumbent providers may be entrenched by the economics of the situation. For example, bitcoin miners appear to be natural monopolies (or at least oligopolies), given that they have converged on a handful of large mining concerns. This is likely due to the large fixed costs of capitalizing the power plant for a mining operation. Similarly, a particular digital currency (e.g., bitcoin versus bitgold) might become a natural monopoly through network externalities. A common public policy response to limit monopoly-power rent seeking is to institutionalize the monopoly as a public utility with democratic governance, like a local water and sewer commission. Some argue that public utility treatment can stifle the emergence of competition that would ameliorate a monopoly situation. Not coincidentally, the bitcoin mine starts to look like a central bank; indeed, central banks, which have extensive experience as governance mechanisms for monetary stability, have taken an active interest in digital currencies.[33]

At the same time, solidification of the status quo can suppress innovation by entrenching both incumbent providers and existing processes. Such suppression can be a by-product of otherwise well-intentioned regulation. Regulators and their charges coevolve over time, and so the incumbent institutions on one side are typically well adapted to the incumbents on the other. Bank examiners know what to expect from well-run banks, and vice versa. The political reality of crisis avoidance is also a powerful force, particularly involving nascent technologies with unclear consequences.

Enshrining one set of interests or market participants over another can have both positive and negative effects. For example, if ex ante rules designed to ensure proper governance, infrastructure, and resilience have the effect of designating (de jure or de facto) a limited, trusted set of miners or other key participants in a distributed ledger structure, confidence in the system and its resilience and potential resolution may increase. But this same motivation could create a set of unintended consequences such as giving the keys to the system to one set of market participants over another. The result could lead to an undermining of confidence in the system by the very rules designed to bolster that confidence. In any case, policy makers will want to watch how the system evolves with an eye toward facilitating the development of a stable system.

Considerations related to enshrining the interests of one group over another may be necessary for adoption of digital ledger technologies in the financial system, particularly where legal structures have been designed with extant financial intermediaries in mind. For example, derivatives markets are presently subject to a relatively new and comprehensive regime to steer transactions to organized exchanges and central clearing at registered clearinghouses. Centralized markets, such as the Australian Securities Exchange, are already implementing blockchain-based clearing-and-settlement systems to replace legacy infrastructure in their clearinghouses, and entrepreneurs are exploring similar possibilities for over-the-counter markets. If a blockchain technology for clearing and settlement to permit bilateral exchange without the need for centralized trading, clearing, and settlement is widely adopted, changes in law, regulation, and regulatory practice could be required. To avoid regulatory arbitrage, supervisors will need to coordinate, as they have regarding capital requirements for banks or conduct rules for other market participants. Authorities will need to consider how these activities should be governed so that oversight can continue for the protection of the system.

Mitigating wider and secondary effects   Regulation should consider both immediate goals and the potential larger effects of an activity. Legal intervention can promote or hinder specific actions, but it can also seek to create systemic effects including efficiency and distributional fairness.

Good rules typically have the goal of helping the users and providers internalize the costs and benefits of an activity. Good rules also try to avoid unnecessary burden, such as onerous reporting requirements. At the federal level, this principle has been codified in a series of executive orders and OMB Circular A-4 (Office of Management and Budget 2003), which direct the following: "Important goals of regulatory analysis are (1) to establish whether federal regulation is necessary and justified to achieve a social goal and (2) to clarify how to design regulations in the most efficient, least burdensome, and most cost-effective manner."[34]

These principles argue for regulatory restraint. Bitcoin began with the conceit of mimicking a traditional gold standard, which effectively puts its monetary policy on autopilot. Libra's proposal to link to a basket of currencies is reminiscent of the International Monetary Fund's Special Drawing Rights. But cryptocurrencies are gradually learning many of the hard lessons of traditional central banking—for example, that monetary and financial stability are public goods, that both inflation and deflation are important hazards, and that a robust governance framework is critical to a successful monetary system. It is difficult to predict how these forces will evolve, but there is great value in permitting the innovators to experiment, especially at these early stages when the stakes are relatively small.

Rules must also be *socially acceptable*; they must "fit" with cultural norms and conditions. In the United States, traditions of personal autonomy and contractual freedom may make some kinds of otherwise plausible regulatory intervention unacceptable. Indeed, the US income tax system is, in many instances, based on self-reporting, not direct government monitoring of transactions and activities that reflect taxable gains. Thus, for example, even if a blockchain technology could capture income tax revenues through payment systems, it's not clear that society would accept such an intrusion. Likewise, an otherwise efficiency-enhancing rule may be unacceptable because it violates conceptions of "fairness." A related concept is *cognitive acceptability*. The counterintuitive nature of many economic arguments, such as free trade, monetary expansion, and public expenditure in recessions, makes them hard sells to a public not made up of experts. Given their complicated mathematical and technological basis, blockchain technologies, for example, may suffer similar challenges of understanding.

Another important dimension of innovation is *generativity*, meaning the self-referential modularity that allows some systems to support additional outcomes not envisioned when the system was created. A familiar example of this property is LEGO blocks, which allow the generation, through creative assembly, of a nearly limitless set of shapes. A purpose-built scale-model airplane may be more realistic than the LEGO version, but it cannot be readily converted to anything else. In the domain of rules, the generative nature of the open architecture of the internet is part of its success; no one foresaw Facebook or Uber at the start.[35]

Blockchain technology, developed initially for bitcoin, may also be a generative system, insofar as it enables transformation of existing financial systems in ways not necessarily foreseen. Generativity is also a desirable property for the regulation of innovative technologies—rules should be open to beneficial surprises. That said, there are risks in a generative system. Unanticipated consequences are not always benign, and an open system can be more susceptible to predatory capture. The precautionary principle, which limits the new if there is significant uncertainty around possible harm, would discourage generativity, with its possibility of unintended consequences.[36]

What are the government's concerns for financial regulation? In the case of blockchain, in addition to the general goals to prevent harm and to provide frameworks for growth, there are also concerns for systemic stability. Although one or more government bodies (sometimes federal, sometimes state, sometimes both) generally exist to supervise or regulate

each of these areas, no one body supervises the entire system. Two creations from the 2008 financial crisis—the Office
of Financial Research (OFR) and the Financial Stability Oversight Council—do have this system-wide view. Central banks
also often take a systemic view—whether authorized by their
laws or as an outgrowth of monetary policy responsibilities
(the US Federal Reserve has recently started issuing financial
stability reports to the public)—and are members, along with
several market regulators and coordination bodies (including
the US SEC), of the Financial Stability Board in Basel, Switzerland. Through this institutional patchwork, regulators, market
watchers, and global coordination bodies have started to focus
on the systemic impacts of blockchain-enabled technologies.

The various currently conceived implementations of blockchain in the financial system touch on the basic services noted
above (albeit some more than others). In some cases, the
migration to blockchain would disrupt little in the financial
system and its regulatory framework as currently organized.
For example, blockchain as a settlement solution could simply
replace current centralized digital ledgers while still residing
under the control of a central repository. A number of financial-sector companies have experimented with projects of this
kind, but so far most have not resulted in widely adopted services. For instance, Nasdaq joined with other industry partners
and piloted a successful margin call system.[37] While there was
significant coverage of the pilot, no similar notice has been
given of any rollout—at this writing, it appears not to have
occurred. A number of these initiatives have involved the firm
R3.[38] R3 started out in 2014 as a consortium of large financial
institutions seeking to explore blockchain-based applications
and has grown into a service provider whose Corda software
and platform are powering initiatives for customers across a
number of verticals in the financial industry.[39]

On the other hand, blockchain might deeply disrupt other
parts of the system, disintermediating existing participants

(perhaps including key players) and raising questions about how crucial monitoring, risk management, and resolution activities might transpire in the context of stress episodes. Steps in this direction are already being taken in insurance contracting and regulation.

In a report issued since the first publication of this chapter, the Financial Stability Board noted, among other things, that fintech can improve financial stability by increasing transparency and through distributed networks dispersing concentration, but it can also accelerate contagion effects and herding, and move risks outside the regulatory perimeter, where the toolkit for dealing with these risks does not exist or has never been applied.[40]

Concerns about distributed ledgers to support cryptocurrencies have become acute in recent months. In the case of Facebook's Libra, the stablecoin would be backed by a basket of fiat currencies—which theoretically limits the possibility of a monetary policy run amok. But monetary policy is notoriously multifaceted and susceptible to unforeseen consequences, and would be even more difficult if it required coordinated national monetary policy efforts to stabilize a coin linked to multiple currencies. Libra's launch raised concerns from all branches of the US government and leaders of both political parties. Fed governor Lael Brainard laid out concerns for Libra that mirrored many of the Financial Stability Board's generalized concerns for fintech: "Liquidity, credit, market or operational risks—alone or in combination—could trigger a loss of confidence and a classic run. . . . The potential for risks and spillovers could be amplified by potential ambiguity surrounding the ability of official authorities to provide oversight and backstop liquidity and to collaborate across borders."[41]

One issue attracting central bankers' attention is nonfinancial "big tech" companies entering into the highly regulated financial world. This is sometimes referred to as "TechFin" because the primary driver isn't the finance piece but the use of finance to exploit the benefits of the technology piece, like further understanding of customer preferences based on financial transactions or interaction within and with financial markets. While protection of entrenched interests may seem an easy explanation, oversight of banks, brokers, advisers, and other financial intermediaries has fostered transparency and trust and allowed for guardrails that can help contain risks. Recognizing these concerns, Facebook's CEO testified to the US Congress that any Libra system would need regulatory approval or risk abandonment by Facebook itself.[42]

In banking, perhaps more than any other industry, trust is foundational. Deposit insurance, for example, increases that trust. But the government's ability to intervene during a crisis could be challenged if a distributed network doesn't create entry points for the government to intervene in a crisis or simply to adjust monetary policy. Careful system design and governance will be needed. Governments need to intervene in favor of financial stability, to manage risk. The Federal Reserve is monitoring and recalibrating in real time.

5.2.4 Means of Regulating: The Regulatory Toolkit

Traditional systems of regulation and governance often use a relatively well explored "toolkit" of intervention and constraint. These systems can be broadly grouped as those that apply in advance of the activity (ex ante constraints) and those that are applied after the fact (ex post). As fintech innovations such as blockchain or artificial intelligence increasingly underlie a significant portion of our financial transactions, a similarly comprehensive approach can be expected to emerge to govern market players and individual contracts.

The most extreme ex ante intervention is prescription: an outright ban on a particular activity that can be linked to a civil or criminal penalty to give it teeth. This ban can be either a general one or a targeted injunction applied in a particular set of circumstances. Less stringent ex ante approaches include regulation, qualification, and oversight, often linked to re-quired "best practices." These ex ante governance approaches can especially discourage generative innovation, because they typically set an intentionally constrained framework of pos-sible actions and techniques, with little room for maneuver or discovery.[43] This may be appropriate in high-risk or high-consequence circumstances. Ex ante constraints on behavior also carry strong protections for incumbents, whose processes are typically well adapted to the rules—indeed, incumbents and the rule sets governing them will often coevolve to a comfortable equilibrium. However, if fintech innovations are indeed symptomatic of disrupted traditional processes, we should expect fintech to threaten precisely at points in the system where the entrenched equilibrium is suboptimal.

A softer and more flexible form of ex ante regulation involves ensuring that minimal quality or conduct standards are satisfied either by the individual actor (e.g., TSA prescreening) or by the system (a self-regulatory organization with approved conduct rules, such as a sports league). Registration and licensing can have a beneficial chilling effect on misbehavior by providing a mechanism for excluding players from a profitable game. Reg-istration systems can be designed to retain flexibility of practice but are often linked with established approaches. Membership can require respect for the norms of the club. On the other hand, such systems can act to certify the registrants' reputabil-ity to otherwise skeptical users—an example of regulation help-ing to promote an activity. For example, the National Futures Association, a delegated self-regulatory organization, main-tains a registration system to certify firms and individuals for participation. In this case, the industry itself has adopted an ex ante registration mechanism.

Ex post approaches can be more supportive of innovation because they allow activities to proceed, only imposing pen-alties if the *outcome* is bad. Ex post penalties can be located in the criminal law, often linked to outcomes and not to the activity itself. Anonymous digital payments are not illegal; anonymous digital payments to support a money laundering syndicate may well be. Similarly, noncriminal consequences can be levied. Whether publicly or privately instigated, these civil penalties can include damages and/or suspension of the activity, either through the removal of a license, through an injunction, or through some other proceeding.

Regulatory regimes often mix and match these ingredients. The SEC requires registration of issuers, exchanges, and broker dealers. There is licensing, and the possibility of delicensing. There are general prohibitions against fraud, with ex post public and private civil remedies and possible criminal penalties. There are specific requirements for disclosure and reporting, and specific practices approved under safe-harbor rules.

Recently, there have been multinational efforts to develop and disseminate best practices in the form of policy toolkits, particularly for banking and finance regulators. Organizations such as the Commonwealth of Nations and the Asian Development Bank (ADB) have explored how the loose coordination of regulatory policy, whether on the axis of shared legal heritage (Commonwealth) or shared regional concerns (ADB), can lead to a more robust environment for business innovation and expansion, on the one hand, and better protection of consumers and more stable financial systems, on the other.

5.2.5 Internal Regulation through the Technology Itself: Code as Law

Regulating an activity that is essentially technological, such as fintech, has the intriguing possibility of building at least some of the desirable practices of that activity into the technology itself. As Lawrence Lessig famously argued regarding the internet, the architecture of a technological system makes rules about what it can and cannot do.[44] In a very real sense, code is law for such purposes.

One reason that a blockchain application like bitcoin or Ethereum has been able to operate with limited legal intervention is that its technical architecture makes it resistant to a wide range of attacks. At the same time, a blockchain can be a component in a larger system with fraudulent or criminal possibilities. There is room for an outside authority to confirm that the architecture does what it purports to do, or to add a layer of societal punishment for those who would try to abuse the service, and perhaps to protect the stability of the system by insisting on mechanisms that produce resilience and confidence. The hacking of the Ethereum system, discussed in chapter 6, illuminates these concerns.

This property of internal regulation creates both a challenge and an opportunity for regulators: Can they participate in the creation of a system to embed good law into the source code itself? Will the designers welcome the presence of regulators? Under what circumstances would the regulators thus expose themselves to liability for any bugs that arise? Would this sort of complicity defeat their effectiveness as enforcers of the rules? There is precedent for such cooperation, but there is also precedent for a more antagonistic relationship that could make such involvement difficult.

There can also be systemic effects of a particular architecture that warrant society's intervention. Individuals acting optimally in their parochial self-interest can cumulatively create misbehaviors that emerge only at the system level, such as bank runs, pricing bubbles, or concentrated risk exposures. Even a blockchain, for example, is not naturally immune to such emergent systemic pathologies.

The exchanges and wallet providers are another point of vulnerability. The chain may be secure, but the points of entry and exit can be corrupted. For instance, in 2013, early in the history of cryptocurrency, bitcoin's Mt. Gox lost over $400 million of bitcoin to hackers, at a time when Mt. Gox controlled 70 percent of bitcoin trading. In recent years additional theft at these points has occurred. The Selfkey service (admittedly interested) provides a record of hacks. It reports that "$292,665,886 worth of cryptocurrency and 510,000 user logins were stolen from crypto exchanges in 2019."[45] These actors may also rely on outside forces that could (intentionally or not) corrupt their ideals or render them unreliable, such as the exertion of territorial jurisdiction when something of theirs flows through the jurisdiction (e.g., Europe's privacy law, the General Data Protection Regulation) or relies on them (west China's currently cheap source of energy for miners' processors).

Despite the distributed nature of the bitcoin blockchain, market conditions engendered an unhealthy centralization of resources, and bad actors can exploit such weaknesses.

5.2.6 Who Regulates: Federalism, Lawmaking, and Regulatory Agencies

It is worth reviewing where rules originate and how they are enforced. Statutes, enacted by the legislature, are the starting point for most governmentally established regulatory regimes. The United States has a common-law legal system, which means that the legislature shares lawmaking power with courts, which interpret the law to adjudicate specific disputes. This power helps adapt existing legal principles to new circumstances. Thus, even if a statute does not specifically mention a particular fintech application, courts can nonetheless construe existing legal rules to apply to the innovative activity. The backbone of law serves as the authority for flexible and specific rules, either those created by governments or those created by private actors themselves. For instance, the early stock exchanges formed before the regulatory agencies that currently oversee them even existed.

Many regulatory regimes, including most of those related to finance, are assigned for oversight to a regulatory body, such as the SEC or the Federal Reserve. The legislature typically delegates power to these bodies, allowing them to elaborate specific rules to implement the more general mandates defined in the statutes. This rule-making process is another means for adapting existing governance regimes to fintech applications. Regulators are also frequently the implementation agents for registrations, licensing, inspections, certifications, and other oversight activity, both ex ante and ex post. When civil or criminal laws have been broken, the Justice Department may also help with enforcement.

In the United States the jurisdictions of states and territories also have lawmaking power. Much of the underlying contract and commercial law relevant to fintech is state law. For example, important initiatives at this level include the blockchain enabling law recently adopted in Wyoming and Vermont, and Delaware has launched a blockchain initiative that aims to develop a similarly innovation-friendly legal environment.[46] Where law gets made and enforced is an important element of its possible effects on fintech applications.

5.3   LAWS OF GENERAL APPLICABILITY; CONTRACTS AND INSTRUMENTS

Against this background, we can now examine how law and regulation may apply to future developments in our financial system. Particular fintech innovations will have domain-specific areas of interaction with regulation. They will also often interact with widely shared principles of legal specification.

In this section, we first consider some of the wider principles with the potential for broad application, with particular attention to those affecting financial instruments and contracts. In later sections we will consider more specific use cases of trading markets, identity, and systemic monitoring. Although fintech is applicable to a number of important areas within financial services, these selected examples should help the reader extrapolate to broader principles of the interaction between regulation and financial technology—particularly in the context of the "why and how" of regulation, discussed above. We reiterate the caution: reading the future is inherently speculative. Some of what we suggest will come to pass; other aspects will not. Our analysis is only a starting point, not a confident road map.

5.3.1 Enabling Legislation I: Existing Provisions

Many financial transactions are constructed around contracts and instruments. These are both creatures of legal recognition, and there are well-developed bodies of law to deal with paper-based examples. In the United States, much of the basic framework on these questions comes from state law. Contracts, property, corporations, and negotiable instruments all depend on laws of states such as New York, California, Massachusetts, or Delaware for their creation as enforceable rules. Financial markets also have a critical overlay of federal rulemaking, such as the US securities, currency, and banking laws and regulations.

In the case of blockchain, its trust-creating nature can substitute for *some* of what law has traditionally done, but we believe that law and regulation will continue to play an important role for blockchain applications. This section will consider examples of legal intervention that will enable blockchain activity by codifying its legal effect. Legal regulation will also aim to accomplish the traditional and linked goals of harm prevention and trust building; this section will examine these as well. In both cases, it will look at existing law and its possible application, along with changes that can be anticipated to deal with concerns specific to a blockchain and its operations.

One question is the degree to which these existing rules may apply to versions created, stored, or even executed via blockchain-enabled digital interaction. A critical existing law is the Uniform Electronic Transactions Act (UETA), promulgated by the Uniform Law Commission.[47] This 1999 draft law has been adopted, sometimes with some local variation, by most states; notable holdouts include New York and Illinois. UETA provides recognition for transactions recorded and "signed" in digital form, moving beyond paper to authorize digital originals. UETA's prefatory note explains its goals and purpose:

> It is important to understand that the purpose of the UETA is to remove barriers to electronic commerce by validating and effectuating electronic records and signatures. It is NOT a general contracting statute—the substantive rules of contracts remain unaffected by UETA. Nor is it a digital signature statute. To the extent that a State has a Digital Signature Law, the UETA is designed to support and complement that statute.

While not explicitly aimed at the fintech applications considered here, UETA's scope would cover much of the world of contracts and instruments to be recorded or executed through a blockchain system, including the execution scripts often called "smart contracts." UETA would not necessarily apply to the recording of one-party declarations that lack all the characteristics of a transaction.

In the world of corporations and other business enterprises, some states specifically authorize the bylaws and shares of a corporation, or the operating agreement of a limited liability company, to be expressed in digital originals. For instance, § 2.06 (b) of the Vermont Business Corporations Act provides that the bylaws "may be stored or depicted in any tangible or electronic medium."[48] Vermont and Wyoming are actively updating their laws to enable blockchain activity. More recently, Vermont adopted a subcategory of the limited liability company, the BBLLC, which explicitly addresses issues related to giving a legal framework to blockchain activities. The BBLLC has been used to create the first legally recognized decentralized autonomous organization (DAO) in the United States. Vermont has also enacted a statute to give explicit evidentiary recognition to blockchain recording.

5.3.2 Enabling Legislation II: Provisions That Could Be Added

Enabling provisions, such as those described in the preceding section, may usefully apply to contracts and instruments relying on a blockchain platform, but most such provisions emerged outside of a fintech context. Targeted (fintech-specific) laws are likely to prove useful in unleashing the full potential of fintech for economic commerce and finance. There is widespread use of "tokens" as objects of blockchain commerce. A token can be a strictly *on-chain asset*, like a bitcoin, taking its existence and value entirely as a matter of the operation of the distributed ledger in which it is specified. A token can also be a representation of an *off-chain asset*, such as a parcel of land. This idea is not strictly a new one. For many years, parcels of land have been represented by *deeds*, effectively paper-based tokens. Significant operational problems have emerged in these paper-based title registration systems, but blockchain-based replacements have not been problem-free either.[49] Shares of stock, checks, and the bills of lading used in international trade are other examples of this kind of legacy "tokenization." There are well-developed laws governing paper tokens, but most of them interact with their physical, documentary nature and will fit badly with their digitized descendants.

For instance, the Uniform Commercial Code (UCC) is a widely adopted state-law approach to recognizing and structuring a variety of commercial practices for these legacy tokens, including their use as negotiable instruments. "Negotiability" is the property of an instrument, such as a check or note, intended to be passed from one owner to the next by a process of assignment. Traditionally, this required that the obligation be owed initially to "the order" of a particular person or company. That person, in turn, can make the instrument payable or due to a new holder by endorsement (typically through signature) and a direction that the instrument is now payable to the order of that new holder. The magic words "to the order of" create this progressive negotiability, until an eventual holder cashes the check, demands payment under the note, or otherwise calls in the underlying bargain contained in the instrument.

A blockchain might manage much of this mechanism of successive token ownership. For instance, ownership transfer of a token representing virtual or actual currency on a blockchain could do much of what a check accomplishes, without needing to involve a bank. Here the blockchain substitutes a somewhat different process for classic negotiation. To get better legal recognition and to avoid a mismatch with existing law, the digital ledger practices would benefit from a specific set of rules in the UCC, either as an amendment to the existing provisions on negotiation or, perhaps more fruitfully, as a new article under the UCC itself.

Smart-contract-based escrow arrangements through a blockchain could also benefit from specific recognition. If you layer a digital triggering mechanism of some kind onto a blockchain currency transfer, you have created something that looks a lot like a traditional escrow agreement. As with negotiation, however, full implementation cries out for a set of rules tailored to the blockchain, and not just borrowed from other contexts with resulting gaps and compromises.

As these examples demonstrate, capturing the potential of blockchain as a vehicle for expressing and executing contracts and instruments will benefit from drafting and enacting well-thought-out enabling provisions. Rather than standing away from traditional law, blockchain proponents should seek to collaborate with law-drafting bodies to develop intelligent solutions that could be enacted broadly in the United States and beyond.

5.3.3   Harm Prevention and Trust Building I: Applications of Current Law

Again, the tasks of building trust in an application and of preventing harm in its use, whether through predation or carelessness, often go hand in hand. The workings of financial markets can be opaque, even to relative experts. Blockchain technology can compound the challenges of opacity. Both trust building and harm prevention can be seen as *credence goods*, which require that users believe in the honesty of providers, without the capacity to monitor them competently.[50] The intervention of a respected regulatory structure can often enhance, rather than impede, markets in credence goods. Much of the regulation of the issuance and trading of financial contracts and instruments targets this domain of harm prevention and trust enhancement. Large portions of this existing regulatory regime should apply to fintech innovations for these purposes.

Fraud—active predation through the use of misleading facts or the suppression of relevant information—is a classic target for preventive regulation in financial markets. The antifraud provisions of the US securities laws are numerous and have wide application. Some are ex ante requirements for filings, disclosures, and approvals for the initial offering and subsequent trading of covered securities. Some are classic ex post punishments for fraudulent activity in the sale or purchase of a security.

The entry-level question is whether the object being traded is a security. This term covers a wide range of financial contracts and instruments, and it can include both blockchain-based and paper-based versions. The *Howey* test usually determines whether something is a security by asking whether "a person invests his money in a common enterprise and is led to expect profits solely from the efforts of the promoter or a third party."[51] In 2017 the SEC released *Report of Investigation Pursuant to Section 21(a) of the Securities Exchange Act of 1934: The DAO* (Exchange Act Rel. No. 81207, July 25, 2017). This report warns that cryptocurrency activities could trigger application of the US securities laws, but it also finds, given the facts and circumstances of this particular case, that the SEC would not bring charges in the case of the DAO and its sale and exchange of DAO tokens. When a cryptocurrency is being organized and marketed by specific promoters and purchased by investors with the expectation of gain from the promoters' efforts, as in the case of many ICOs, the currency is likely to be a security. Once the currency becomes an independent system operating without central control or promotion, it can stop having the characteristics of a security and fall outside the SEC's jurisdiction. An offering might also be exempt if the coins constitute "utility tokens," representing a redeemable right of some kind, like a prepaid drink ticket at a charity event.

In 2017 and 2018 there was a boom in selling new cryptocurrency tokens. According to Cointelegraph (using data supplied by ICObench), 2017 saw 966 ICOs, and in 2018 this number jumped to 2,284.[52] Only a handful of these have attempted compliance with the normal SEC-mandated processes of registration, whether on a full-blown S-1 or via Regulation A. Most either (1) sought out some exemption, such as the broad opening for sales to accredited investors under Rule 506 of Regulation D, (2) claimed *not* to meet the *Howey* test, (3) avoided US jurisdiction on the initial token sales, or (4) just ignored the SEC and plowed ahead. These strategies have met with mixed success.

Early on, the SEC did provide some guidance on whether a particular token was a security, ruling in 2017 that "tokens offered and sold by a 'virtual' organization known as 'The DAO' were securities and therefore subject to the federal securities laws."[53] Staff speeches and actions revealed that established cryptocurrencies, however, such as bitcoin and ether, would probably not be treated as securities.[54]

The SEC introduced an outreach program to help deal with advances in technology. In 2018 it launched a "FinHub" initiative, with the goal of providing "a resource for public engagement on the SEC's Fintech-related issues and initiatives, such as distributed ledger technology (including digital assets), automated investment advice, digital marketplace financing, and artificial intelligence/machine learning."[55] On May 31, 2019, the FinHub staff hosted a public forum focusing on distributed ledger technology and digital assets, which drew considerable interest.[56] Policy clarity is still a work in progress.

Ironically, for some time the strategy of seeking compliance with the SEC rules was among the least successful. Until 2019, attempts at registration simply stalled in the SEC review process. In July 2019, a request by Blockstack to be allowed to make an ICO under Regulation A+ (effectively an abbreviated approach to a public offering) and under Regulation S to foreign buyers was finally approved after months of regulatory to and fro. The offering closed in November 2019 for a total of $23 million. It remains to be seen whether this really represents a serious thaw in the SEC's willingness to approve cryptocurrency ventures.

The tactic of ignoring the SEC and plowing ahead has been the most dangerous because it may expose promoters to a number of channels for ex post punishment. The most general of these comes under Section 10b of the 1934 Exchange Act and the related Rule 10b-5, which provides the following:

> It shall be unlawful for any person, directly or indirectly, by the use of any means or instrumentality of interstate commerce, or of the mails or of any facility of any national securities exchange,
>
> (a) To employ any device, scheme, or artifice to defraud,
> (b) To make any untrue statement of a material fact or to omit to state a material fact necessary in order to make the statements made, in the light of the circumstances under which they were made, not misleading, or
> (c) To engage in any act, practice, or course of business which operates or would operate as a fraud or deceit upon any person,
>
> in connection with the purchase or sale of any security.

To the extent that any of the persons involved in a blockchain-based securities transaction are located in the United States, the blockchain itself would probably count as an "instrumentality of interstate commerce," as would any other technology-based market or transaction platform. This rule creates liability for civil and criminal penalties by the government as well as a civil cause of action for the individuals and businesses harmed by the conduct. There is little doubt that a fraudulent blockchain transaction for securities that met the definitions and jurisdictional requirements of 10b-5 could and would be prosecuted under current law.

Rule 10b-5 is hardly the only law that could apply in the case of blockchain fraud. The general federal law against "wire fraud" (18 U.S. Code §1343) would probably apply (the internet or other vehicle for the chain providing the wire), as well as a number of state antifraud provisions.

As of early 2020, SEC application of its antifraud provisions to ICOs has been spotty. The SEC has charged a few high-profile targets, but all the investigations to date have led to relatively light terms of settlement. For instance, in the 2018 case of the Airfox tokens, sold under the label "AirTokens," the goal was a system for mobile telecommunications companies to offer rewards that customers could redeem in a variety of ways. The ICO raised approximately $15 million, which was intended to establish the technology and business arrangements to support this ecosystem. While purchasers needed to agree that they "were buying AirTokens for their utility as a medium of exchange for mobile airtime," the facts showed that the reality of the transaction was quite different, and that the anticipation of appreciation was an important element in the investor motivation. The agreed remedial actions included a $250,000 fine, registration of the AirTokens as securities under the Exchange Act, together with the reporting involved, and an offer of rescission and repurchase to purchasers of the tokens. No criminal penalties were assessed; private causes of action by token holders were preserved.[57]

The case of Paragon, described in the same release with Airfox, was similarly decided. Here, the tokens were "ParagonCoins," which would be useful in an ecosystem intended to help the "cannabis community" become more accepted in the mainstream. Elements in this process included providing coworking spaces and various blockchain-based apps to support cannabis sales. The ICO raised approximately $12 million. Although the tokens were to have useful value in exchange for services organized by Paragon, the SEC concluded that the prospect of appreciation was a critical factor in their purchase and sale. The remedial actions were similar: a $250,000 fine, registration of the ParagonCoins as securities under the Exchange Act, together with the requisite reporting, and an offer of rescission and repurchase to purchasers of the tokens. Here, too, no criminal penalties were assessed, and private causes of action by token holders were preserved.

In more recent examples, the SEC in 2019 moved to enjoin sales of tokens being offered by Telegram Group Inc. and its wholly owned subsidiary TON Issuer Inc. The total at stake was reported to be $1.7 billion.[58] And in February 2020, the SEC settled charges against yet another blockchain technology start-up, Enigma MPC, based in San Francisco and Israel. The ICO conducted by Enigma was deemed an unregistered offering of securities. In a now-familiar pattern, Enigma agreed to a claims process that would return funds to its investors, register its tokens as securities, file periodic reports with the SEC, and pay a $500,000 penalty.[59]

How has the SEC been doing? On the one hand, this enforcement has had serious consequences for the enterprises and investors involved; on the other hand, they represent a relatively small slice of the ICO activity that went forward with such ebullience in the cryptocurrency boom. As discussed earlier, one commissioner has suggested that the way to solve this uncertainty is to provide for a "safe harbor" for ICOs so that they can get to the circulation stage and function as currencies rather than investments.

A further tactic taken under existing securities law approaches involves requiring and certifying structures of private governance. This approach to "self-regulatory organizations" was set up under the Securities Exchange Act of 1934 and originally applied to stock exchanges such as the New York Stock Exchange and to the National Association of Securities Dealers. More recent mergers and reorganizations have led to other organizations such as the Financial Industry Regulatory Authority. The idea is to let the organizations propose and report on their operations and governance rules and regulations, subject to the approval of the SEC. The premise is that the organizations will know their business needs better than a regulator would, and should therefore be the source of the governance approach. Indeed, because many of these self-regulatory organizations are now commercial actors that compete with one another—for example, the market exchanges or central clearing houses—they are incentivized to offer competitive products that are also viewed as safe and fair to the market participants who could choose to do business in a competitor's market. The regulator, on the other hand, can keep an eye out for abusive or otherwise objectionable practices that might find their way into the operations notwithstanding the alignment of interests. Flexibility and generativity are provided for, while still avoiding predation and building trust.

While it has not yet happened, one could imagine the extension of this approach to blockchain providers, with the on-chain structures of process and operation for major tokens that have achieved utility status providing the rules of a self-regulating organization, but still subject to regulatory oversight and review. The Libra Association has conceived something close to this, but oversight of a regulatory organization on a global basis is difficult; and watchers have raised concerns that the association is nevertheless so tied to Facebook that it lacks real independence and objectivity. One such effort involves the identification of some 1.5 million legal entities through a Global Legal Entity Identifier (LEI) System, managed by a private foundation that adheres to rules laid out and monitored by an informal ("charter based") group of regulators from dozens of countries.

5.3.4   Harm Prevention and Trust Building II: Developing New Law

Existing laws and regulations cannot do the entire job here either. New rules for preventing harm and building trust will be needed to deal with fintech-specific challenges. For instance, the ability to set up automatically executing contracts that cannot be rescinded is sometimes offered as an advantage that fintech could provide. That said, there may be circumstances of fraud or a mistake where it may be necessary to undo a nonrescindable contract. How do you build a "reset button" into a fintech platform and keep the integrity that is a core part of it? Would it involve air gaps (physical separation of computers from network connections) and "ask the human to execute it" moments? What is the legal review and intervention that might be needed to trigger such a circumstance? Contracts frequently contain *severability* clauses, which allow the contract to survive even where a particular offending clause is struck by virtue of a court decision. In such a case, could the code be written to allow the contract to function even without that clause? If not, could the contract be opened to have the rest rewritten so that it operates as newly intended? These questions are explored more fully in section 5.3.6.

As new products emerge, new rules may be needed. We still often envision financial innovations, such as blockchain technology, as better ways of doing things we already understand. We are only just beginning to anticipate the really novel possibilities for setting up and executing agreements and legally active instruments. Disruptive change is happening, but it is hard to predict in advance. What we can anticipate is that law will be called on to do many of the things it already does to make a new technology trustworthy.

5.3.5   Coordination and Standard Setting

A final area for government activity at a general level is providing mechanisms for coordination and standard setting on the software that can be used to power the platforms and to express the terms of contracts and instruments in executable code. While simply mandating such standards could be attempted, by and large the government seeks to be a catalyst and convener to help private actors agree on common standards. The National Institute for Science and Technology plays such a role, and this kind of activity with respect to the financial markets is part of the mandate of the OFR. Regulatory reporting (financial supervisors' required information collections, in many cases republished for transparency) can itself be a form of standardization. On a global basis, the International Organization for Standardization (ISO) is a private body that develops standards but whose members include governments and whose standards are often baked into official mandates. The LEI, discussed above, adheres to ISO standard 17422, and ISO 20022 covers many financial messaging standards.

A possible step in this direction is the development of a "legal specification language" with the capacity to express and execute the permutations of event and consequence, which are central to many contracts and instruments. Such a language could move blockchain technology, for example, from being a relatively passive ledger for establishing records of transactions to a platform on which their design and execution are carried out. "Smart contracts" and "smart securities" would become quickly computable objects in an ecosystem of like specifications. Elements of this language and system exist; creating the complete package will take not only time and effort but also the kind of coordination and standard development processes in which government can take an active and useful role.

5.3.6 Techno-legal Aspects of Smart Contracts

The internet technical community has taken an interest in smart contracts, for a number of their promising capabilities. Although smart contracts do not, in general, require a blockchain platform, they are often viewed as an extension of the basic blockchain system found in the bitcoin system. A smart contract today is seen as an *executable code* that is designed to run on specific computing architectures. A given smart contract may be executed on one computer (i.e., one node in the blockchain system), or it may be designed to run concurrently with other related copies of itself, or other smart contracts that are related to (or derived from) itself. The execution of a group of smart contracts may be designed to occur simultaneously, or the contracts may be executed in a cascading or interleaved fashion. These modes of execution may have dramatic ramifications for the outcome of the contract as a unit.

Another dimension of the smart contract paradigm is the fact that multiple parties are typically involved in the actual execution of the contract, including the originator of the smart contract, the computer/node owner or operator where the contract runs, external data sources, and the counterparty in the contract. These various entities need not reside within the same legal jurisdiction.

Today there are a number of open technical issues with regard to smart contracts that may carry legal implications, such as authenticated data sources, correct and complete execution, forensics and postevent evidence, and cross-jurisdiction smart contract executions. All of these are possible targets for the kind of standard-setting activity in which government can play an important role.[60]

NOTES

The views of the authors are their own and not necessarily those of their institutions.

1. O. R. Goodenough, "Legal Technology 3.0," *Huffington Post*, February 4, 2015, http://www.huffingtonpost.com/oliver-r-goodenough /legal-technology-30_b_6603658.html?utm_hp_ref=tw.

2. For convenience, we refer to distributed cryptographic ledgers generically as "blockchain" or "blockchain technology," even though certain variants, such as R3/Corda, don't use blocks.

3. Some discussions of "regulation" limit this term to the more narrow class of rules made by governmental agencies such as the Environmental Protection Agency or the Securities and Exchange Commission (SEC). In this chapter, we use the term in the broader context of governmentally originated rules as described in the text.

4. M. Flood, H. V. Jagadish, and L. Raschid, "Big Data Challenges and Opportunities in Financial Stability Monitoring," Banque de France *Financial Stability Review*, no. 20 (April 2016): 129–142.

5. R. Chase, *Peers Inc: How People and Platforms Are Inventing the Collaborative Economy and Reinventing Capitalism* (New York: PublicAffairs, 2015), 72.

6. Visionary Future, *Commonwealth Fintech Toolkit*, draft report, London, 2019.

7. "Central Bank Heads Keen to Benefit from Fintech Toolkit," Secretariat of the Commonwealth of Nations, 2018, https://thecommonwealth .org/media/news/central-bank-heads-keen-benefit-fintech-toolkit.

8. S. E. Dudley and J. Brito, *Regulation: A Primer*, 2nd ed. (Arlington, VA: Mercatus Center at George Mason University, 2012); R. A. Posner, *A Failure of Capitalism: The Crisis of '08 and the Descent into Depression* (Cambridge, MA: Harvard University Press, 2009); C. R. Sunstein, "Disrupting Voluntary Transactions," in *Markets and Justice: Nomos XXXI*, ed. John W. Chapman and J. Roland Pennock (New York: New York University Press, 1989), 279–302; O. Goodenough, "Governance for Cloud Computing: The Role of Public and Private Rulemaking

in Promoting the Growth of a New Industry" (Vermont Law School Research Paper No. 34-13), http://ssrn.com/abstract=2342594.

9. "Circular A-4," Office of Management and Budget, 2003, https://obamawhitehouse.archives.gov/omb/circulars_a004_a-4/.

10. "Paul Romer," speaker biography, Leigh Bureau, 2012, http://web.archive.org/web/20120606014844/http://www.leighbureau.com/speakers/promer/romer.pdf.

11. A. Greenberg, "Silk Road Creator Ross Ulbricht Sentenced to Life in Prison," *Wired*, May 29, 2015, https://www.wired.com/2015/05/silk-road-creator-ross-ulbricht-sentenced-life-prison/.

12. I. Magaziner, "Creating a Framework for Global Electronic Commerce," *Future Insight*, Progress and Freedom Foundation, July 1999, http://www.pff.org/issues-pubs/futureinsights/fi6.1globaleconomiccommerce.html.

13. J. A. Drobac and O. R. Goodenough, "Exposing the Myth of Consent," *Indiana Health Law Review*, 2015, http://ssrn.com/abstract=2559341.

14. See S. Shifflett and C. Jones, "Buyer Beware: Hundreds of Bitcoin Wannabes Show Hallmarks of Fraud," *Wall Street Journal*, May 17, 2018, https://www.wsj.com/articles/buyer-beware-hundreds-of-bitcoin-wannabes-show-hallmarks-of-fraud-1526573115; S. Dowlat, "Cryptoasset Market Coverage Initiation Network Creation," July 11, 2018, https://research.bloomberg.com/pub/res/d28giW28tf6G7T_Wr77aU0gDgFQ; "Cryptocurrency Anti-Money Laundering Report 2019 Q4," CipherTrace, 2020, https://ciphertrace.com/q4-2019-cryptocurrency-anti-money-laundering-report/.

15. J. Condos, W. H. Sorrel, and S. L. Donegan, *Blockchain Technology: Opportunities and Risks*, Vermont General Assembly, January 15, 2016, https://legislature.vermont.gov/assets/Legislative-Reports/blockchain-technology-report-final.pdf; Vermont General Assembly, "The Vermont Statutes Online. Title 12: Court Procedure; Chapter 081: Conduct of Trial,"https://legislature.vermont.gov/statutes/section/12/081/01913.

16. Vermont General Assembly, "An Act Relating to Miscellaneous Economic Development Provisions," bill as passed by the House and Senate, H.868, 2016, https://legislature.vermont.gov/bill/status/2016/H.868.

17. Vermont Law School, *Financial Technology Report*, 2017, https://legislature.vermont.gov/assets/Legislative-Reports/Vermont-Report-Final-Version-December-7.pdf.

18. Vermont General Assembly, "Blockchain-Based Limited Liability Companies," 11 V.S.A. § 4173 et seq., 2018, https://legislature.vermont.gov/statutes/section/11/025/04173.

19. J. Tashea, "Wyoming and Vermont Hope to Attract Tech Entrepreneurs by Passing Laws Favorable to Blockchain," *ABA Journal*, March 1, 2019, https://www.abajournal.com/magazine/article/blockchain-wyoming-vermont-regulations-laws.

20. T. Delahunty, "Wyoming Sets Standard for U.S., Passing 13 Blockchain Laws in 2019," News BTC, 2019, https://www.newsbtc.com/2019/11/20/wyoming-sets-standard-for-u-s-passing-13-blockchain-laws-in-2019/.

21. "Hester Peirce Proposal for Treatment of Cryptocurrency," Anthony L.G., PLLC, March 3, 2020, http://securities-law-blog.com/2020/03/03/hester-peirce-proposal-for-treatment-of-cryptocurrency/.

22. Arizona State Legislature, "Regulatory Sandbox Program," A.R.S. §41-5601 to 41-5612, 2019, https://www.azleg.gov/arsDetail/?title=41.

23. Arizona Attorney General, "Welcome to Arizona's Fintech Sandbox," 2020, https://www.azag.gov/fintech.

24. Arizona Attorney General, "Sandbox Participants," 2020, https://www.azag.gov/fintech/participants.

25. P. Goldstein, "What Is Behind Delaware's New Blockchain Deal with IBM?," State Tech, July 26, 2018, https://statetechmagazine.com/article/2018/07/what-behind-delawares-new-blockchain-deal-ibm.

26. New York State Department of Financial Services, "Virtual Currency Business Activity (BitLicense)," 2020, https://www.dfs.ny.gov/apps_and_licensing/virtual_currency_businesses.

27. New York State Department of Financial Services, "Financial Services Superintendent Linda A. Lacewell Announces New Proposed Regime for Listing Virtual Currencies," press release, December 11, 2019, https://www.dfs.ny.gov/reports_and_publications/press_releases/pr1912101.

28. Financial Conduct Authority, "Regulatory Sandbox," 2020, https://www.fca.org.uk/firms/innovation/regulatory-sandbox.

29. Concerns regarding competition in laxity go back at least a century. See E. White, "'To Establish a More Effective Supervision of Banking': How the Birth of the Fed Altered Bank Supervision," in *The Origins, History, and Future of the Federal Reserve: A Return to Jekyll Island*, ed. M. Bordo and W. Roberds (Cambridge: Cambridge University Press, 2011), 7–54; E. Meyer Jr., "Financing Agriculture" (address before the State Bank Division of the American Bankers Association, New York, October 2, 1922), https://archive.org/download/financingagricu00meye/financingagricu00meye.pdf.

30. D. Shrier, "Helping to Level the Playing Field for Regulators—Introducing the Commonwealth Fintech Policy Toolkit," Commonwealth Secretariat, October 7, 2019, https://thecommonwealth.org/media/news/blog-helping-level-playing-field-regulators-introducing-commonwealth-fintech-policy.

31. Internal Revenue Service, "Virtual Currencies," 2020, https://www.irs.gov/businesses/small-businesses-self-employed/virtual-currencies.

32. Internal Revenue Service, "Rev. Rul. 2019-24," 2019, https://www.irs.gov/pub/irs-drop/rr-19-24.pdf.

33. B. Broadbent, "Central Banks and Digital Currencies" (speech at the London School of Economics, March 2, 2016, Bank of England), https://www.bankofengland.co.uk/speech/2016/central-banks-and-digital-currencies; Bank for International Settlements, *Digital Currencies*, November 2015, http://www.bis.org/cpmi/publ/d137.pdf; European Central Bank and Bank of Japan, *Project Stella: Balancing Confidentiality and Auditability in a Distributed Ledger Environment*, technical report, February 2020, https://www.boj.or.jp/en/announcements/release_2020/rel200212a.htm/.

34. Office of Information and Regulatory Affairs, "Regulatory Impact Analysis: A Primer," 2016, https://www.whitehouse.gov/sites/whitehouse.gov/files/omb/inforeg/regpol/circular-a-4_regulatory-impact-analysis-a-primer.pdf.

35. J. Zittrain, *The Future of the Internet and How to Stop It* (New Haven, CT: Yale University Press, 2008).

36. O. Goodenough, "Generativity: Making Law a More Open Institutional 'Ecosystem' for Productive Innovation" (Vermont Law School Paper No. 4-15, 2015), http://papers.ssrn.com/sol3/papers.cfm?abstract_id=2589263.

37. M. Huillet, "Nasdaq Blockchain Pilot Handles Margin Calls and Collateral Delivery 'within Minutes,'" Cointelegraph, June 20, 2018, https://cointelegraph.com/news/nasdaq-blockchain-pilot-handles-margin-calls-and-collateral-delivery-within-minutes. See also Nasdaq, "Building on the Blockchain: Nasdaq's Vision of Innovation," 2016, https://www.nasdaq.com/articles/building-blockchain-2016-03-23.

38. R3, "Building the Future of Frictionless Commerce," 2020, https://www.r3.com/wp-content/uploads/2020/02/R3_Corporate_Brochure_Letter_Digital_feb_2020.pdf.

39. R3, "Customers," 2020, https://www.r3.com/customers/ works.

40. Financial Stability Board, *Financial Stability Implications from FinTech: Supervisory and Regulatory Issues That Merit Authorities' Attention*, June 27, 2017, https://www.fsb.org/wp-content/uploads/R270617.pdf.

41. L. Brainard, "Digital Currencies, Stablecoins, and the Evolving Payments Landscape," October 16, 2019, https://www.federalreserve.gov/newsevents/speech/brainard20191016a.htm.

42. U.S. House Financial Services Committee, "An Examination of Facebook and Its Impact on the Financial Services and Housing Sectors," Hearing Memorandum, October 23, 2019, https://financialservices.house.gov/calendar/eventsingle.aspx?EventID=404487.

43. L. Kaplow, "Rules versus Standards: An Economic Analysis," *Duke Law Journal* 42 (1992): 557–629, http://scholarship.law.duke.edu/dlj/vol42/iss3/2.

44. L. Lessig, "Codev2," 2005, http://codev2.cc/download+remix/Lessig-Codev2.pdf.

45. Selfkey, "A Comprehensive List of Cryptocurrency Exchange Hacks," February 13, 2020, https://selfkey.org/list-of-cryptocurrency-exchange-hacks/.

46. Delaware Office of the Governor, "Governor Markell Launches Delaware Blockchain Initiative," *PR Newswire*, May 2, 2016, http://www.prnewswire.com/news-releases/governor-markell-launches-delaware-blockchain-initiative-300260672.html.

47. Uniform Law Commission, "Uniform Electronic Transactions Act (1999)," National Conference of Commissioners on Uniform State Laws, 1999, https://www.uniformlaws.org/HigherLogic/System/DownloadDocumentFile.ashx?DocumentFileKey=2c38eebd-69af-aafc-ddc3-b3d292bf805a.

48. Vermont General Assembly, "Vermont Business Corporations: Incorporation: Bylaws," 11A V.S.A. § 2.06, 2010, http://legislature.vermont.gov/statutes/section/11A/002/00002.06.

49. On the challenges of paper-based title registration, see J. P. Hunt, R. Stanton, and N. Wallace, "US Residential-Mortgage Transfer Systems: A Data-Management Crisis," in *Handbook of Financial Data and Risk Information*, vol. 2, *Software and Data*, ed. M. Brose, M. Flood, D. Krishna, and W. Nichols (Cambridge: Cambridge University Press, 2014), 85–132. On blockchain-based alternatives, see V. L. Lemieux, "Evaluating the Use of Blockchain in Land Transactions: An Archival Science Perspective," *European Property Law Journal* 6, no. 3 (December 2017): 392–440, https://doi.org/10.1515/eplj-2017-0019.

50. A. Wolinsky, "Competition in Markets for Credence Goods," *Journal of Institutional Theoretical Economics* 151 (1995): 117–131.

51. SEC v. W. J. Howey Co., 328 U.S. 293 (1946), 299, https://scholar.google.co.uk/scholar_case?case=12975052269830471754&q=SEC+v.+W.+J.+Howey+Co.,+328+U.S.+293+(1946)&hl=en&as_sdt=2006&as_vis=1.

52. D. Pozzi, "ICO Market 2018 vs 2017: Trends, Capitalization, Localization, Industries, Success Rate," Cointelegraph, January 5, 2019, https://cointelegraph.com/news/ico-market-2018-vs-2017-trends-capitalization-localization-industries-success-rate.

53. Securities and Exchange Commission, "SEC Issues Investigative Report Concluding DAO Tokens, a Digital Asset, Were Securities," press release, July 25, 2017, https://www.sec.gov/news/press-release/2017-131.

54. B. Pisani, "Bitcoin and Ether Are Not Securities, but Some Initial Coin Offerings May Be, SEC Official Says," CNBC, June 4, 2018, https://www.cnbc.com/2018/06/14/bitcoin-and-ethereum-are-not -securities-but-some-cryptocurrencies-may-be-sec-official-says.html; Securities and Exchange Commission to Jacob E. Comer, re: Cipher Technologies Bitcoin Fund, October 1, 2019, https://www.sec.gov /Archives/edgar/data/1776589/999999999719007180/filename1.pdf.

55. Securities and Exchange Commission, "SEC Launches New Strategic Hub for Innovation and Financial Technology," press release, October 18, 2018, https://www.sec.gov/news/press-release/2018-240.

56. Securities and Exchange Commission, "SEC Staff Announces Agenda for May 31 Fintech Forum," press release, April 24, 2019, https://www.sec.gov/news/press-release/2019-59.

57. Securities and Exchange Commission, "Two ICO Issuers Settle SEC Registration Charges, Agree to Register Tokens as Securities," press release, November 16, 2018, https://www.sec.gov/news/press-release /2018-264.

58. Securities and Exchange Commission, "SEC Halts Alleged $1.7 Billion Unregistered Digital Token Offering," press release, October 11, 2019, https://www.sec.gov/news/press-release/2019-212.

59. Securities and Exchange Commission, "ICO Issuer Settles SEC Registration Charges, Agrees to Return Funds and Register Tokens as Securities," press release, February 19, 2020, https://www.sec.gov /news/press-release/2020-37.

60. A detailed discussion of these elements is beyond the scope of this chapter. We may address them in a future document.

6 POLICY AND FINTECH, PART II: USE CASES

Oliver R. Goodenough, Mark Flood,
Matthew Reed, David L. Shrier,
Thomas Hardjono, and
Alex Pentland

6.1 SPECIFIC USE CASE I: TRANSACTION RECORDS AND TRADING MARKETS

Several efforts have been made to use new technologies to change how securities are issued and traded, but thus far these efforts have failed to deliver a sufficiently compelling value proposition to induce widespread change. With the rise of blockchain-based technologies, even the leaders of the world's largest incumbent stock exchanges are now acknowledging a threat to the status quo. This section examines a few critical issues related to technological innovation in the issuance and trading of securities and explores possible regulatory responses to these challenges.

6.1.1 Issuance and Trading in a Blockchain Context

Most stocks and bonds are issued as securities with known and recorded ownership. This is certainly the case since the Tax Equity and Fiscal Responsibility Act of 1982 (TEFRA) prohibited the issuance of US bearer bonds.[1] Security ownership recordation is, at its core, a process of recording a "fact" with distributed, shared agreement on its truth. Because a blockchain manages a consensus version of the truth, an appropriately designed blockchain could, in principle, be well suited to the tasks of securities transfer and ownership recording and

have the potential to make the process more accurate and efficient. In addition, the distributed nature of blockchain could
create a greater sense of trust in the system, as any participant
in the market can validate a transaction. Moreover, regulatory
oversight would become easier because an irrevocable ledger is
readily accessible. After issuance, much of the life of a security
exists in secondary markets. Thus, demonstration of exclusive
ownership and transfer becomes paramount, tasks for which
cryptocurrency blockchains have shown capability. Later in
the chapter we address the related issue of *identity*, which must
also be solved for a recordation system to make sense.

Permissioned blockchains can solve for issues of identity of
participants and exclusivity of ownership. The bitcoin blockchain (BCBC) protocol is less well suited to this purpose, as it
strives to maintain the anonymity of participants in an effort
to mimic old-fashioned cash (specie or paper currency) payments. Apropos of the TEFRA note above, ownership identification is required for numerous purposes, including property
taxes and taxes on capital gains, so a permissioned/identified
system will be needed. However, systems have already been
proposed (by the Massachusetts Institute of Technology,
among others) for privacy-protected, traceable transactions.
Identity in these systems could be managed by a trusted third
party, while the identity of a particular participant in a transaction could be cryptographically shielded. This system would
allow for anonymous trading of beneficial ownership until
the occurrence of an appropriately permissioned event (e.g.,
a warrant is issued by a duly recognized court of authority), at
which point the guardian entity managing the identity could
selectively release the required information. Similar anonymity requirements are commonplace in brokered financial markets, where the broker hides participants' identities (from each
other) as a way to limit information asymmetries.

How do we decide who is "inside the wall"—that is, who
gets to write blocks to the blockchain? Given that advance

knowledge of the index is valuable (tradable) information, who gets to read the blocks on the chain as the consensus is being formed? Some versions of permissioned blockchains allow a small set of trusted participants to trade with each other, akin to a private trading network. Yet, this would have an exclusionary effect on small investors. It is also possible to create a permissioned, public blockchain where only some have "write access" but anyone can "read" the transaction stream, and this may provide for the balance required between competing objectives.

What do we do in the case of errors of execution? The BCBC and most other blockchains do not have a convenient "undo" mechanism when mistakes are made. For example, a minor programming error forced Knight Capital to sell itself after losing $440 million at a rate of $10 million a minute.[2] To avoid such scenarios, one might impose stringent authentication of participants, but this too would deviate from the original BCBC protocol of user anonymity. In the case of error, it is possible to inject a "correcting entry," but the counterparties would need to agree to this—if Snidely decided he liked his erroneous transfer, it would be difficult to undo absent a court order (and even then, that simply creates a legal claim). In cases where anonymity is less critical, other options are available. For example, institutional participants in wholesale funding markets typically have an "investigations" office for semiformal arbitration of mistakes and disagreements with regular counterparties. Blockchain technology does not preclude a similar approach.

The need for an "undo" tool is illuminated by a dramatic blockchain failure that occurred in June 2016. In this case, Ethereum was the context for an attack by a hacker using the *nom de fraude* "the Attacker."[3] This would-be bandit exploited a programming flaw in a digital currency fund—the decentralized autonomous organization (DAO)—to direct the transfer of 3.6 million ETH (then worth about $53 million) into his or her account. The cofounder of Ethereum countered by freezing the DAO tokens. The Attacker then added insult to injury by asserting, through a post on Pastebin, that he or she had a valid claim to the money, arguing that the record in the Ethereum chain was the only source for the title and that any attempt to change the record would be a breach of the rules. Even though the Attacker threatened to unleash lawyers on those seeking to correct the fraud, reverse hackers allied to the platform managed to recapture most of the funds.[4]

Resorting to the use of cybervigilantes to battle back from predatory exploitation of the system's architecture suggests that trusting in the technology is not a substitute for authoritative governance. Rather, creating some kind of reconciliation or correction capability looks increasingly to be a necessary element of a blockchain-based trading system. Such a capacity ultimately needs an adjudicator; in a traditional market or contract we look to choice of law and choice of forum provisions to set up the correction system. We can also specify *private* adjudication, through arbitration or some kind of market-specific committee. The choices are several; the need to have one in place is critical.

6.1.2 Settlement and Hypothecation

The settlement of a trade is an area currently burdened with several layers of a process. Much of this process predates the advent of electronic records and thus has the potential to be automated using blockchain technology. A good deal of securities settlement involves statements of ownership—of stocks, bonds, and so forth. This is broadly consistent with the original BCBC, which tracks uninterrupted ownership of specific coins through time. In part, this works because the individual coins are clearly defined and identified, and ownership is rivalrous. It makes sense that, at every instant, there is a one-to-one mapping between a coin and its owner, and that one should be able to track an individual coin's ownership relationships uninterrupted through time. Moreover, to the extent that a registrar's blockchain uses a distributed ledger, the BCBC has a mining cost that can be calibrated to encourage truthful voting under a distributed consensus protocol. A number of blockchain variations would be capable of managing such a distributed ledger of ownership.

For some legal applications, a document's chain of custody is important. An analog is the chain of obligation for reused or rehypothecated collateral. Unmanaged rehypothecation chains—the Lehman collateral hairball—were an important factor in the September 2008 run. Collateral rehypothecation frequently occurs in bilateral over-the-counter (OTC) markets. A trusted, decentralized registration point for OTC collateral pledges could therefore be an especially valuable application for an appropriately managed blockchain. However, the ability for accurate identification and authentication (which permissioned blockchains can require but which are absent from the BCBC) would be crucial to make this work reliably.

Scalability is also a critical issue. The BCBC protocol manages a distributed transaction ledger, so the current state of an individual's "account" must be calculated by rolling forward all historical transactions. Because current inventories of cash and securities are key variables in the settlement process, this calculation would need to be performed often. It is not clear that this process will scale adequately, especially in equities markets, where high-frequency trading is dominant.[5] Some solutions to blockchain scalability have suggested creating "sub-consensus" nodes that aggregate to a larger consensus, but this only exacerbates the coordination issue noted above. Financial reform legislation moved most derivatives to clearinghouses, in part so that the regulators could have access to comprehensive information from the clearinghouses. It is not clear how this can be accomplished by a distributed system without some sort of coordinated reporting mechanism.

Similarly, the BCBC protocol does not directly support fungibility of cash and securities, relying instead on a relatively clumsy process of excessive lump-sum transfer, followed by a mining and return of "change" in the appropriate amount. This introduces a coordination burden to ensure that these two messages are recognized as countermanding components of the same legal transaction. In principle, this should be straightforward and feasible, but *practical experience* shows that financial markets cannot always keep related transactions aligned.[6] Disputes should be expected in practice, and some type of dispute-resolution mechanism will be needed. It would be hypothetically possible to train a machine-mediated dispute resolution system to facilitate efficiency, but it may not be feasible (at least in the near term) to eliminate human intervention entirely.

We have seen occasional flash crashes (precipitously steep declines in market prices) in a range of markets using high-frequency algorithmic trading. In many cases, the trading venue intervened to clamp trading and cancel executed transactions. This involves the unilateral suspension of trading to stem further acceleration of losses and instability and subsequent reversal by a third party (the exchange) of "completed" legal agreements. Clearly, this is not an optimal state of affairs, but conditional on a flash crash, unilateral intervention to cancel contracts is preferable to most alternatives. However, this requires a trusted relationship outside of the relationship between the transacting parties themselves, and some form of effective delegated authority permitting the trading venue to act pursuant to a set of predetermined rules or with the ex post involvement of authorities. Blockchain technologies also have the "undo" issues cited previously. Blockchain was designed as an irrevocable ledger, so unwinding errors becomes cumbersome, to say the least.

6.1.3 Transaction Monitoring

A blockchain defines a consensus version of the truth. In practice, we should expect to see an ecosystem of many blockchains, large and small, defining various "local truths" for specific communities and purposes. The movement to give blockchains legal standing as evidence in contract enforcement is progressing, with the Vermont statutes discussed in chapter 5 standing as early beacons. In such a world, it is inevitable that two competing blockchain systems will eventually announce conflicting versions of the "truth." It is possible that the blockchain consensus mechanism itself will step in to harmonize the differences. However, this may not happen automatically, because the consensus preference in each community may be to tolerate the inconsistency. Once again, this creates a need for a reconciliation mechanism. Industry coordination efforts such as those by Hyperledger and Interledger need to take into account the nuances of financial-securities-specific implications, and/or a new coordinating action will need to be taken around securities transactions to allow for reconciliation.

Suppose that industry blockchains successfully record much of the low-level data validation work that is currently handled by traditional double-entry bookkeeping and back-office confirmation and reconciliation processes. These blockchains could then be central staging points for supervision by regulatory bodies, archival recording, and enforcement of market manipulation laws. This raises issues such as the following: how much access should systemic supervisors have to these details without intruding on individual privacy, under what circumstances should supervisors be allowed to escalate their access, and who gets to decide whether escalation is permitted.

6.2   SPECIFIC USE CASE II: IDENTITY, TRUST, AND DATA SECURITY IN A BLOCKCHAIN ENVIRONMENT

As noted elsewhere in this chapter, the financial services industry must be able to provide its core services to the rest of the economy, and the stability of the system needed to provide these services relies on trust in the system, resilience and reliability, and robustness to manipulation. Blockchain technology alone promises much, but many use cases will require integration with other existing and emerging fintech components, for example, for enhanced identity management and information security.

6.2.1 Current Infrastructure

The infrastructure of our financial system relies on an often-disparate network of networks and systems that have been built up over time. These networks must identify instruments and parties precisely and unambiguously in order to move money or settle securities. One such network is the payment system managed by the Society for Worldwide Interbank Financial Transfers (SWIFT), which moves massive sums of money among major financial institutions, including central banks. Like so many infrastructures underpinning our financial system—whether they are designed to facilitate trade or investment, payment systems, or risk transfer platforms—the SWIFT system relies on precise, unambiguous, and robust-to-fraud identification of counterparties and transactors.

SWIFT uses the Business Identifier Code (BIC) for this purpose. But the financial system more broadly lacks an unambiguous and ubiquitous means of identity management. For decades, disparate identification systems built up in our financial markets. Vendors provided proprietary partial solutions, such as the Committee on Uniform Securities Identification Procedures (CUSIP) number, which identifies individual securities; the Dunn and Bradstreet DUNS number; and the Markit Red Code, which identifies reference entities in credit default swaps. These vended solutions, each of which is different and covers a portion of the world's financial market participants, have proved costly and to be of limited use outside of internal systems, because of intellectual property limitations.

In other markets, a superior product may emerge as an effective market standard. For financial entity identification, no superior product emerged organically, as parochial financial interests encouraged the various proprietary systems to remain proprietary, with the identifiers' owners capturing most of the economic rents. Although all end users would benefit from a common, open identification standard, no individual player examining the costs and benefits could unilaterally justify the costs of creating such a global system. Moreover, because a global system would be a natural monopoly with large network externalities, individual players would be unlikely to cooperate without external compulsion. A recent effort of authorities from around the globe has sought to solve this problem by creating the Legal Entity Identifier (LEI), which has now been adopted by over 1.5 million entities in 195 countries.[7] This development is a good example of a productive use of the convening power of government.

In the case of these identity management systems, whether a closed, proprietary system (such as the BIC) or an open system (such as the LEI), the ability to rely on the identifier is paramount. Market participants and the authorities that oversee them must know "who is who" in our markets. Also critical is the need for identification systems that interoperate, especially as markets become more interconnected. This interoperability will aid oversight and risk management systems by supporting aggregation and netting of exposures, reducing opportunities for error or fraud, and generally improving confidence in markets and other infrastructures. But how does this confidence arise? How do we become confident that we are dealing with the intended "whom"?

Different solutions are available for this problem. One approach is self-identification. This may work well where the incentives to self-identify accurately are high and the costs of remedy low. Self-identification may also work where a counterparty has the opportunity to conduct due diligence to manage the risk of misidentification (or other counterparty attributes, such as credit risk). This approach may be sufficient where the costs of remedy (such as expensive litigation) are high. Likewise, self-identification may also work in a closed system with repeat transactions, where the incentives to self-identify accurately and the costs of inaccurate identification are sufficiently high.

But self-identification is also often coupled with a trusted source. That source could come from the government (a driver's license or Social Security card) or an institution (such as the SWIFT system, a credit provider with skin in the game, or perhaps a distributed system of verification). A trusted source of entity verification can be a proxy for the expensive due diligence regime described above. In practical cases, the level of assurance necessary, given the risks and costs of remediation, is measured against the level of proof of trust provided.

In a distributed system, what would be the source of proof, and would it be sufficient given the risks and costs of remediation? Again, different approaches are available, including limited blockchain networks (much like the SWIFT network), where some level of proof is a condition of entry into the system. Who should be the gatekeeper for such a system, and how can we establish trust in this gatekeeper? An analogy is the registration system our markets currently deploy, where exchanges and other market infrastructures must meet regulators' quality and fairness conditions before gaining registration authority. Oversight, via inspections, examinations, heightened sanctions regimes, and books and records requirements, ensures both ongoing compliance with the trust rules and confidence in the system.

In other regimes, economic forces and liability regimes support the trust infrastructure. Dark pools, where closed networks of large traders operate in an opaque-by-design framework that protects anonymity, provide an example. The dark pool's host has sufficient regulatory and legal exposure to give participants confidence in posted bids and offers, despite not knowing their counterparties' identities. Blockchain implementations could use similar mechanisms to manage counterparty identification.

What about more open systems that are not centrally managed or regulated but instead operate as peer-to-peer (P2P) networks—as many blockchain advocates envision? Such systems can rely on self-identification but counterparties will typically want additional assurances. The distributed network might provide proof of identity, perhaps using a hierarchal system of agreed-upon, standard, third-party, proof-checking sources. In such cases, self-identification is possible, but it presents problems ranging from simple fraud exposure to tactics for concealing beneficial ownership to avoid market shifts. These forces can significantly complicate the jobs of risk managers and regulators.

At a minimum, authorities and courts will require a blockchain platform operating in a regulated market to be able to reveal the identity of "anonymous" participants in certain circumstances. The technology must provide this flexibility of counterparties' ensured legitimacy, even in an anonymous transaction, coupled with the ability to reveal the identity of participants. This naturally raises the question of who has permission to unlock this information, under what circumstances, and how authorities (courts, regulators, or self-regulatory institutions) can acquire both the keys and certainty that those keys will work. All of this also runs against certain expectations for "deputized" law enforcement agents—the banks and other intermediaries that are required to file "suspicious activity reports" with the Treasury—if they must rely on identity information from a third party instead of the agent itself, which bears the regulatory burden. Without careful design, the result could be further "derisking" by banks that find it cheaper to avoid certain clients than bear the risk that they might be associated with bad actors.

Understanding networks of counterparty connections is critical for counterparty and systemic risk management, for supervision and market monitoring, and to value investments. These interconnections can explain the propagation of risks and reveal structural points of risk concentration and potential failure. A market crisis—for example, in the overnight funding market—might affect one firm directly but affect its counterparties indirectly. These networks of exposure are critical for financial stability oversight.

Network data—linking identified entities to their corporate sisters through regulatory filings, or linking them to counterparties through (traded or illiquid) instruments—can address questions of "who owns whom" and "who owns what." Fintech platforms, such as blockchain storage or smart-contract representations of derivatives agreements, may be natural technology solutions in this context. Just as entity identification requires identification standards and governance frameworks, representations of counterparty networks will need common standards and governance mechanisms in order to provide certainty for both firms and supervisors that the network data reveals precise and actionable information.

These arrangements have numerous complexities. For example, ownership may derive from clear language in a regulatory filing or corporate ownership agreement, but it could also exist by virtue of a springing interest triggered, for example, by external factors or demands, or a minority shareholder interest that regulators deem to be a controlling interest.[8] If a public blockchain is the storage platform for counterparty network data, that system would need to be dynamic and might also need to support selective revelation of network details to appropriate network participants or regulators. These complexities reveal difficult questions of governance, which authorities will likely translate into formal system requirements.

6.2.2 Security within Blockchains: Regulatory and Market Needs

Just as market participants and supervisors need assurance that the information in the financial system is accurate and actionable, they also require that the information technologies that undergird the system be resilient and secure. US financial markets have a strong reputation for fairness and transparency, but even these markets sometimes suffer from concerns about unequal access and treatment. Blockchain-based systems will need to provide trustworthy security and resilience, but the built-in redundancy of distributed ledgers, properly managed, might offer improvements over existing infrastructures that suffer from single points of failure and "weakest link" problems.

The 2016 penetration of the SWIFT interbank payment system highlights the hazards of potential weak links. According to press reports, hackers penetrated SWIFT's client software, diverting money from the Bangladesh Bank's (the central bank) account at the New York Federal Reserve Bank to accounts in Sri Lanka and the Philippines. The heist attempted to transfer almost $1 billion, but the New York Fed (alerted by a spelling error) thwarted most of these transfers. The hackers ended up stealing over $100 million, much of which was subsequently laundered through casinos in the Philippines. SWIFT and Bangladesh Bank have since recovered much of the stolen money, but a significant amount is believed to be missing. In addition to stealing huge sums, cyberfraud also potentially threatens financial stability by endangering the credibility of the backbone of our financial system. Fortunately, both the three thousand institutions that own SWIFT and its eleven thousand users have strong motivation to prevent further damage. SWIFT is a closed system, designed to be secure. But the weak point was the Bangladesh Bank's SWIFT software portal, which the fraudster(s) compromised with the use of stolen credentials.

Resilience to cyberattacks is particularly important for blockchain platforms, especially public blockchains, which must limit the ability of one node to disrupt the whole system, through penetration, malware, denials of service, and other means.

A registration regime, such as a permissioned blockchain, may provide assurance of cyberattack resilience to participants, but regulators will also require assurance, as well as full access to the critical nodes of the system. Securities and Exchange Commission disclosure laws require that public companies disclose material risks. Annual reports are now full of discussions of the impact of cyberthreats, although a firm's need to address ongoing threats may legitimately weaken such disclosures. Nonpublic firms do not have such disclosure requirements.

Public blockchains may also face free-rider challenges. For a blockchain system under attack, who has the necessary authority, responsibility, and access to fight back? The law may authorize a regulator to intervene, but this authority may be inadequate if parts of the distributed network reside outside regulatory reach. Blockchain participants themselves may welcome supervision and a demonstration of adherence to understood rules, as a form of public assurance that the system is both safe and fair. This puts more pressure on authorities to understand fintech innovations and their proponents, and to provide clear guidance on security and resilience.

6.2.3   Identity within Blockchains: Current Limitations and Possible Solutions

Managing digital identities is a challenge, especially for public (permissionless) blockchains such as the bitcoin system and blockchain. Bitcoin uses *self-asserted* identities, meaning that any participant can simply create a public key pair and join the blockchain pseudonymously. Self-asserted identity is partly a way for individuals to assert control and maintain data privacy in an increasingly connected world.

However, self-asserted identity has an inherent limitation in terms of scalability. This limitation is not unique to the BCBC; it is also present, for example, in the PGP (Pretty Good Privacy) system where users self-issue PGP key pairs.[9] Key holders (PGP users) must provide their PGP public key directly to friends and colleagues, either in person or through a public "key ownership declaration" event, such as the "PGP key-signing parties" at face-to-face meetings of the Internet Engineering Task Force.

Most current self-asserted digital identities (in the form of self-generated public key pairs) do not scale well, because they lack integration with existing digital and real-world infrastructures. A complete and scalable identity management system needs to ground identity in the physical world, and it should not rely solely and unconditionally on existing identity/service providers.[10] We believe a new model is needed for "self-sourced identities" that would preserve privacy while ensuring scalability at the global internet level. Specifically, a scalable identity model must allow entities in the ecosystem to (1) verify the "quality" of an identity, (2) assess the relative "freedom" or independence of an identity from any given authority (e.g., government, businesses), and (3) assess the source of trust for a digital identity.

If anonymity is a requirement for self-asserted identities, then self-issuance of a public key pair (the case in the BCBC) is inadequate. True anonymity requires that identity be unlinkable across transactions, to prevent identity leakage through correlation attacks. Even if a digital identity is anonymous and unlinkable, counterparties must also still accept that identity. Parties relying on an anonymous, self-asserted identity will still need to assess its provenance and source of trust. To meet such requirements, a future self-asserted identity system would need to incorporate the notion of the varying degree of quality of the identity as a function of the veracity of the underlying provenance information (i.e., source of trust).

6.2.4   Digital Identities and Attributes for Future Blockchain Systems

Several avenues for scalable identity management and federation are available. These new approaches may require the introduction of new blockchain technologies and components, including new remuneration models for participants in the ecosystem, as well as more efficient proof-of-work schemes. New identity technologies include the following:

1. *Verifiable pseudonymous identities and attributes*: Anonymous and verifiable identities have been a topic of research for over two decades.[11] Some of these schemes have been implemented in systems such as U-Prove and IdeMix, and some limited deployments have been carried out.[12] These proposed systems have not seen broad deployment on the internet because of a number of constraints (e.g., lack of use case or business model). The arrival of the bitcoin system and the potential of new forms of blockchain-based systems may provide use cases of the deployment of these existing anonymous and verifiable identities.

2. *Smart contracts for binding and revealing attributes*: A node on the blockchain P2P network can compute smart contracts, which are sequences of computations that map to legal agreements (e.g., between two transacting entities). The same computation model might bind attributes—regarding a pseudonymous identity—to a contract that names the pseudonymous identity. The computation could begin with attributes that are "blinded" and then subsequently release one or more of the attributes during the multiround smart-contract exchange protocol. The multiround negotiations would build toward a release of all the relevant attributes regarding both sides of the transaction. An example of such contracts is bidding at auctions, which could start with an anonymous or pseudonymous buyer/bidder accompanied by attributes of the buyer (e.g., buyer financial worth, history of bidding).

One innovation that could contribute to reliable identity management in future blockchain systems is data-driven distributed computation to derive attributes. In this approach, the P2P distributed nodes on a blockchain would each collect data regarding an identity and perform analytics based on the data available to each node. Each node would first arrive at a "subattribute" value or parameter (e.g., single credit score) independently of the other nodes. Collectively the nodes would then contribute their respective subattributes to a group computation process, such as a multiparty computation (MPC) algorithm, which would result in a complete attribute. If a privacy-preserving algorithm is used for the MPC, this will have the added benefit of no single node knowing the subattributes of the other nodes.[13] Proposed solutions, such as Enigma, can provide a foundation for deriving attributes.[14] Attribute derivation, of course, would need to be reversible, for the reasons articulated above.

Another opportunity lies in the legal aspects of identities and attributes on the blockchain—namely, the introduction of a legal trust framework that uses automated contracts exchange (smart contracts or otherwise) to reduce friction in using digital identities through the blockchain. Such frameworks aim to reduce risks and liabilities of entities in the ecosystem through a set of agreed principles, operating rules, and mechanisms for legal recourse. Legal trust frameworks are crucial to the acceptance of digital identities and attributes in the real world. Some examples of legal trust frameworks for identity management and federation are the Federal Identity, Credential, and Access Management program, OpenID Exchange, and Safe-BioPharma.[15]

6.2.5 Scalable Digital Identities: Addressability, Source of Trust, and Verifiable Attributes

A number of desirable characteristics for digital identities can help guide future blockchain innovation around identity management. If satisfied, these characteristics could meet many of the regulatory needs described above.

1. *Addressability*: The notion of addressability refers not only to the uniqueness of an identity string at a global scale but also to any semantics embedded within the identity

structure that make it usable in practice. For example, the current "email identity" consists of a name (unique within the namespace of the domain) followed by a fully qualified domain name. These semantics enable the Simple Mail Transfer Protocol and Post Office Protocol v3 to interpret the identifier as a routable email address.

2. *Source of trust*: The source of trust of an identity (within a namespace) is derived or bequeathed from the authoritative entity that owns and/or manages that namespace. In essence, the source of trust vouches for the existence of the named identity and is associated with an individual or entity. For example, the Social Security number (SSN) of a US citizen is bequeathed by the government as the authoritative entity governing the SSN namespace. An email service provider vouches for an email address as the legal entity that owns the corresponding domain namespace. A public key infrastructure (PKI) service provider legally signs and issues a digital certificate to a user under the PKI provider's authority as specified in the service contract, commonly referred to as the certificate practices statement. A source of trust could also be established through recurring interactions with other trusted sources, such as banks that have performed "know your customer" on clients and then issued credit cards. A source of trust is crucial for the legal acceptability of the digital identity within online transactions, especially when transactions cross boundaries between the digital world and the real world. A formal legal trust framework typically expresses the legal aspects of identity management within a given application ecosystem. The trust framework is a set of legal processes and operating rules for the issuance, management, and accreditation of identities and identity providers within that ecosystem.

3. *Verifiable attributes*: Related to an identity's source of trust is the source of trust or *attribute authority* for attributes

associated with the digital identity. The attribute authority "binds" (often cryptographically) an attribute to a digital identity. In many instances, an attribute may have several authoritative sources, each making assertions with different degrees of veracity. The *relying party* in a transaction is the entity that ultimately decides whether to accept or reject a given assertion regarding an identity. For example, a state government in the United States may be an attribute authority for a person's residency status (e.g., "Joe is a legal resident of Massachusetts"). A private banking consortium may be the attribute authority for some financial information regarding an identity ("Joe has a FICO score above 500 pts").

4. *Privacy preserving*: In many cases, a digital identity scheme should preserve the privacy of its owner. Currently, identities in the form of email addresses are designed for addressability at the expense of privacy. Self-asserted identities in a bitcoin or PGP system provide a degree of privacy, but at the expense of scalability. New paradigms, such as the ability to create an opt-in anonymous identity on a permissioned blockchain, with anonymous verification and the ability of a regulator following due process to reveal identity, help bridge these schemes.

6.3   SPECIFIC USE CASE III: BLOCKCHAIN, STABILITY, AND SYSTEMIC OVERSIGHT

Our discussions so far have focused on the needs of authorities and market participants in their direct activities, and on rules that can help facilitate the adoption of fintech platforms, such as blockchains, in a productive and protective way. We argued in the introduction above that fintech innovations are new technologies emerging to address the exponential big data challenges in financial services. These forces are especially relevant for systemic oversight to monitor financial stability, where the full financial system is in scope and the implications of systemic externalities can be severe.

It is important that these technologies and the legal framework be adaptable to permit authorities, market participants, and the courts to address or avoid failures during periods of stress to the stability of the system. Big data challenges are impinging on systemic financial stability monitoring at every point of the data life cycle.[16]

For example, latency reductions in high-frequency trading (HFT) continue to increase both the velocity of trading messages generated and the ability of systems to process those messages. HFT algorithms are themselves a form of fintech, but their intensive focus on latency minimization seems to leave little room for time-consuming proof-of-work processes associated with many blockchains. Clearinghouses for HFT venues will need to balance complex trade-offs among competing priorities—for example, between the scope of access to market data and its staleness. The paperwork crisis of the 1960s led to a dramatic redesign of clearing and settlement processes, and a similar rethink may be in store now.

More generally, supervisory solutions include suitable points of entry for policy tools such as liquidity infusions, protocols to coordinate industry support in a crisis to backstop or restart market activities, and the possibility to unwind transactions and resolve failed institutions, markets, or processes.

We focus on two broad challenges: (1) the abstraction, evaluation, and analysis of data from a systemic perspective and (2) mechanisms for crisp and effective systemic intervention, particularly in times of stress or crisis. In traditional financial markets and transactions, these two functions have been the domain of a small group of regulatory bodies, such as central banks and analytical teams like the Office of Financial Research (OFR).

Particularly in the domain of cryptocurrencies, concerns are emerging about their potential to disrupt the traditional monetary and financial stability policies of central banks. To date, blockchain-based digital currencies have operated as small-scale payments media without the backing of central banks. They thus lack the traditional monetary governance mechanisms to achieve inflation or unemployment targets or to stabilize financial systems. Perhaps because of this, together with the absence of adjustments such as legal tender recognition, no blockchain currency has thus far grown big enough to present stability concerns in a major economy. Nonetheless, central banks and others are paying attention to this issue.[17]

We address the intervention question first, before turning to the more complex issue of data.

6.3.1 Intervention Mechanisms

It is useful to consider financial crises, as these episodes are likely to expose important operational bottlenecks and gaps in supervisory authority. In a crisis, official intervention can be necessary, for example, to replace vanishing private-sector liquidity, to clamp the runaway feedback of a flash crash, or to otherwise mitigate the potential long-term harms of a short-term breakdown.

Liquidity intervention by central banks is a critical tool for crisis management, benefiting from many decades of hard-earned experience. In a liquidity crisis, central banks provide funding to critical nodes in the system, typically by lending against good collateral. It is unclear how best to translate such a protocol to a possible future world in which the payment system is centered on a cryptocurrency founded on a decentralized blockchain. For example, would a legal-tender fiat currency, managed by a central bank, be a useful recourse for a panicked flight to quality that might ensue in a crisis? Would authorities or market participants be able to restart private payment systems that are suffering from technical failures or a loss of confidence? Might a fully digital system, particularly one not linked to a fiat currency but nevertheless universally accepted, provide an accelerant to a crisis? And could authorities intervene to tamp down any such accelerants? Would holders of a cryptocurrency further devalue that currency in a flight to a perceived more stable fiat currency, particularly where a government was injecting cash into the system to stabilize it? Answering such questions is an important (but open) research challenge.

In another context, flash crashes and associated trading halts can lead to voided transactions as trading venues triage their systems to limit the damage. But such transactions, particularly in derivatives markets, may have been intended as critical hedges for one or more counterparties. Voiding such transactions may thus expose large risks by removing a hedge in the midst of a very volatile market. Should markets coordinate transaction cancellations across trading venues? If so, who should make this decision, and how should coordination occur? For example, if each exchange clearinghouse uses a local blockchain as its system of record, what are the standards and procedures for integrating data across blockchains in a crisis? How should one resolve disputes regarding information recorded on the blockchain system(s) of record, noting that time for resolution may be very limited?

Market participants may require that the unwind protocol be incorporated in the same blockchain. But this may create a central point of failure. Technical issues (e.g., a denial-of-service attack or a mutating computer virus) may erode confidence in the blockchain and the market that relies on it. Again, what should be the protocol for restarting such a system and rebuilding confidence? What should be the entry points for human and/or supervisory intervention? It is important to clarify these issues in advance, thus avoiding paralysis or power grabs in a crisis.

Once again, answering such questions is an open research challenge. While these concerns exist for all aspects of business and regulation, they are particularly critical for financial stability in the context of resolving firms, central counterparties, and financial market utilities. Should a critical node of the system fail, the existence of immutable blockchain transactions or contracts could hinder or thwart the ability of supervisors to resolve institutions, in much the same way that the International Swaps and Derivatives Association's master agreements cross-default provisions hindered the ability to transition swaps from failing or failed counterparties.[18]

6.3.2 Data: Extraction, Evaluation, and Analysis

Since 2008 there has been increased attention to the cumulative, systemic effects of individual actions in the financial markets. Individual actions that are acceptable assumptions of risk or failures of payment in a single transaction can, if taken in the aggregate, create the equivalent of a heart attack in the system as a whole. Any attempt to understand, anticipate, and ameliorate systemic effects must start with identifying and collecting the relevant data about transactions and markets. New data sets are emerging from many sources, ranging from official collections such as supervisory stress tests to informal access to public corpora of news reports. Culling this massive information resource for patterns of concern will require correspondingly massive efforts at data collection, integration, and analysis.

It is common to classify big data scalability challenges according to the predominant bottleneck that materializes. These are the "Vs" of big data: volume, velocity, variety, and veracity. All these dimensions are relevant to fintech.[19] For example, both market participants and their regulators are turning to cloud storage systems to help address challenges associated with rapidly growing data volumes. We touched briefly on issues of velocity in our discussion of HFT above. Similarly, integration of identifiers—for example, in the LEI framework—addresses a fundamental problem with variety. In the remainder of this subsection, we will focus on blockchain platforms, which can help address challenges with data quality (veracity). Although blockchain systems can improve data quality, they can also introduce new challenges.

Privacy and anonymity are entry-level concerns in this process. The decentralized ledger built into the first-generation blockchains presupposes all-or-nothing transparency in the record of transactions. This helps establish the consensus needed for a valid blockchain ledger, but it creates problems when participants wish to record a transaction privately. Even in more general implementations, the distributed ledger must be open at least to validators (and potentially others), presenting questions about who knows what about transactions—for example, for supervisory or risk management purposes—under what circumstances, and in what format. Conversely, many early adopters of cryptocurrency have valued anonymity, displaying a range of motivations from the innocent to the malign.

The BCBC, in particular, goes to great lengths to anonymize (or psuedonymize) the identities of blockchain participants. Although bitcoin's anonymity can be useful in certain cases, for many financial transactions the unambiguous disclosure of the true identities of obligors and obligees matters very much. Bitcoin's pronounced anonymity posture highlights the question of blockchain transparency. Again, who gets to see what? Particularly in a crisis, financial stability supervisors will have a sharply heightened need for information, which suggests the need for adjustable transparency in key blockchains.

Even outside of a crisis, there will be valid requirements for partial information revelation. For example, since the 2008–2009 global financial crisis, numerous financial stability indexes have emerged, such as the OFR's Financial Stress Index or the various SRISK indexes at New York University's V-Lab.[20] A key goal of these indexes is to provide aggregated signals of accumulating risks to market participants. In many cases, these signals may depend directly or indirectly on the identities of key participants in the financial system, putting participant anonymity and financial stability in tension. In general, then, the law or its regulatory implementation should make credible levers available to supervisors to adjust policy in the face of changing risks. A key question is how the governance framework will intervene to stabilize the system during stress periods. The law must be capable of enforcing rights established and represented in blockchain.

Another attribute of a distributed (public and permissionless) ledger—whether to support a currency, a payment system, a clearing or settlement regime, or secure contracting—is the absence of a central node for collection of information about the system or its actors or transactions. The many benefits of such an approach have been celebrated, including (potentially) anonymity, reduction of costs, avoidance of reuse (rehypothecation) of collateral, and others.[21] Removal of a common ledger, however, could have consequences for both access to information and the quality of that information. In all instances, it is important to understand the implications of the permission rules for the ledger in question.

The BCBC, for example, builds in two forms of latency that are central to its process for building a consensus version of the truth into the distributed ledger. First, there is a mining latency for the brute-force calculations needed to establish the right to add a new block to the chain. It is theoretically necessary that this process be computationally costly—when signaling is costless, arbitrary nonsense (e.g., spam) or malicious misinformation can swamp the ledger. Currently, the BCBC mining costs periodically increase relative to reward, by intrinsic design (the *halving*, a process where the mining incentive decreases by 50 percent). In theory, a different blockchain with a higher reward, or a blockchain that touches a financial instrument worth considerably more (say, a trading blockchain that deals with transactions in the hundreds of millions or billions of dollars), could incentivize pursuit of fraudulent activity.

Depending on the consensus mechanism, a "consensus latency" in addition to the mining latency may be needed for an adequate number of affirming votes to accumulate for a particular version of the blockchain to proceed as the consensus truth. Both forms of latency imply a temporal delay, which could create tension, for example, if the goal is to support HFT operations. Although early implementations, such as the BCBC, have strongly favored a decentralized ledger and distributed consensus in establishing the agreed-upon version of the truth, the possibilities under alternative centralization assumptions have not yet been thoroughly explored, either from a legal perspective or from a technical perspective.

Alternatively, consider the example of the US wholesale payment system, which handles trillions of dollars in transactions each day. Presently, access to information about that system, its operations, and the flow of dollars through it can be understood by surveying a relatively small number of clearing banks, including the Federal Reserve Bank of New York, and financial market utilities (FMUs) that provide the settlement infrastructure.[22] A distributed ledger system could involve the same basic participants exchanging obligations, and thus result in the same basic access to information about the system as can be gathered now through the clearing banks and FMUs. As a result, the introduction of a blockchain-based system of record need not disrupt the ability of supervisors and market participants to monitor the system.

On the other hand, a decentralized ledger could diffuse this currently concentrated system with many implications. First, not enough is known about low-latency blockchain systems. Just as mining and consensus latency may recommend against a blockchain to support HFT, they may turn out to be an awkward choice for monitoring the financial system as a whole. Timely information gathering may be impossible in a highly diffuse financial system during rapidly changing, fluid situations, such as a market stress event. Capturing information about millions of disaggregate transactions and attributing them to central nodes or participants from perhaps thousands of servers would take computing power, time, and specialized tools that do not yet exist. This could also complicate efforts to identify failures and subsequently restart the system in the event of a cyberattack such as a denial of service against multiple nodes of the distributed ledger.

Access to information in a distributed ledger could be further complicated by a lack of resources (reliable power grids and/or communications infrastructure), misaligned incentives (key miners who stand to lose from full information revelation amid a crisis), or incompatible legal frameworks (privacy and information sharing laws) in key jurisdictions. Any of these forces could motivate regulations that ensure cooperation and fair play.

Additionally, simple access to distributed information about the system does not imply the feasibility of integrating data sets from various venues and jurisdictions effectively. The technologies and standards for payment information exchange, particularly across borders, will require coordination. There are alternatives to coordinated information integration for purposes of monitoring, regulation, and resolution—an ad hoc patchwork of local systems or a set of isolated silos—but any solution will present implementation challenges.

As noted above, anonymity or pseudonymity of transactors in a blockchain could raise other supervisory (and law enforcement) concerns. For example, given the traditional role of nodes in the system, such as banks' use of nodes to file suspicious activity reports, information flow could be limited by a distributed ledger network. Anonymity was a low-level requirement for the BCBC, but it is not clear how crucial this feature is, or what other possibilities open up if this constraint is eased. Although law enforcement concerns are generally beyond the scope of this chapter, regulators will surely seek to have means to identify market actors and their actions both to protect its participants and to preserve trust in the system itself. This should be balanced, however, against the legitimate need for some degree of anonymity to protect proprietary trading activity or avoid front running ahead of large market-moving activities (which created the need for dark pools).

On the other hand, pretrade anonymity is a crucial feature of many dealer markets, where knowledge of who is trading or whether they have come to buy or sell can, by itself, be sufficiently revelatory to drive trading away from the market altogether. The blockchain ledger would represent a new information source in these intricate environments, and the implications for existing microstructures are far from absolute. It is not clear that a blockchain would necessarily disrupt existing relationships, nor is it clear whether such disruption would be good or bad, on net. One should acknowledge, however, that the potential for disruption exists, and stay attuned to its ramifications as innovations are introduced. For example, the possible loss of anonymity might drive trading away from central nodes of the system and into bilateral markets, which in turn could have implications for firms' internal risk management systems, particularly if they lack the information necessary to monitor risk exposures.

This concern touches the regulatory system in several respects. Since 2002, the Sarbanes-Oxley law has required that corporate executives in the United States certify the adequacy of internal controls for risk management systems. Gathering the information necessary to meet this compliance requirement could be even more challenging in a distributed system if transactions are recorded and positions are reflected on multiple, dynamic platforms. The costs of maintaining internal risk management systems that ingest information from distributed ledgers could prove high. A similar concern arises in the context of the stress testing of banks now required for compliance with the Dodd-Frank Act. Risk management systems may need retooling to comply with the requirements of the law, and supervisors—in this case, the Federal Reserve and the Federal Deposit Insurance Corporation—will likewise need to adapt to identify the source of and standards for the data necessary to perform their supervisory functions.

Supervisors have invested significant effort to align reporting and transaction standards to improve the quality of information about the financial system. A good example is the creation of swaps data repositories, central counterparties, and swap execution facilities, where the OFR and other regulators are working to align data standards for entities, products, transactions, and myriad other data fields. As previously discussed, a possibly transformative application of blockchain technology would be for messaging, settling, clearing, and reporting the transaction using a single decentralized ledger. Here again, blockchain technology is not a panacea, however. Without common standards to reflect the legal and economic terms of the transactions and their counterparties, the precrisis opacity overlaying our derivatives markets would persist, regardless of the promise of blockchain technology. What remains, then, are questions of who will develop these standards, and how. Will competitive forces drive narrow, proprietary blockchain systems? Or will early steps be taken to avoid a disjoined collection of specific, one-off blockchain implementations that suffer from the kinds of classic collective-action problems that have hamstrung financial markets for years?

Finally, blockchain technology presents a significant opportunity to improve on many aspects of our financial infrastructure. One critical area is access to information by appropriate authorities, and the ability to securely share that information. In making design decisions, technologists could consider the benefits of improving the ability of supervisors to govern such that they can perform their critical role in overseeing orderly markets, protecting investors, testing the soundness of institutions at the core of the financial system, and building trust and confidence in our financial markets. Hopefully this will be a taken opportunity rather than a lost one.

6.4   CONCLUSIONS AND STEPS FORWARD

We are only at the dawn of realizing the potential of disruptive financial technologies. The coming years will see new applications emerge, new kinds of organizations develop, and new consequences arise that will need to be dealt with by a diverse community of stakeholders.

The technological and application developments for financial innovation will inevitably be accompanied by developments in government rule setting and oversight: in short, *regulation*. Some of this will involve applying existing rules and oversight structures; some will involve creating new provisions that will better fit the particular needs of a technologically based application. In this chapter we have sought to provide a framework for imagining what this future interaction of financial innovations such as blockchain with government may look like, along with our admittedly speculative vision of some of the possible points of contact.

We hope that this combined exercise will be a useful starting point for further deliberation and consideration as the process goes forward. We also note the emergence of various toolkits for policy makers and encourage those toolkit creators to consider the architectural principles that we have outlined herein.

Our thinking so far has largely focused on the *substance* of the applicable rules. In closing, we also wish to speculate on the *process* by which they will be developed. We strongly urge technology advocates such as the blockchain user community to get involved, and in some cases seek partnerships, with the various points of contact in government as this goes forward. For the most part, this engagement will lead to better outcomes. The modern regulatory process often invokes a model of multistakeholder dialog, with the goal of eliciting approaches that best serve the industry as well as the public and the needs of government itself. The technical complexity of blockchain applications makes this need for engagement even more critical. Indeed, regulatory and policy bodies such as the Organisation for Economic Co-operation and Development, the European Union, and the UK government have various formal and informal consultative engagements with private-sector actors to strive for policy that considers a variety of perspectives, including that of enterprise, alongside representatives of consumer advocacy, academia, and government.

Indeed, we note that the regulatory sophistication of technology market participants varies considerably. We admonish tech start-ups to engage in a proactive rather than reactive dialog with the applicable regulators for their respective businesses— the first contact with a regulator should not be the enforcement letter. They should also be open to hearing from those who have learned hard lessons from our financial markets even while they usefully disrupt. We also hope that those so-called entrenched interests use their positions and wisdom about financial markets carefully and avoid pushing out newcomers just to limit competition. Arguments that like activities should be regulated alike make sense if the regulation still makes sense, even if it means increased costs of entry.

A similar admonition can be aimed at governmental actors. As envisioned in such principles as those set out in Circular A-4, where possible, governmental intervention should consist of light-handed regulation, based on market and self-governing principles developed in consultation with those most affected. We favor the toolkit approach, where select actions can be chosen to address a given circumstance, as not all interventions are suitable for all domiciles, and every country must adapt its approach to optimize the benefits for its particular set of consumers, enterprise, and society.

Such a collaborative process can never be fully harmonious; there are simply too many diverging interests between and within the various classes of players. And the fractious and often tumultuous atmosphere of national government coinciding with the Trump presidency adds a layer of uncertainty. But dialog can nonetheless be far more productive than contentious processes based on hostility, mutual suspicion, and avoidance. We hope that this chapter will help catalyze the next stages in the process.

ACKNOWLEDGMENTS

The authors are grateful for the research and conceptual contributions of Josh Jackson, which have informed portions of this chapter.

NOTES

The views of the authors are their own and not necessarily those of their institutions.

1. Federal Deposit Insurance Corporation (FDIC), "Role of the Transfer Agent," Section 11 in *Trust Examination Manual*, 2005, https://www.fdic.gov/regulations/examinations/trustmanual/section_11/rta_manualroleoftransferagent.html.

2. N. Popper, "Knight Capital Says Trading Glitch Cost It $440 Million," *New York Times*, August 2, 2012, http://dealbook.nytimes.com/2012/08/02/knight-capital-says-trading-mishap-cost-it-440-million/?_r=0.

3. M. A. Russon, "The Curious Tale of Ethereum: How a Hacker Stole $53m in Digital Currency and Could Legally Keep It," *International Business Times*, June 20, 2016, http://www.ibtimes.co.uk/curious-tale-ethereum-how-hacker-stole-53m-digital-currency-could-legally-keep-it-1566524.

4. A. Quentson, "Ethereum Devs Hack the Hacker, Price Skyrockets," *Crypto Coins News*, June 22, 2016, https://www.cryptocoinsnews.com/ethereum-devs-hack-the-hacker-price-skyrockets/.

5. The parable of Shlemiel the road painter is apt in this context. See, for example, https://discuss.fogcreek.com/techinterview/default.asp?cmd=show&ixPost=153.

6. "How to Clean TRACE Data," Copenhagen Business School Department of Finance, 2016, http://sf.cbs.dk/jdnielsen/how_to_clean_trace _data.

7. Global Legal Entity Identifier Foundation website, as of October 30, 2019, https://www.gleif.org/en/lei-data/global-lei-index/lei-statistics.

8. A *springing interest* shifts ownership in the event that a particular event occurs.

9. D. Atkins, W. Stallings, and P. Zimmerman, PGP Message Exchange Formats, IETF RFC1991, Internet Engineering Task Force, August 1996.

10. A. Pentland, D. Shrier, T. Hardjono, and I. Wladawsky-Berger, "Towards the Internet of Trusted Data," in *Trusted Data*, 2nd ed., ed. T. Hardjono, D. Shrier, and A. Pentland (Cambridge, MA: MIT Press), 15–40.

11. See, for example, D. L. Chaum, "Untraceable Electronic Mail, Return Addresses, and Digital Pseudonyms," *Communications of the ACM* 24, no. 2 (February 1981): 84–88; S. Brands, "Untraceable Off-line Cash in Wallets with Observers," in *Advances in Cryptology— CRYPTO'93: 13th Annual International Cryptology Conference, Santa Barbara, California, USA, August 22–26, 1993, Proceedings*, ed. D. Stinson (Berlin: Springer-Verlag, 1993), 302–318; S. Brands, *Rethinking Public Key Infrastructures and Digital Certificates* (Cambridge, MA: MIT Press, 2000); J. Camenisch and E. Van Herreweghen, "Design and Implementation of the Idemix Anonymous Credential System," in *CCS '02: Proceedings of the 9th ACM Conference on Computer and Communications Security*, ed. V. Athuri (New York: Association for Computing Machinery, 2002), 21–30; A. Lysyanskaya, R. L. Rivest, A. Sahai, and S. Wolf, "Pseudonym Systems," in *Selected Areas in Cryptography: 6th Annual International Workshop, SAC'99, Kingston, Ontario, Canada, August 9–10, 1999, Proceedings*, ed. H. Heys and C. Adams (Berlin: Springer, 1999), 184–199; B. Rosenberg, ed., *Handbook of Financial Cryptography and Security* (Boca Raton, FL: CRC Press, 2011).

12. See "Overview," U-Prove, February 25, 2012, https://www.microsoft .com/en-us/research/project/u-prove/; J. Camenisch, M. Dubovitskaya, P. Kalambet, A. Lehmann, G. Neven, F.-S. Preiss, and T. Usatiy, *IBM Identity Mixer: Authentication without Identification*, 2015, https://www.zurich

.ibm.com/pdf/csc/2015-11-12-Idemix-Presentation.pdf; ABC4Trust, "ABC4Trust: Attribute-Based Credentials for Trust," March 28, 2012, https://abc4trust.eu.

13. For an overview of privacy-preserving MPC, see M. Flood, J. Katz, S. Ong, and A. Smith, "Cryptography and the Economics of Supervisory Information: Balancing Transparency and Confidentiality" (OFR Working Paper No. 0011, September 2013), http://financialresearch .gov/working-papers/files/OFRwp0011_FloodKatzOngSmith_Cryp tographyAndTheEconomicsOfSupervisoryInformation.pdf.

14. G. Zyskind, O. Nathan, and A. Pentland, "Enigma: Decentralized Computation Platform with Guaranteed Privacy," submitted June 10, 2015, https://arxiv.org/abs/1506.03471.

15. See Federal Identity, Credential and Access Management (FICAM) Program, https://www.idmanagement.gov/manage/; OIX, OpenID Exchange, http://openidentityexchange.org; SAFE-BioPharma Association, Trust Framework Provider Services, https://www.safe-biopharma .org/infocenter/Trust_Framework_Provder_Services.pdf.

16. See M. Flood, H. V. Jagadish, and L. Raschid, "Big Data Challenges and Opportunities in Financial Stability Monitoring," *Financial Stability Review of the Banque de France*, April 2016, 129–142, https:// publications.banque-france.fr/sites/default/files/medias/documents /financial-stability-review-20_2016-04.pdf.

17. See, for example, R. Ali, "Innovations in Payment Technologies and the Emergence of Digital Currencies," *Bank of England Quarterly Bulletin*, 2014, http://www.bankofengland.co.uk/publications/Documents /quarterlybulletin/2014/qb14q3digitalcurrenciesbitcoin1.pdf; T. Adrian and T. Mancini-Griffoli, *The Rise of Digital Money*, Fintech Notes, Note/19/01, International Monetary Fund, July 2019, https://www.imf .org/~/media/Files/Publications/FTN063/2019/English/FTNEA2019001 .ashx; International Monetary Fund, "Fintech: The Experience So Far" (IMF Policy Paper, June 2019), https://www.imf.org/en/Publications /Policy-Papers/Issues/2019/06/27/Fintech-The-Experience-So-Far -47056/.

18. ISDA, "Major Banks Agree to Sign ISDA Resolution Stay Protocol," press release, October 11, 2014, http://www2.isda.org/news/major -banks-agree-to-sign-isda-resolution-stay-protocol.

19. See Flood, Jagadish, and Raschid, "Big Data Challenges and Opportunities in Financial Stability Monitoring," for a fuller discussion of these issues.

20. Office of Financial Research, "OFR Financial Stress Index," https://www.financialresearch.gov/financial-stress-index, accessed July 13, 2021; V-Lab, "Global Volatility," https://vlab.stern.nyu.edu, accessed July 13, 2021.

21. McKinsey & Company, "Beyond the Hype: Blockchain in the Capital Markets" (McKinsey Working Paper No. 12, December 2015), http://www.mckinsey.com/industries/financial-services/our-insights/beyond-the-hype-blockchains-in-capital-markets; M. Mainelli and A. Milne, "The Impact and Potential of Blockchain on the Securities Transaction Lifecycle" (SWIFT Institute, Working Paper No. 2015-007, May 2016), http://www.swiftinstitute.org/wp-content/uploads/2016/05/The-Impact-and-Potential-of-Blockchain-on-the-Securities-Transaction-Lifecycle_Mainelli-and-Milne-FINAL.pdf; D. He et al., "Virtual Currencies and Beyond: Initial Considerations" (International Monetary Fund SDN/16/03, January 2016), https://www.imf.org/external/pubs/ft/sdn/2016/sdn1603.pdf.

22. Payments Risk Committee, *Intraday Liquidity Flows*, technical report, Federal Reserve Bank of New York, March 30, 2012, https://www.newyorkfed.org/medialibrary/microsites/prc/files/prc_120329.pdf.

7 DIGITAL BANKING MANIFESTO 2.0

Alex Lipton, David L. Shrier,
and Alex Pentland

Banks are trying to be cool and hip and build super cool digital front ends. . . . But it's like putting lipstick on a pig—ultimately it's still a pig and the new front end is still running into an awful digital back end.

—Mark Mullen, chief executive of Atom,
Durham, United Kingdom

7.1 INTRODUCTION

We wrote the original version of the Digital Banking Manifesto in 2016 when the economy as a whole, including the banking system, was on the mend after the fairly traumatic experiences of the global financial crisis (GFC). We are updating the manifesto amid an economic crisis of arguably more massive proportions ignited by the COVID-19 virus. The GFC was a wasted opportunity to reorganize the world financial ecosystem. If history has taught us anything, it's that the current crisis will likely fall into the same category. Already in the midst of the COVID-19 crisis, digital banking technology adoption is accelerating all over the globe.

Yet, reform is badly needed. In the past decade, too-big-to-fail banks became bigger rather than smaller, massively increasing their share of the banking business. For instance, J.P. Morgan has nearly twice as many assets now as it had at the end of 2006 just before the onset of the crisis; over the same period, assets of China's four systemically essential banks more than tripled. Although better capitalized, banking institutions have become so complicated that it is tough to ascertain their stability and creditworthiness with certainty. Their balance sheets are opaque and have complexity risks that are not well understood by regulators, depositors, investors, or even internal management. This complexity can reach high levels and may become too big to manage.

Moreover, in periods when large-scale lending is necessary (as it is at the moment), banks are not relied on; instead, central banks change their usual lender-of-last-resort modus operandi and become buyer-of-last-resort instead.

The general public's frustration with the status quo manifests itself in many ways—in politics, in general discourse, and, most directly, in the incredible rise and more recent fall of bitcoin and other cryptocurrencies. However, not all is lost. The introduction of new technologies is unleashing competitive threats to the existing players and will reshape the entire financial ecosystem. In our estimation, the following areas will see the fiercest competition: (1) fractional-reserve banks versus narrow banks, (2) digital cash versus physical cash, (3) fiat currencies versus unpegged cryptocurrencies versus asset-backed cryptocurrencies, (4) centralized payment systems versus distributed payment systems, and (5) centralized identity versus decentralized identity.

We are entering a new era of innovation that will reshape consumers' relationships with their banks. To understand how banking will evolve in the digital age, we need to understand its basic premise. While reasonable people can disagree about nuances, at heart, the art of banking is one of skillful record keeping in the double-entry general ledger. At the micro level, banks can be thought of as dividend-producing machines seeking deposits and issuing loans. At the macro level, they are creators of credit money.[1]

The main determinants of banks' quality and reliability are the amount of capital and the level of liquidity (mostly central bank money and government paper) they keep. In general, a bank would like to maintain the right levels of both—if it has too little, it becomes fragile; if it has too much, it becomes unprofitable and hence unable to fulfill its purpose of paying dividends. Some of the loans issued by the bank will be repaid as expected, and some will default. In general, when loans are repaid, the bank's capital grows; and when they default, the bank's capital diminishes. If the bank's capital falls below a certain fraction of its risk-weighted assets, the bank defaults. This setting is the premise behind a fractional-reserve bank. However, in principle, one can build a bank with assets comprising solely marketable low-risk securities and central bank cash in the amount exceeding its deposit base. Short of operational failures, such a bank cannot default and is by far more resilient than its fractional-reserve brethren.

Banking as we know it originated in the High Middle Ages and blossomed during the Renaissance and the early modern period, mostly in the form of fractional-reserve banking firms, which were naturally prone to collapse. On occasion, legislative attempts to convert banking from fractional reserve to narrow style have been undertaken—for instance, in Venice and Amsterdam. Over time, banks became much narrower than they had been, or are today. During the nineteenth century, British and American commercial banks, pursuing their self-interests, followed the real bills doctrine (where they only issued currency fully backed by hard assets), and in harmony with that approach lent predominantly for short maturities. Bank loans financed mostly short-term working capital and trade credit, with maturities of two to three months, and were collateralized by the borrower's wealth or the goods in transit. After the creation of the Federal Reserve Bank in 1913, commercial banks drifted away from the real bills doctrine. They started to lend for much longer maturities and instituted revolving lines of credit for some of their borrowers, thus sacrificing prudence and overemphasizing their maturity transformation ability. The Great Depression of 1929 showed the inability of the banks to meet their obligations successfully, which pushed the idea of a narrow bank to the fore.

The practical conversion of fractional-reserve banks into narrow banks did not occur in the 1940s, owing to enormous political pressure from fractional-reserve banks, not to mention a need to boost inflation in order to evaporate the war debt. However, the idea has stayed close to the surface. It gained considerable popularity during and after the savings and loan crisis of the 1980s and 1990s, and, not surprisingly, it became prevalent again during and after the GFC. We show below that technological developments make the creation of narrow banks an attractive and highly desirable possibility.

Good bankers differ from bad ones by their ability to attract a large pool of reliable borrowers, so that default levels stay close to their expected values. (Some defaults are inevitable and are accounted for by charging interest.) At the same time, good bankers need to attract long-term depositors and serve them well so that depositors do not suddenly withdraw their deposits. If the latter were to happen, the bank could exhaust its liquid reserves and default through a different route. In principle, if its less liquid assets are sound, the central bank, which is called the lender of last resort for a reason, can come to the rescue and provide additional liquidity. It is clear from the above description that banking activity is mostly technological and mathematical. Hence, it is well suited to be digitized.

Yet, the prevalence of legacy systems and legacy culture inhibits banks from embracing innovation as much as they should, if they wish to survive and thrive in the digital economy of the twenty-first century. The root causes of banking malaise are not difficult to understand—traditional banks are far behind the latest technological breakthroughs; they also have a weak handle on the risks on their books. While most industries, including retail, travel, communications, and mass media, have undergone revolutionary changes in their business models over the past thirty years or so, banking has remained static at its core, living on its past glories and ignoring the winds of change. Existing banks suffer from numerous drawbacks because competition among them is relatively weak.

Moreover, their customers are generally not happy with the level of customer service they receive. In addition, customers are at risk of losing their deposits (above and beyond the regulatory guaranteed minimum) should their bank default. Zero or negative deposit rates, which became prevalent in most developed countries in recent years, make keeping money in the bank both risky and unprofitable. Yet, at present, customers do not have viable alternatives. And there are whole strata of people and small and medium-size enterprises (SMEs), especially in developing countries, that are either underbanked or unbanked, since traditional banking methods are not flexible enough either to solve the "know your customer" (KYC) problem for them or to assess their creditworthiness.

7.2   CURRENT FINTECH TRENDS

Numerous fintech trends will shape the emerging banking landscape over the next few years. Fintech start-ups build their businesses based on banking application programming interfaces (APIs); partner with banks, which allows them to act as ersatz banks; differentiate themselves by offering an ever-expanding basket of retail banking products and services; and change their modus operandi from being unbundlers of banking services to becoming aggregators of these services. Large social-media-oriented platforms want to build or expand their fintech companies. Finally, large financial institutions want to develop their fintech capabilities so that they can compete with both small but agile fintech start-ups and tech heavy-weights. New digital-asset-centered banks will begin to appear.

The emergence of open banking legislative initiatives greatly facilitates these developments. Open banking is a reality in Europe, and it is gradually taking hold in the rest of the world as well. Relying on the new legislation, fintech companies can create plug-and-play APIs, which leverage open financial data. Previously, each bank held its own consumers' financial data, while at present, consumer financial data held by different financial institutions is callable via a single API. The ready availability of this data is creating new competition for the incumbents by allowing fintech companies to use such APIs as building blocks for their emerging business models.

Thanks to new developments in data technology and mobile telecommunications adoption, we see the potential rise of an unstoppable third wave of innovation in banking. We will outline the key features, benefits, and strategic imperative of the digital bank of the future (DBF).

To understand the opportunity that is promulgating this third wave, we explore the first two waves of digital innovation in banking.

7.3 FIRST–WAVE COMPANIES: DIGITAL INCREMENTALISTS

Digital technologies have been used in the banking industry for years. They have been added incrementally to existing operations, either as an overlay or as a minor extension. We term these the "incrementalists" or first-wave companies.

In the mid-1970s, Citi began experimenting with the automated teller machine (ATM). Former MIT chairman John Reed led the development of Citi's efforts in this area, revolutionizing retail banking. The story of the ATM is a landmark study in corporate innovation.[2] The concept was simple: deploy machines that could process transactions such as cash withdrawals and check deposits. What was revolutionary was what followed. Banks historically had limited business hours, such as from 9:00 a.m. to 3:00 p.m., which was inconvenient for people who worked from 9:00 a.m. to 5:00 p.m. However, in the 1950s, most households in the United States had a single earner, and the stay-at-home wife was able to handle banking needs during the day. Mapping to a behavior change in society, as more and more women entered the workforce, the United States saw a rise in two-income households, and thus fewer people could take advantage of daytime banking services. Thanks to electronic banking, executives could see exactly when people used banking services. Evening use of ATMs surged. Banks in turn began extending their hours into the evening to accommodate the working professional. By 2014, there were 524,000 tellers in the United States, up from 484,000 in 1985.[3]

Online banking, likewise, was piloted in the 1980s by Citibank and Chemical Bank, through Minitel (France) and Prestel (United Kingdom), but didn't take off until the 1990s in conjunction with soaring internet usage. Simple browser-based tools gave consumers access to many principal banking transactions, such as money transfer, bank statements, and electronic bill payment. While the incumbent commercial banks initially were the purveyors of online banking, the rise of the internet also saw the appearance of the internet bank— most prominently NetBank in 1996.

7.4   SECOND-WAVE COMPANIES: DIGITAL HYBRIDS

We term the second-wave companies, like NetBank, as "digital hybrids." Frequently taking advantage of front-end systems to better market to and connect with consumers, they remain shackled by legacy back- and middle-office infrastructure, risk modeling systems, and sometimes labor models. Often these hybrid banks will have an incumbent bank as their back end. For example, Simple Bank, which was founded in 2009, introduced many innovations to streamline account management and costs but uses Bancorp as the back end. Other emergent hybrid banks, such as Fidor Bank (Germany), Atom Bank (United Kingdom), LHV Pank (Estonia), and DBS Digibank (Singapore), enjoy a purpose-built IT infrastructure that is 60–80 percent less expensive to build and 30–50 percent less costly to maintain than that of legacy banks. Head count is also considerably lower, about 10–15 percent of the levels of a traditional bank. However, these digital hybrids still use centralized databases, cloud-based storage, and primitive user data protocols. They represent a bridge solution between the Main Street bank of yesterday and the fully digital bank of the future.

7.5 THIRD-WAVE COMPANIES: DIGITAL NATIVES

A new set of technologies is emerging that facilitates close integration with consumers' lives. These technologies promise access to financial services for the 2.5 billion unbanked or underbanked consumers globally.[4] They also offer greater financial flexibility to the over 45 million SMEs around the world that are currently underbanked.[5]

DBFs will take advantage of these technologies and will be designed around the needs of digital natives—the fifty-and-under crowd who grew up with computers as a part of their daily lives. For the millennials, a mobile-first strategy will drive ease of access and rapid adoption through seamless integration with their lives.

Taking a breakthrough approach to data security, DBFs will eschew a central data repository, easily attacked, in favor of a secure, encrypted, distributed data system. Personal data stores permit not only better digital wallets but also greater security around personal biometric data, which is integral to the digital bank's security protocols.

The new technology paradigm prompts the question: What role do banks genuinely have in the new world? Have we reached the end of banks in the way we know them? Is it possible that fractional banking is on its last legs and the introduction of government-issued digital cash, which can be stored in a digital wallet outside the banking system, will put the final nail in its coffin?

We will now look at the essential requirements for a digital bank from three perspectives: customer, investor, and the bank itself.

7.6 KEY REQUIREMENTS FOR A DIGITAL BANK: CUSTOMER PERSPECTIVE

The consumer's view of the digital bank is shown in figure 7.1. At a minimum, on the retail side, the DBF should be able to offer the following:

1. *Holistic and customizable experience.* Provide a holistic, interactive, and intuitive overview of the customer's money and, more broadly, their financial life, including information on their current account and deposit balances, transactions, outstanding loans, recurring payments, pension contributions, and accumulation as well as securities accounts. Tailor its services for different customer segments such as small and informal merchants, mass affluent, youth market, international travelers, or low-income customers. Offer a trusted and relatively inexpensive source of credit for its customers.

2. *End-to-end digital.* Provide a holistic, fully digital experience for customers, including paperless application and passing of the KYC process. Also, provide an interactive and intuitive digital financial planner to organize customers' economic lives and optimize their resources: immediate cash flow requirements, savings (including tools for automatic

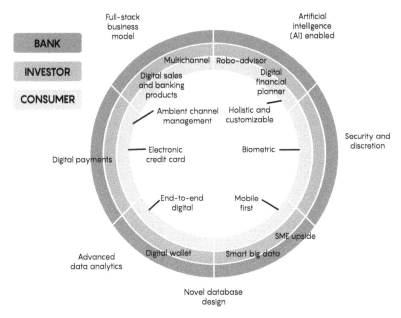

FIGURE 7.1
Consumer's view of the DBF.

savings), medical expenses, education, retirement (including robo-advisory with services previously available only to high-end investors), and investments, including tools for trading securities. Empower customers to electronically apply for a mortgage or loan. Offer competitive insurance contracts for home, liability, medical, and travel insurance, with credit checking procedures expanded to social media. Provide reporting documentation related to bank activity, including tax statements. Provide access to personal data store (PDS).

3. *Mobile first*. Enable natively driven mobile e-payment solutions, including domestic and international payments and remittances, automatic bill payments, and peer-to-peer (P2P) payments and money transfers. Rather than having mobile as an afterthought or an added capability, start with

mobile and build out from there—not just user experience but fundamental infrastructure and credit analytics.

4. *Foreign exchange services.* Deliver seamless and inexpensive foreign exchange services, including protection against exchange rate fluctuations, by providing multicurrency accounts. Potentially, a full range of instruments for hedging against foreign exchange risk, including forward contracts, spot contracts, swaps, and exchange-traded options, can be offered.

5. *Digital assets.* Offer efficient tokenization, handling, custody, and storage of digital assets.

6. *Biometrics technology.* Offer biometrics technology such as face and voice biometrics, already actively used at airports and international border controls, to customers as a way of logging in to their accounts. Behavioral biometrics, which is being developed at the moment, is a promising avenue for achieving an extra degree of protection.

7. *E-credit card.* Implement bank e-credit card based on customer preferences with preset limits and permitted transactions, consumption-related patterns, and a comprehensive digital wallet and PDS, which includes, at the minimum, electronic ID, e-card for secure online purchases, and tools to view, pay, organize, analyze, and archive e-bills and generate relevant tax documents.

8. *Access to P2P world.* Provide access to "crowd-everything," including P2P payment and lending opportunities.

7.7   KEY REQUIREMENTS FOR A DIGITAL BANK: INVESTOR PERSPECTIVE

A digital bank is an exciting investment opportunity and an inevitable business step because legacy banks are no longer able to adequately service their customers' needs in the digital age. Customer requirements simply cannot be met by traditional banks unable to catch up with the digital revolution.

With neither real estate overhead nor massive maintenance spending on legacy IT systems, digital banks expect to grow multibillion-dollar balance sheets in several years of operations with a fraction of full-time staff compared with traditional banks. For instance, Atom Bank in the United Kingdom intends to grow into a £5 billion balance sheet business in five years with just 340 full-time staff, while legacy bank Metro has that size balance sheet with 2,200 people. It is clear, however, that the majority of digital banks' personnel will be engineers and data scientists, although, as always, the role of sales and marketing should not be underestimated.

Monetization and capturing value are of paramount importance for investors. Compared with legacy banks, digital banks can generate value in numerous ways:

1. *Digital payments.* Digital payments form the core of monetization. They include mobile and online payments, both domestic and foreign, as well as mobile P2P interactions. Digital payments enable banks to boost fees and interest income and reach a broader set of customers with more diverse services; digital banks can process digital payments more cost effectively than incumbent banks can, allowing market share gains through competitive pricing and accessing the 2.5 billion unbanked and underbanked.

2. *Digital wallet.* Digital wallet is essential for digital commerce and ecosystems built on value-added services. In addition, it optimizes transaction costs for customers and funding costs for banking operations.

3. *Digital sales and banking products.* AI-assisted sales of banking products, such as deposits, loans, and mortgages, are conducted through direct channels, including social media. This is in line with shifting consumer preferences and behavior trends in e-commerce, mainly directed at Generation Y and tech-savvy customers.

4. *Multichanneling.* An integrated and seamless multichannel approach to sales increases the bank's share of customers'

wallet and boosts customer loyalty, thereby making a significant difference in customer adoption rates.

5. *Digital financial planner and robo-advisory.* An AI-based digital financial planner manages monthly income, recurring payments, savings, and investments, increasing the interaction between the digital bank and customers. The bank acts as a trusted shepherd defining customer life-cycle financial needs. This represents the logical continuation of the circle of trust between the digital bank and customers. In this model, customers rely on robo-advisory services to optimize investment portfolios based on individual goals and preferences, regularly adjust them and record incremental results, and properly allocate resources for each phase of the customer's voyage toward all things digital.

6. *Smart big data.* Advanced analytics allows the digital bank to transform its data into more personalized client service aimed at data monetization.

7. *SME emphasis.* AI- and big-data-based credit models enable risk-managed provisioning of credit access to SMEs, banking the 45 million underbanked SMEs globally. As of 2018, banks in Scandinavia, the United Kingdom, and Western Europe were forecast to have half or more of new inflow revenue coming from digital-related activities in most products, such as savings and term deposits, and bank services to SMEs.[6]

7.8 KEY REQUIREMENTS FOR A DIGITAL BANK: BANK PERSPECTIVE

Banks are mired in the legacy of old IT systems that are bad. . . . Coutts introduced the first automated banking system in 1967. The joke is that they are still running on it today.

—Anthony Thomson, founder, Atom Bank

Banks are not unique in their use of legacy systems. For instance, the US nuclear weapons force still relies on a 1970s-era computer system and 8-inch floppy disks.

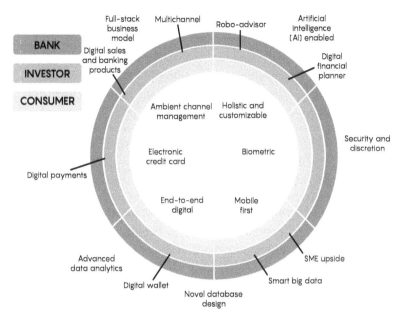

FIGURE 7.2
The investor's view of the DBF.

Note the investor's lens on the digital bank, as illustrated in figure 7.2. By its very nature, a digital bank has to be a cross between a fintech company and a bank. While a digital bank, similar to a conventional one, can be organized into five divisions (retail banking, private and business banking, analytics and IT, finance management and operations, and risk management), the relative importance of these departments is not the same. Moreover, the relationship map between various divisions is different in digital and legacy banking, with analytics and IT being the cornerstone of the digital banking edifice. In general, the success or failure of a bank is measurable by technologies and analytical methods adopted, such as the following:

1. *Novel IT infrastructure.* Building a digital bank from scratch enables creation of a flexible IT infrastructure, which

provides state-of-the-art risk management, helps optimize the bank's balance sheet to achieve a return on capital that is significantly higher than that of incumbents, and guarantees compliance with continually changing banking regulations in real time, which is achieved via building modern regulatory technology capabilities.

2. *Database design.* A digital bank's IT is based on state-of-the-art database technology, which can cope with the exponential growth in data, new internet technologies, and analysis methods. This technology uses a distributed ledger framework.

3. *Advanced-data analytics.* Since banks own abundant reserves of raw behavioral data, which can provide valuable insights into future customer choices, the value proposition offered by digital banking can be extended. Following the example of internet powerhouses such as Google, Amazon, Alibaba, and Facebook, the bank should consolidate data across deposits, consumer finance, and other transaction accounts for a unified view of customer activities. For instance, customers' in-store payments are far more accurate than conventional profile data (e.g., age, income, geography) in predicting their future financial activities and creditworthiness. Customers' geospatial mobility among stores provides further improvements. In addition, by using customer data, digital banks can create offerings ranging from payment solutions and information services, savings, and deposit-taking right through to online banking, advisory services, and simple financing. It is imperative to evaluate collected customer transactions in real time and connect them for prediction of future customer behavior using deep learning and other probabilistic algorithms. It is essential to build in safeguards of customer privacy per their preferences and legal requirements.

4. *AI.* Autonomous selection of the best methodology, when presented with arbitrary data, enables banks to adapt to novel information and dynamically build a full financial profile of their customers, including creditworthiness, debt

capacity, and risk appetite for financial planning. Additionally, AI can rapidly adapt to customer needs and present the best offers at the right time, changing dynamically as the customer evolves. A *smart bank* can more quickly capitalize on shifts in a customer's life cycle and help the customer achieve their financial goals.

5. *Full-stack business model.* The full-stack business model is crucial to the total client experience. This approach facilitates the bank's compliance with the regulatory framework, which enforces the prevention of money laundering and fraud and guarantees customers' protection. In general, intelligent fraud detection and remediation systems can function in a far more superior fashion than conventional methods.

6. *Security and discretion.* If implemented correctly, bulletproof security and customer protection offer digital banks a significant competitive advantage over other financial services providers. These features are embedded in a secure IT architecture from the onset and preclude both data misuse and data sales to third parties. They naturally include the implementation of new cryptographically secured distributed data management.[7]

7. *Distributed ledger.* Using the distributed ledger reduces financial transaction costs, improves the resilience of the system as a whole, and mitigates operational risks. Without a doubt, the distributed ledger will become intertwined with the operational procedures of a digital bank and its interactions with other digital, legacy, and central banks.

7.9 DIGITAL CUSTOMER SEGMENT

A digital bank must be able to attract enough customers to be viable in the long run. According to a recent consumer behavior survey, 43 percent of respondents would consider moving their money to an independent digital-only bank, 5 percent have already done so, and 52 percent are not ready yet (the bank's view of the digital bank is shown in figure 7.3).[8] Digital banks have several natural constituencies in both developed and, especially, developing economies:[9]

1. *Professionals.* Consumers with at least an undergraduate college education.

2. *Middle classes.* Digitally educated middle-upper and mass-affluent professional and managerial consumers.

3. *Digital banking natives.* Gen Y (students and young professionals in their twenties and thirties) individuals, who are exceedingly digitally savvy. They will form the foundation of the customer base for the digital bank.

4. *SMEs.* SMEs that go mainstream using a digital banking platform designed for their needs, potentially banking 45 million underbanked or unbanked SMEs globally.[10]

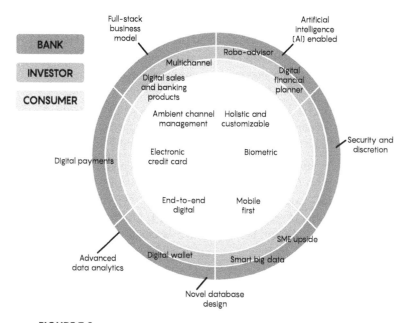

FIGURE 7.3
The bank's view of the DBF.

7.10   UNLEASHING DIGITAL CURRENCY

Digital banking of the future is unimaginable without using digital currency.[11] Currently, both central and private banks are actively pursuing the creation of digital currencies. Some considerations for this dimension can be summarized as follows:

1. *Nonbank digital currencies.* While the best-known digital currency is bitcoin, its low-transactions-per-second capacity makes it unsuitable for high-volume transactions. Thus, other digital currencies based on consensus achievable by means other than proof of work will be used in digital banking. One should not forget that bitcoin is not the first digital currency to emerge, nor will it be the last. Digital cash, invented by David Chaum more than thirty years ago, is likely to make a comeback at the next level of efficiency.

2. *Central bank digital currencies.* Several central banks are investigating whether a state-backed digital currency could reduce capital outflow, money laundering, and tax evasion and make economic activity more transparent and efficient. For instance, People's Bank of China, the Bank of England, and the Bank of Russia are all actively looking in this direction. In this scenario, the "free" (or inexpensive) deposits that commercial banks have been benefiting from will evaporate.

3. *Private bank digital currencies.* The idea of banks issuing currency by themselves is ancient, as dozens of banks in the United States were doing so in the nineteenth century. Advances in digitization have made this idea viable again. For example, the bank of Tokyo Mitsubishi UFJ (MUFJ) is developing its digital currency, MUFG coin, and the corresponding smartphone application prototype to authenticate digital tokens on a P2P platform. The bank expects to rein in financial transactional costs, including cheaper international remittances and money transfers. Moreover,

in the future, the bank might potentially issue its digital currency to customers.[12] Similar motivations are behind the development of the JPM coin.

4. *Stable coins.* While the term "stable coin" is self-explanatory to some extent, there is a need for a precise definition. The European Central Bank offers an attractive one: "[Stable-coin are defined as] digital units of value that are not a form of any specific currency (or basket thereof) but rely on a set of stabilization tools which are supposed to minimi[z]e fluctuations of their price in such currency(ies)."[13] These coins are a natural answer to the inherent volatility of non-bank digital currencies and can serve as a much-needed tokenized medium of exchange.[14]

5. *Trade coins.* Trade coins are a particular type of stable coins backed by assets. Such coins were envisaged by a team of MIT researchers in the Connection Science group in 2018.[15] The MIT Connection Science team proposed a practical mechanism combining novel technological breakthroughs with well-established hedging techniques for building an asset-backed transactional oriented cryptocurrency. They showed that in its mature state, the digital trade coin could serve as a much-needed counterpoint to fiat reserve currencies of today, which are routinely manipulated by central banks. Subsequently, the creators of Libra liberally used the main elements of the MIT design for their coin.[16]

7.11   NARROW BANK

Earlier we mentioned an attractive concept of a narrow bank,[17] and in this section we discuss it further. The main characteristic of a narrow bank is its assets mix, including solely marketable low-risk government securities and central bank cash in the amount exceeding its deposit base. By construction, such a bank can be affected only by operational failures.

State-of-the-art technology can minimize, but not eliminate, operational failures, thus providing a maximally safe payment system. As a result, deposits held at a narrow bank are functionally equivalent to currency, thus abolishing the need for deposit insurance with all its perverse effects on the system as a whole, including, but not limited to, the associated moral hazards.

This fact makes narrow banks ideal emitters of fiat-backed and asset-backed tokens. Indeed, the only way to keep a one-to-one parity between the fiat currency and digital tokens is to keep the exact amount of the fiat in escrow. However, one cannot put the requisite amount in a fractional-reserve bank and expect it to be safe at all times. Thus, one has to either use a narrow bank or open an account directly at the central bank. A central bank, while happy to accommodate licensed banking institutions and a small, select group of trusted nonbanking financial firms, such as central clearing counterparties, cannot and will not allow a broader range of corporate or individual participants (particularly if they wish to be anonymous) to have an account with them. There are several reasons for this, including, but not limited to, being unable to solve the KYC/AML (anti–money laundering) problem, not to mention potential political complications.

Narrow banks will be key ingredients of the financial ecosystem of the future. In the buildup to the GFC, banks simultaneously reduced their capital ratios and chose a progressively riskier asset mix in an effort to stay as leveraged as possible. However, after 2008, their group behavior changed dramatically, and banks became much narrower than before. At the same time, the Federal Reserve radically altered its modus operandi by massively expanding its balance sheet. Recent dramatic events caused by the COVID-19 pandemic accelerated the Federal Reserve transformation even further. We are observing exciting and somewhat perplexing developments: until the onset of the GFC, central banks were narrow banks, and commercial banks were fractional-reserve banks; while after the crisis, the situation almost completely flipped.

A suitably designed narrow bank is a natural repository of funds for those who highly value their funds' stability (either by predilection, such as wealthy individuals and organizations, or by necessity, such as central clearing counterparties). Besides, the narrow bank, being a neutral custodian, can provide value-added services and be a beneficial source of digital identity.

If banking institutions all become narrow, then credit creation will be performed by lending affiliates and other lenders—for instance, mutual funds or hedge funds, which will become money creators of the future.

In fact, after the GFC, a considerable portion of the credit has been issued by nonbanks, while many banks keep massive excess reserves with central banks, thus becoming de facto more narrow and reducing their money-creation capacities. Incumbent fractional-reserve banks can become much more cost-efficient, agile, and stable by splitting themselves into transaction-oriented narrow banks and lending affiliates (fractional-reserve banks and narrow banks are compared in figure 7.4).

After this transformation, narrow banks can use technological advancements such as distributed ledgers technology and AI to provide excellent transactional banking services and compete with transactionally oriented fintech start-ups. At the same time, uninsured lending affiliates of narrow banks, unencumbered by the requirement to offer utility-like transactional services, can better serve the needs of the real economy by providing traditional as well as innovative credit financial products. Given that lending affiliates would not be able to draw cheap sources of funding in the form of deposits, they would have to maintain healthy capital cushions and choose the quality of assets that align with their risk appetite, thus attracting savings and other types of funding from investors.

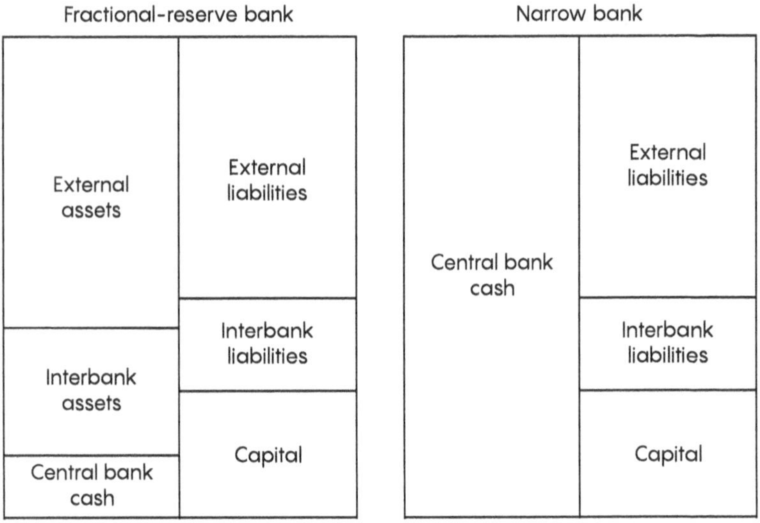

FIGURE 7.4
A fractional-reserve bank versus a narrow bank. The difference is in the choice of assets.

Lending affiliates would be naturally stratified depending on the level of their speculative activities, have skin in the game, and be open to scrutiny by their investors. Thus, splitting fractional-reserve banks into narrow banks and lending affiliates would increase the investment value of both enormous energy releases caused by nuclear fission.

7.12   SHAPING ECOSYSTEMS

It is natural to expect that a well-designed digital bank will become the cornerstone of a much bigger financial ecosystem— or even a set of interconnected ecosystems. As critical constituent parts of such an ecosystem, digital service providers can be thought of as insurers, brokers, wealth managers, robo-advisors, credit card issuers, cross-border payment providers, currency exchanges, and P2P lenders. The ability of these companies to satisfy the financial needs of their clients will be significantly enhanced by their access to a broader financial system through the digital bank. At the same time, the bank will benefit by getting additional information about customers' demands and habits, thus closing the information feedback loop. It is necessary to provide customers with proper privacy safeguards.

Moreover, digital cash issued by the bank can serve as a lubricant allowing the wheels of commerce to spin faster and much more efficiently than is currently feasible. It is possible to imagine a DBF in the center of the internet of things, which can be thought of as the bank of things. For instance, if a bank's client informs him or her that the roof needs repairs, the bank can immediately recommend several contractors, organize bids, help the client choose the most suitable one, and arrange to finance it. Thus, in addition to financial businesses, a DBF can incorporate various nonfinancial actors into its ecosystem. All these developments will enhance the social utility of the bank and its appreciation by the public while at the same time increasing its profitability. Banks have to keep in mind that there is no time to lose, because the competition for their customers' digital wallets from current digital champions Google, Amazon, Facebook, and Alibaba will be fierce.

7.13 BEYOND BANKS

The unsatisfactory state of affairs with existing banks presents a unique opportunity to build a digital bank from scratch. Such a bank will fulfill its mission by utilizing the most advanced technologies, including cryptography and distributed ledger techniques, AI, big data, and deep learning. From the very beginning, it will be based on balance sheet optimization; deployment of digital, distributed ledger–inspired infrastructure; and comprehensive automation and digitization of the

middle and back office, as well as heightened security employing the most advanced cryptographic techniques throughout
the entire organization. By design, this bank will be highly
efficient, profitable, and agile. And its infrastructure will be
flexible enough to handle both private digital currencies (such
as bitcoin) and potential government-issued currencies (such
as Britcoin). If so desired, this bank will be capable of issuing a digital currency by itself. The bank will liberally apply
AI and big data analytics to create an unparalleled customer
experience, automate personal and SME credit issuance, and
improve risk management. By design, such a bank will be valued by investors, customers, and regulators alike.

And yet, by building such a bank, are we trapped in the old
paradigm? If you look at WeChat or Sesame, you will see what
is scaring the C-level of even leading-edge companies like
Facebook and Google, to say nothing of the fright induced at
leading telecommunications companies. Perhaps surprisingly,
many legacy banks seem to be more sanguine. WeChat is rede-
fining what financial services means in relation to the broader
suite of consumer services with which individuals engage.

The key is to have customer-centric data across all areas of
life, which is held in a standard format with standard APIs that
work across the entire digital ecosystem and not just its financial services or products corner. (In this way, it is like a universal PDS, but customers don't own or manage the data; the
PDS does.) Using this central, panoptic data, WeChat can integrate services from the range of life opportunities (e.g., enter-
tainment, work, finance, family) seamlessly and consistently.
This gives customers fully integrated payments, credit and
banking, unbelievable advising capability, and amazing KYC/
AML, all in a completely transparent form. Users just wander
around online and in person, find exciting things, and buy,
sell, and trade seamlessly. WeChat and Sesame are also integrating health, lifestyle, and employment services with money
services and are doing so completely transparently, with no

separate apps or web pages. Consumers can just take care of those things that will help them live better lives. However, this is conditional on consumers' ability to secure credit as necessary. Given the somewhat uncertain and limited capacity of P2P networks to provide credit, digital banks have to come to the rescue.

A similar future is unfolding for SMEs: customers are shepherded to buy, and money-flow issues like credit, payments, and KYC/AML are almost nonexistent. WeChat reportedly reached over 1 million SMEs integrated into its services in the first few months of operations.

Is there a future that is effectively one where there is "no banking" versus "digital banking"? Instead of having digital banking as a discrete service, banking functions are just integrated invisibly everywhere. Several immediate challenges come to mind with this model:

1. *Money creation.* Because of the exclusive and unique role of banks in credit money creation, nonbank actors simply do not have the necessary capacity to satisfy the financial needs of their customers.

2. *Regulatory constraints.* There are numerous constraints around offering banking services that may be too limiting for companies in western Europe and the United States. If China begins to adopt more restrictive financial regulations to better protect consumers, these regulations will also create a less hospitable business environment for these kinds of services.

3. *Stock market pressure.* Will WeChat (or the next WeChat) want to take its high-flying tech stock market multiple and burden it with a financial services discount?[18] The more successful it becomes at financial services, the more acute this question becomes. However, if the financialization of a tech company is done in a deliberate and measured way, it can increase the shareholder value.

Despite these challenges, is there a model that we could call "invisible banking" that integrates into our daily lives without friction? The answer is yes and no—the legacy banking model will unquestionably disappear over time. Some believe that the integration of artificial intelligence into cryptocurrency could provide a pathway to this invisible banking future (DeFi, or decentralized finance); others believe that Big Tech, such as Amazon, Apple, or Ali Baba, will facilitate it and profit from it. Still, in the transition period, digital banks will have a role in daily life as transaction lubricants and enablers.

NOTES

1. A. Berentsen and F. Schar, "The Case for Central Bank Electronic Money and the Non-case for Central Bank Cryptocurrencies," *Federal Reserve Bank of St. Louis Review* 100, no. 2 (2018): 79–106, https:// research.stlouisfed.org/publications/review/2018/02/13/the-case-for -central-bank-electronic-money-and-the-non-case-for-central-bank -cryptocurrencies. This chapter provides a detailed explanation of how money is created and destroyed by the banking system as a whole and by individual banks. It also shows that different banks become naturally interconnected in the process.

2. E. Florian, D. Burke, and J. Merro, "The Money Machines," *Fortune*, July 26, 2004, https://archive.fortune.com/magazines/fortune /fortune_archive/2004/07/26/377172/index.htm.

3. Bureau of Labor Statistics, *Occupational Outlook Handbook*, 2015, https://www.bls.gov/ooh/.

4. I. Chaia, T. Goland, and R. Schiff, "Counting the World's Unbanked," *McKinsey Quarterly*, March 1, 2010, https://www.mckinsey.com/industries /financial-services/our-insights/counting-the-worlds-unbanked #:~:text=Fully%202.5%20billion%20of%20the,unserved%20doesn't%20 mean%20unservable.

5. O. Alper and M. Hommes, "Access to Credit among Micro, Small, and Medium Enterprises," World Bank Group, 2013, https:// openknowledge.worldbank.org/handle/10986/21726.

6. A. Broeders and S. Khanna, "Strategic Choices for Banks in the Digital Age" (McKinsey & Company, January 1, 2015), https://www.mckinsey.com/industries/financial-services/our-insights/strategic-choices-for-banks-in-the-digital-age.

7. G. Prisco, "Enigma, MIT Media Lab's Blockchain-Based Encrypted Data Marketplace, to Launch Beta," *Bitcoin Magazine*, December 22, 2015, https://bitcoinmagazine.com/business/enigma-mit-media-lab-s-blockchain-based-encrypted-data-marketplace-to-launch-beta-1450810499.

8. Data is from the February 2019 "Marqeta Consumer Behavior Survey" as cited by Axios. One thousand, two hundred US internet users aged eighteen to sixty-five were surveyed online by Propeller Insights during January 16–17, 2019.

9. For example, in Asia the number of digital banking customers was estimated at more than 800 million out of a global total of 1.9 billion (source: "Number of Active Online Banking Users Worldwide in 2020 with Forecasts from 2021 to 2024, by Region," Statista, https://www.statista.com/statistics/1228757/online-banking-users-worldwide/, accessed July 12, 2021), as stated in J. Chen, C. V. Hv, and K. Lam, "How to Prepare for Asia's Digital-Banking Boom," McKinsey & Company, 2014) https://www.mckinsey.com/industries/financial-services/our-insights/how-to-prepare-for-asias-digital-banking-boom.

10. D. Shrier, J. Larossi, D. Sharma, and A. Pentland, "Blockchain & Transactions, Markets and Marketplaces" (MIT White Paper, 2016), https://www.getsmarter.com/blog/wp-content/uploads/2017/07/mit_blockchain_transactions_report.pdf.

11. D. Shrier, G. Canale, and A. Pentland, "Mobile Money & Payments: Technology Trends" (MIT White Paper, 2016), https://www.getsmarter.com/blog/wp-content/uploads/2017/07/mit_mobile_and_money_payments_report.pdf.

12. S. Das, "Japanese Banking Giant Reveals Plans for a Digital Currency," *Cryptocurrency News*, February 2, 2016, https://www.ccn.com/japanese-banking-giant-reveals-plans-for-a-digital-currency/.

13. D. Bullmann, J. Klemm, and A. Pinna, "In Search for Stability in Crypto-assets: Are Stablecoins the Solution?" (European Central Bank

Occasional Paper Series, 2019), 3, https://www.ecb.europa.eu/pub/pdf
/scpops/ecb.op230~d57946be3b.en.pdf.

14. A. Lipton, "Towards a Stable Tokenized Medium of Exchange," in
Cryptoassets: Legal, Regulatory, and Monetary Perspectives, ed. C. Brum-
mer (New York: Oxford University Press, 2019); A. Lipton, F. Schar,
A. Sardon, and C. Schupbach, "From Tether to Libra: Stablecoins and
the Future of Money" (white paper, Hebrew University, 2020), https://
arxiv.org/pdf/2005.12949.pdf.

15. A. Lipton, T. Hardjono, and A. Pentland, "Digital Trade Coin:
Towards a More Stable Digital Currency," *Royal Society Open Science* 5,
no. 7 (2018): 180155, http://dx.doi.org/10.1098/rsos.180155; A. Lipton and A. Pentland, "Breaking the Bank," *Scientific American*, January
26–31, 2018.

16. Libra Association Members, "An Introduction to Libra" (white
paper, Libra Association, 2019), https://sls.gmu.edu/pfrt/wp-content
/uploads/sites/54/2020/02/LibraWhitePaper_en_US-Rev0723.pdf.

17. A. Lipton, A. Pentland, and T. Hardjono, "Narrow Banks and
Fiat Backed Digital Coins," *Capco Institute Journal* 47 (2018): 101–116,
https://www.capco.com/capco-institute/journal-47-digitization
/narrow-banks-and-flat-backed-digital-coins.

18. It is possible that both tech premium and financial discount are
temporary in nature.

III FINTECH POSSIBILITIES

8 REGULATORY SANDBOXES

Oliver R. Goodenough
and David L. Shrier

8.1 INTRODUCTION

The technology industry operates under the mantra of "move fast and break things." While this approach has some merits for innovating a new kind of mobile phone or a new piece of software, it famously falls apart when applied to critical systems. Fintech regulatory sandboxes can bridge the gap between the tech start-up attitude of "build fast" and government needs to provide for consumer protection and financial stability.

There's a well-known joke in computer (and auto) circles that describes an imaginary conversation between Microsoft founder Bill Gates and the CEO of General Motors, where Gates says, "If GM had kept up with technology like the computer industry has, we would all be driving twenty-five dollar cars that got 1,000 miles/gallon," and GM's CEO replies, "Yeah, but would you want your car to crash twice a day?"[1] The issue becomes equally sensitive in the financial services context, where a family's ability to buy food and pay for housing is governed by their access to financial services or, at a minimum, cash. A digital cash wallet, for example, that had a bug and erased someone's account could spell homelessness for a family relying on it. A new kind of securities trading and settlement system could destabilize markets if it went awry.

In addition, new regulations around data privacy and data portability, such as the General Data Protection Regulation, the California Consumer Privacy Act, and UK Open Banking, can be complex in application and difficult for companies to comply with. At the same time, the path for monetizing open data, the fine details of which are still unclear, has opened up,[2] and a number of companies are pursuing opportunities in the banking sector as a result.

The high degree of complexity and sensitivity to change that the financial sector presents has given rise to regulatory sandboxes, environments in which companies and governments can collaboratively explore the issues and impacts of new technologies in a safe environment. Regulators and policy makers need to understand how to design, build, and apply these tools, and the private sector needs to understand the benefits of capitalizing on this close access to regulators.

8.1.1   What Is a Regulatory Sandbox?

A regulatory sandbox is a tool that governments can use to foster innovative approaches to commercial activity, such as the development and deployment of fintech applications. These innovative approaches can come from both established players and early-stage companies. The sandbox is permissive, in that it creates opportunities for experiments that might not fit within existing regulatory frameworks; it is also supervisory, in that it invites innovators to work within regulatory oversight, rather than ignoring it and asking for forgiveness later. Such a sandbox "allows FinTech startups and other innovators to conduct live experiments in a controlled environment under a regulator's supervision."[3]

A number of jurisdictions around the world have established these testing grounds. The United Kingdom is a leader in this movement. In 2015 its Financial Conduct Authority (FCA) issued a report[4] setting out both the rationale for a sandbox and suggestions for its shape and operations.

8.1.2 Rationale and Goals

Existing sandbox initiatives have identified a number of rationales and goals for their existence. We discuss a few of these below.

Speeding productive innovation Legacy regulatory regimes, however well intentioned, have necessarily been tailored to a set of practices and concerns growing out of the established customs of the targeted industry. As a result, they often mandate approaches that will block truly innovative steps. The process of removing these impediments through traditional legislative and regulatory revision is generally cumbersome. A lighter touch, which involves controlled, supervised experimentation, can be a quicker route to permitting—and regulating—productive innovation.

Bringing innovation out of the dark If the regulatory barriers remain high, innovators may be tempted to "seek forgiveness and not permission." The example of Uber's assault on the traditional taxi industry illustrates such a strategy. This approach is not optimal, either for society or for the companies involved. Rather, it is important that innovators and regulators engage in a productive dialog as new applications and business models are developed. The sandbox approach should be designed to encourage such an interchange.

Regulatory education A more collaborative approach will allow the regulators to learn directly about the functioning of the innovative companies and their creative applications and products. This will allow a government to be more nimble and accurate in allowing productive innovation and short-circuiting harmful practices. Rooting regulatory approaches in experience will also produce improved frameworks.

Benefits to the consumers The new products and services that become possible through fintech applications should not benefit just their suppliers. To be successful over the long haul, they should also benefit consumers. Internet banking, while not a perfect application, has been adopted by millions of Americans because of its convenience and ease of use. Other innovations now entering the pipeline, or indeed not yet imagined, will have similar impacts. The process of speeding them to market, while continuing to protect the public interest, can be accelerated through the supervised experimentation that a sandbox permits.

Financial inclusion A common impact of technologically mediated innovation is the extension of benefits previously available only to the well-off to the more general public. This can be true in finance as well. By way of example, well-intentioned protective regimes have created a private marketplace for accredited investors that often makes much-higher-yield investments available to the wealthy than the vanilla deposits and returns available to nonaccredited investors. While the need for safeguards continues, tokenization and other technologies can assist in opening well-vetted investment opportunities with higher-yield possibilities to less well-heeled populations. The sandbox approach would allow exploring initiatives toward this goal.

Jurisdictional head start and economic development In addition to these directly related benefits, there is no question that there is jurisdictional competition over the direct economic development and the indirect benefits, such as increased tax revenues, that being a center of innovative commerce can bring to a domicile. If a government is seeking to host blockchain and fintech solutions, a sandbox would allow it to be at the front edge of the process. Demonstrating this capacity in turn signals to interested innovators both within and outside the country its receptivity to innovation.[5]

8.1.3 Concerns and Responses
Legitimate concerns can arise when designing and implementing a blockchain/fintech sandbox. It should be designed

to maximize the benefits of innovation while minimizing the chance of serious harm arising. A good summary of these concerns and some potential solutions to them is offered by the Consultative Group to Assist the Poor in its discussion of sandbox approaches:

> While there are good reasons to explore regulatory sandboxes, policy makers should be prepared to face challenges. Most importantly, operating a regulatory sandbox requires adequate human and financial resources to select proposals, provide guidance, oversee experiments and evaluate innovations. Regulators may lack these resources in many EMDE [Emerging Market and Developing Economies] countries. Therefore, policy makers need to pay attention to details and carefully consider their options. These may include various sandbox designs and other pro-innovation approaches that have been used successfully. For example, the test-and-learn approach enables a regulator to craft an ad hoc framework within which an innovator tests a new idea in a live environment, with safeguards and key performance indicators in place. A wait-and-see approach allows a regulator to observe how an innovation evolves before intervening (e.g., person-to-person lending in China).[6]

8.2 EXISTING INITIATIVES AND MODELS

There are a number of existing fintech sandbox initiatives around the world, most with a wider mandate than a purely blockchain-based initiative. The British initiative is perhaps the most developed sandbox. In the United States, Arizona has established a sandbox; Illinois proposed one in its last legislative session, but it was not enacted. At the federal level, the Consumer Financial Protection Bureau (CFPB) announced a sandbox initiative in July 2018.[7] The CFPB has announced plans to implement this through an existing program on "trial disclosure programs."[8] The regulatory action was adopted September 10, 2019, and the sandbox is accepting applicants.[9]

A survey administered by Davis Wright Tremaine offers a useful background.[10] The following sections provide a brief summary on some of these sandbox initiatives that are up and running.

8.2.1   The United Kingdom

The impetus for the United Kingdom's adoption of the sandbox approach seems to have come from its FCA as part of its preexisting Project Innovate. The City of London has long been an international leader in the financial industry, and the financial community has been concerned about the need to digest and deploy fintech as a means of keeping that leadership. The idea of a sandbox was formally floated in a 2015 report by the FCA, titled *Regulatory Sandbox*.[11] The report was generally well received. The approach was formalized in 2016, and the first cohort accepted in 2017.[12] Twenty-four firms were accepted into that cohort, and eighteen tests were carried to completion. The program has been deemed sufficiently successful that five additional cohorts have been accepted, and the sixth cohort accepted applications through December 2019.[13] In 2017 the FCA declared that "early indications suggest the sandbox is providing the benefits it set out to achieve with evidence of the sandbox enabling new products to be tested, reducing time and cost of getting innovative ideas to market, improving access to finance for innovators, and ensuring appropriate safeguards are built into new products and services."[14]

With this track record, the FCA has learned some lessons from the experience and has, to some degree, refined its approach in each of the cohorts.[15] If a government is actively considering a fintech sandbox, a study of the UK approach would be a worthwhile exercise.

8.2.2   Arizona

The first US application of the fintech sandbox approach was adopted by Arizona in 2018.[16] It was authorized by a legislative enactment (A.R.S. § 41-5601) and will be overseen by its attorney general, who is a supporter of the initiative.

Details on its operation are available on the website of the Arizona attorney general (https://www.azag.gov/FinTech). Its announced purpose, explained on that site, is familiar: "The Sandbox enables a participant to obtain limited access to Arizona's market to test innovative financial products or services without first obtaining full state licensure or other authorization that otherwise may be required." The program is seeking applications at this time. (The application form is available at https://www.azag.gov/FinTech/application.)

Interestingly, securities trading, insurance products, and services that provide solely deposit-taking functions are not eligible to enter the Arizona sandbox. These exceptions may reflect turf conflicts within the Arizona regulatory and business communities. Some of these gaps, particularly the gap on insurance products, may leave an opening for a government to be an early mover.

8.2.3 Singapore

Singapore has a history as a financial center in Asia. Like the United Kingdom, it is actively seeking to protect and foster its status by staying at the forefront of fintech innovation. Its enthusiastic embrace of blockchain applications is one aspect of this; the adoption of a fintech sandbox is another. The Singapore sandbox initiative is under the authority of the Monetary Authority of Singapore (MAS). Its statement of purpose is as follows:

> MAS is encouraging more FinTech experimentation so that promising innovations can be tested in the market and have a chance for wider adoption, in Singapore and abroad. The regulatory sandbox will enable FIs as well as FinTech players to experiment with innovative financial products or services in the production environment but within a well-defined space and duration. It shall also include appropriate safeguards to contain the consequences of failure and maintain the overall safety and soundness of the financial system.[17]

MAS has taken a nuanced approach, with a regular sandbox as well as an "express" version with fast-track approval for instances where "the risks are low and well understood by the market."[18] A description of its guidelines is available on its website (https://www.mas.gov.sg/development/FinTech/regulatory-sandbox).

8.2.4   Other Countries and the Global Financial Innovation Network

A number of other countries have announced similar initiatives, and the Global Financial Innovation Network (GFIN) involving many of these has been announced.[19] Jurisdictions and NGOs listed as members include the following:

Abu Dhabi Global Market

Australian Securities & Investments Commission

Autorité des marchés financiers (Canada)

Central Bank of Bahrain

Consultative Group to Assist the Poor

Consumer Financial Protection Bureau (United States)

Dubai Financial Services Authority

Financial Conduct Authority (United Kingdom)

Guernsey Financial Services Commission

Hong Kong Monetary Authority

Monetary Authority of Singapore (Singapore)

Ontario Securities Commission (Canada)

8.2.5   Conclusions and Takeaways

As this introductory review indicates, the sandbox approach has been considered and adopted by a number of jurisdictions, and their design approaches and experience can be a useful guide to any initiative that a government chooses to establish. Furthermore, the longer-lived versions, such as that in the United Kingdom, have been deemed successes by their regulatory sponsors.

Taken as a whole, the experience of other jurisdictions makes a case for the possibility of a fintech sandbox to meet the complex goals of promoting change while providing protection against predation and other losses to the public.

8.3 POSSIBILITIES FOR A GOVERNMENT TO CONSIDER

8.3.1 Participating Departments/Leadership

In order to be successful, any regulatory sandbox adopted by a government should include the principal regulatory stakeholders for fintech supervision. If these stakeholders can come to a coordinated approach to a sandbox, it will help provide the surety of application that the innovator will need. In addition, other ministries, departments, and/or supervisory bodies may need to be included. For example, national governments may wish to incorporate their information and communications technology ministries in addition to finance, because of the pervasiveness of digital finance and the growth of platform companies that use mobile communications for fintech.

8.3.2 Market Segment Targets

A government should decide which market segments would be productive to target. The targets should be considered broadly as an initial matter, which could lead to a wide variety of projects being submitted under the sandbox. Deciding which projects to pilot would provide a chance to explore a government's capacity to evaluate and oversee the experiments as they go forward. The point of the exercise in any sandbox effort is to be *surprised* by the creativity of the fintech and distributed ledger sectors, and not to artificially constrain the creativity in advance. That said, targets could include the following:

• InsureTech

• Real estate

• Securities, including "smart securities"

- Banking, settlement, "know your customer"
- Cryptocurrencies
- Tokenization and blockchain in noncurrency areas
- Recordation in property, collateral, and other areas
- Privacy/data protection
- Food and agriculture supply chains
- Energy generation, distribution, and conservation
- Health-care data
- Other categories of personal data; data self-sovereignty

8.3.3 Project Elements/Criteria

A government desiring to establish a sandbox will need to have a reasonably well-defined set of goals and specific project elements that will inform whether to select a particular project. At a general level, a project should answer yes to the following questions:

- Does it truly foster innovation, or is it just a request for regulatory relief on existing approaches?
- Is there a strong likelihood of consumer or other public benefit from the proposed innovation?
- Will the proposed innovation provide utility to the company proposing its adoption, such as a good use case for testing the technology?
- Would the risks associated with the proposed innovation be adequately contained?
- Will the proposed innovation create economic activity and development for the citizenry of that domicile?

Other criteria, or different versions of the above, are set out in the various sandbox proposals already described, and those proposals should be considered when determining the goals for a sandbox initiative.

At the level of specific project applications, the following elements should be present:

- The proposal should be made with sufficient specificity so as to constitute an implementable project and not a general fishing expedition.
- The proposal should relate to a specific project and not seek a general variance.
- The project should be suitable to testing through a sandbox approach and not be a part of a full-blown rollout.
- The company should have both the financial and the managerial capacity to effectively carry out the proposed test.
- Consumer protection criteria should be clearly specified.
- There should be an appropriate nexus to the domicile, with a particular attention to economic activity. Connection with local governments could be encouraged.
- The time frame for the project and its test should be limited to a reasonably short horizon.

If a government develops a sandbox, the criteria established in other jurisdictions can provide a useful guide to its thinking.

8.3.4 The Application Process

In considering the application process, the government can create priority avenues for projects coming from verified supply channels. These could include projects vouched for by one of the various incubator programs, coworking locations, or maker spaces in the jurisdiction. The government could also give priority to projects emerging from its colleges and universities.

It can be useful to have a phased application process, with a first-stage initial inquiry to prequalify an idea as at least generally meeting the goals and criteria, followed by the second stage of an actual request, which would contain significantly greater detail. Application forms for existing programs can provide guidance for this part of the process.

Attention should also be given to the number of projects that can be productively overseen in the sandbox, with the winnowing-down process aimed at getting to and maintaining that target.

8.3.5 Benefits and Opportunities
The sandbox should provide the following possibilities, which will benefit the applicants:

- Unified application across participating departments
- Quick response
- Where appropriate, relief on a "no action" basis within existing rules
- Where appropriate, waivers or exemptions from existing rules, which can be limited by restrictions that are more appropriate to the tested approach
- Collaboration between the company and the regulator on the consideration for permanent rule-making/qualification criteria

8.4 NEXT STEPS

For governmental stakeholders interested in seeing such an initiative go forward, the following is a possible road map for further action.

8.4.1 Form an Intra- and Interagency Consultation Group
As mentioned above, a working group allowing such consultation should be formed and convened.

8.4.2 Determine Regulatory/Legislative Authorization
Relatively early in the process, the group should determine what can be done at the agency level without legislation and

what will need legislative authorization. To the extent that legislation is necessary, it should be drafted in collaboration with the appropriate legislative committees. Some designated funding may also be needed, which would require legislative approval.

8.4.3   Obtain Stakeholder Input

A range of private and public stakeholders should provide information on opportunities and concerns that can help guide this process. Neutral third parties, such as university researchers with expertise in the area, can help balance competing interests and provide unbiased perspectives on the approach as it develops.

8.4.4   Design the Program

The program should be designed with careful consideration given to the goals and criteria described in this memorandum and further developed in the process. Existing sandbox programs in other jurisdictions can be mined to assist in the design process. Once a design is agreed upon, it should be adopted through the appropriate regulatory and legislative processes.

8.4.5   Implement the Program

Implementation of the program should include an allocation of resources for developing the website and other necessary resources to gather the applications, evaluate them, and work with the selected programs to maximize effectiveness and consumer protection. The government should also allocate resources for outreach into the technology and innovation communities and for publicity into the wider world of innovators.

8.4.6   Determine Collaborations

A government needs to carefully evaluate collaborators, which could include other governments; multigovernmental bodies such as the GFIN, the Organisation for Economic Co-operation and Development, or the Commonwealth; and commercial entities, foundations, academic institutions, and others that might bring value to the effort.

8.4.7   Evaluate the Program

The program's outcomes should be evaluated periodically, with intentional determinations made as to whether to continue the program or modify it in light of experience.

8.5   CONCLUSIONS

The fintech sandbox approach has been adopted by a number of jurisdictions worldwide and has proved successful in advancing the goals of promoting innovation while attending to consumer protection and assisting governments in their efforts to attract more jobs-creating innovative new firms to their jurisdictions. It offers governments a safe means of facilitating innovation, and offers start-up companies a mechanism to engage with governments that was previously unattainable because of the expense and expertise involved in a full-press government affairs program. Fintech sandboxes are powerful tools to create innovative new offerings for consumers and enterprises.

NOTES

Portions of this chapter appeared in an earlier form as a research paper for the Distributed Ledger Governance Association, Inc.

1. D. Mikkelson, "General Motors Replies to Bill Gates," Snopes, 2010, https://www.snopes.com/fact-check/car-balk/.

2. P. Papamichael, C. Evagorou, and C. Antoniades, "Anticipating the Challenges and Opportunities of PSD2," Deloitte, 2017, https://www2 .deloitte.com/cy/en/pages/financial-services/articles/anticipating -challenges-opportunities-psd2.html.

3. BBVA Research, "What Is a Regulatory Sandbox?," https://www
.bbva.com/en/what-is-regulatory-sandbox/, accessed April 26, 2018.

4. Financial Conduct Authority, *Regulatory Sandbox*, 2015, https://
www.fca.org.uk/publication/research/regulatory-sandbox.pdf.

5. Additional information on the sandbox approach is available at the
following locations: *American Banker*: J. Henrichs, "Fintech Needs More
Regulatory 'Sandboxes,'"April 26, 2018, https://www.americanbanker
.com/opinion/FinTech-needs-more-regulatory-sandboxes. US Treasury:
"Treasury Releases Report on Nonbank Financials, Fintech, and Innovation," press release, July 31, 2018, https://home.treasury.gov/news
/press-releases/sm447; and "A Financial System That Creates Economic
Opportunities: Nonbank Financials, Fintech, and Innovation," July
2018, https://home.treasury.gov/sites/default/files/2018-08/A-Financial
-System-that-Creates-Economic-Opportunities---Nonbank-Financials
-Fintech-and-Innovation.pdf.

6. I. Jenik, "Regulatory Sandboxes: Potential for Financial Inclusion,"
Consultative Group to Assist the Poor (CGAP) blog, August 17, 2017,
http://www.cgap.org/blog/regulatory-sandboxes-potential-financial
-inclusion.

7. Consumer Financial Protection Bureau, "Bureau of Consumer
Financial Protection Announces Director for the Office of Innovation,"
July 18, 2018, https://www.consumerfinance.gov/about-us/newsroom
/bureau-consumer-financial-protection-announces-director-office
-innovation/.

8. Consumer Financial Protection Bureau, "CFPB Office of Innovation Proposes 'Disclosure Sandbox' for Companies to Test New
Ways to Inform Consumers," September 13, 2018, https://www.con
sumerfinance.gov/about-us/blog/bcfp-office-innovation-proposes
-disclosure-sandbox-FinTech-companies-test-new-ways-inform
-consumers/.

9. Consumer Financial Protection Bureau, "Policy to Encourage Trial
Disclosure Programs," policy guidance and procedural rule, 2019,
https://files.consumerfinance.gov/f/documents/cfpb_final-policy-to
-encourage-tdp.pdf.

10. Davis Wright Tremaine LLP, "Fintech Sandboxes—Update on State Approaches" JD Supra, April 16, 2018, https://www.jdsupra.com/legalnews/FinTech-sandboxes-update-on-state-80891/.

11. Financial Conduct Authority, *Regulatory Sandbox*.

12. Financial Conduct Authority, "Regulatory Sandbox—Cohort 1," June 15, 2017, https://www.fca.org.uk/firms/regulatory-sandbox/cohort-1.

13. Regulatory News, "FCA Regulatory Sandbox Open for Applications to Cohort 6," Moody's Analytics, October 23, 2019, https://www.moodysanalytics.com/regulatory-news/oct-23-19-fca-regulatory-sandbox-open-for-applications-to-cohort-6.

14. Financial Conduct Authority, "Regulatory Sandbox Lessons Learned Report," October 20, 2017, https://www.fca.org.uk/publications/research/regulatory-sandbox-lessons-learned-report.

15. Financial Conduct Authority, "Regulatory Sandbox Lessons Learned Report."

16. A. Stanley, "Arizona Becomes First U.S. State to Launch Regulatory Sandbox for FinTech," *Forbes*, March 23, 2018, https://www.forbes.com/sites/astanley/2018/03/23/arizona-becomes-first-u-s-state-to-launch-regulatory-sandbox-for-fintech/?sh=559a61591372.

17. Monetary Authority of Singapore, "Regulatory Sandbox," updated August 7, 2019, https://www.mas.gov.sg/development/FinTech/regulatory-sandbox.

18. Monetary Authority of Singapore, "Regulatory Sandbox."

19. Financial Conduct Authority, "Global Financial Innovation Network (GFIN)," updated February 27, 2020, https://www.fca.org.uk/firms/innovation/global-financial-innovation-network.

9   LEAPFROGGING WITH NEXTGEN FINTECHS AND EMERGING TECH FOR THE GROWTH OF AFRICA

Michelle Chivunga

9.1   AFRICAN CONTEXT

The African continent, which constitutes fifty-five countries and has a population set to reach 2.2 billion people by 2050,[1] is facing unprecedented change with the emergence of the fourth industrial revolution, characterized by a vibrant digital economy that has many transformative digital tools that can change Africa as we know it today. These digital tools are being heralded as game changers for Africa's development, industrialization, growth, and transformation. Growth projections for the continent continue to be positive, with GDP predicted to reach 4.1 percent as of 2020 according to the African Development Bank's "African Economic Outlook 2019."[2] However, high levels of global uncertainty, rising indebtedness, a slower pace of economic recovery, and poor domestic reforms in some key countries are threatening this level of growth. In addition, the fluctuations of local currencies, rising interest rates, and difficulty in accessing affordable liquidity pose some major challenges for many countries across the continent. This has weakened investor confidence and will hinder further growth if not addressed. External factors including global trade tensions, political turf wars, post-Brexit challenges, and other significant unexpected global issues have further exacerbated the threat to the level of growth. It is important for Africa to explore and strategically plan for how it can be cushioned from the unexpected consequences of such global challenges. African nations need to be particularly cautious about rising debt levels and unmanageable long-term borrowing, which is squeezing some nations and limiting financial flexibilities that are necessary to diversify economies.

The heavy reliance on foreign exchange and the US dollar further limits accessibility and choice. The lack of diversification around currency, fiat or otherwise, is an important factor—indeed an opportunity for new financial instruments to enter the markets and boost liquidity, which is desperately needed to bring forward the industrialization and growth required in Africa. African countries need to carefully navigate the environment to ensure minimal unintended consequences and take advantage of the opportunities available, including tapping emerging technology, forming new trading relationships on equal footing, increasing investments, boosting collaborative partnerships internally and externally, and boosting internal private-sector engagement. In particular, monitoring progress with China is an important consideration given that China, with about $2 trillion worth of trading activity, is Africa's largest trading partner,[3] surpassing the United States and Europe. As the African continent is becoming more widely recognized as a focal region for future investment opportunities and potentially the next growth phenomenon, Africa must strengthen its capacity to meet not only the needs of the investment community but also the needs of its internal market, in particular supporting entrepreneurs and micro, small, and medium enterprises (MSMEs), which make up over 70 percent of the African business community. The source of GDP production for many economies in the future can be derived from fully supported MSMEs in Africa.

Africa is in a strong position to renegotiate trade relationships after Brexit with both the United Kingdom and the European Union; negotiations should already be in progress. This presents an opportunity for Africa to boost both interregional trade and access to global trading opportunities for MSMEs as significant drivers of economic growth in Africa. Despite some of the core challenges outlined above, now is probably the most exciting and best time for the continent to lead the delivery of internally driven solutions to spur growth. High up on the continent's agenda is the implementation of the Africa Continental Free Trade Area (AfCFTA).[4] The AfCFTA has the transformative potential to introduce the world's largest single market since the creation of the World Trade Organization. This much-anticipated vision would create a single market that allows for seamless intra-Africa trade and free movement of goods, capital, and people among the African member states.

Before digging into the significance of the AfCFTA, it is important to set some context. The development agenda in Africa is particularly key for the future of the continent. First, the continent has taken a different approach by pushing to change the discourse so that Africans themselves are center stage in driving the development agenda and bringing to the fore solutions that are best suited for Africa. Underpinning this is the important alignment with the global Sustainable Development Goals (2030), aimed at leaving no one behind and ensuring fairer economic systems that provide for the many rather than the few. This is in line with the African Union's Agenda 2063, focused on building the "Africa we want." In this context, there are several key important "ingredients," or what we will refer to as growth components (GCs), which need to be given priority and are critical for Africa's successful shift to becoming a production economy and a key driver of growth rather than just a consumer or recipient of growth from other parts of the world. This includes and is not limited to favorable economic fiscal alignment; human-centric, evidence-based policy frameworks; strong leadership; harmonized and secure governance structures; healthy and well-regulated transparent trading environments with access to easy flowing liquidity; accessible labor markets with a variety of job opportunities; investment in a reskilled workforce and talent to service the digital age; a healthy digital economy with robust infrastructure systems; and the creation and retention of productive, innovative high-value chains that MSMEs can access to tap value. These key GCs will spur economic growth and diversification in the continent. A few of the GCs will be picked up and explored in the context of a growing dynamic digital and fintech economy. By no means are these GCs the only factors needed for sustainable development and growth for the region, but they do play a key catalytic role in boosting growth. Many other GCs are explored in further specialist publications and are beyond the scope of this snapshot chapter.

9.2   THE RELEVANCE OF THE AFCFTA AND DIGITIZATION

The launch of the AfCFTA on May 30, 2019, sparked a remarkable and ambitious drive by African Union member states to facilitate seamless trade, particularly interregional trade that today is low in volume[5] but could be boosted through a single market that is projected to significantly contribute up to US$4 trillion GDP to African economies. This will be the world's largest single market when fully operational with all member states, including some of the top ten fastest-growing economies, which are located in Africa.[6] At the time this chapter was written, the AfCFTA had fifty-four members committed to the delivery of this game-changing initiative, which is an opportunity to not only facilitate trade across borders but also to generate, redistribute, and retain wealth within African nations, supporting economic diversification and social capital development and creating value across communities. The World Bank predicts the AfCFTA could lift 30 million people out of poverty and increase real income gains by up to 7 percent by 2035.[7] The AfCFTA combined with a healthy digital economy provides an indispensable platform to boost productivity, create jobs, open access to new markets, and boost MSMEs and entrepreneurship capacity. This is particularly important given that Africa is a youthful continent with many young people, some of whom are facing high levels of unemployment and high barriers of entry to the labor market. The traditional labor market will not generate the number of jobs that are required to tackle the high unemployment levels. In order to stimulate the creation of more jobs, it is important to boost entrepreneurship and direct resources to MSMEs. The emergent technology tools can support this transition.

A range of technological advancements across continents, made possible by the fourth industrial revolution, can and will enable African economies to take the lead not just in using digital solutions from other parts of the world but also in leveraging homemade African technology solutions to leapfrog and help create jobs, liquidity pools, and new trading markets to strengthen wealth access for Africans. The opportunities to leapfrog and tap tailored digital solutions will provide greater choice and access. This is what Africa needs. Digitization is not new to African countries: nations such as Kenya have been leading digital movements through creations such as M-Pesa, a mobile money innovation that has excited the world and motivated other applications to follow. These applications have been founded on data-driven innovations that utilize blockchain, artificial intelligence (AI), 3D printing, drones, and robotics, which are now starting to feature in the corners of African economies. Nigeria, Africa's most populous nation, has seen an increase in fintech investment in the past few years—more than $600 million in funding between 2014 and 2019.[8] A majority of the fintech solutions coming to market in Africa have been in the payments sector, although a growing trend as more awareness builds in the emergent technology sector is the rise of products that are being driven by some of the newer technologies, including AI, blockchain, and the internet of things (IoT). These technologies are automating transactions and processes, helping with efficiency, and creating transformational business models. Driving this further will be a thriving private sector, which needs to have a closer alignment and engagement with governments, civil society, and other key stakeholders to ensure that digital solutions are fit for the marketplaces and aligned to policy frameworks, and that properly managed wide-scale digital education programs are set up. Governments have a key role to play in ensuring that regulatory and policy frameworks that are in place are conducive to innovation and help create a competitive digital economy. Such an economy is key for the future growth of the continent and the world as a whole. The World Economic Forum predicts that by 2022 close to 60 percent of the world's GDP will come from digitized activity.[9]

For Africa, it is essential that investment in infrastructure be prioritized, ensuring that high-speed broadband and internet connectivity can reach a larger pool of people across the continent. This will pave the way for utilization of digital tools and support innovation from more value chains in different sectors, boosting African GDP by as much as $300 billion a year.[10] It might come as a surprise to some that the African continent is the world leader in mobile-enabled digital payment systems and that it hosts some of the most innovative systems, such as M-Pesa (mentioned earlier) and payments systems such as Paystack. But there are many barriers that hinder the scalability of such solutions across the continent. These include challenges around data (accessibility, processing, affordability, and disparities in national data laws), the high costs associated with both cross-border and international settlements, internet inaccessibility, and trade barriers faced by many innovators and potential new entrants into the market. Africa's need for connectivity will grow, especially as the mobile market in the region continues to boom;

the number of smartphones is expected to almost double to reach 678 million by the end of 2025, an adoption rate of 65 percent.[11] Although smartphone adoption is high, internet user penetration levels still lag behind. To capitalize on smartphone adoption, more investment in internet infrastructures and connectivity will be key. In 2013 McKinsey predicted that with continuous infrastructure investment, internet reach will expand at a much larger scale, potentially adding $300 billion a year to Africa's GDP.[12] These developments present a big opportunity for mobile phone innovation—particularly decentralized innovations that can be easily deployed onto mobile platforms. The implementation of the AfCFTA is positioned to alleviate challenges around trade and some of the barriers outlined earlier. At the second e-commerce conference organized by the African Union in Dakar in 2018, the trade commissioner (H. E. Albert Muchanga) outlined three core operational instruments that will enhance digital trade and the digital economy in the African continent: (1) the Pan-African Payments and Settlements System, which will derisk trading across Africa; (2) the Continental Online Mechanism, for monitoring, reporting, and eliminating nontariff barriers to help tackle restrictive regulations; and (3) the African Trade Observatory, which will integrate an online platform that provides more secure, reliable, timely, and accurate data and listing of authorized economic operators. This will help facilitate more seamless, transparent interregional trade, creating a more competitive business environment in which African businesses can build and strengthen their global market positions. A number of countries across Africa are developing national digital strategies that map out the opportunities that come with digital engagements. As this chapter was being written, Senegal[13] was developing a national e-commerce strategy to guide the development of a robust digital strategy to help boost growth in the country. The African Union is collaborating with many actors and national representatives to develop

Africa's digital transformation strategy, which outlines some of the core digital tools. This will be a useful resource for member countries in adopting their own national digital strategies to encompasses innovative plans that leverage emerging technologies for development plans at the country level.

9.3 DIGITIZATION AND FINTECHS TO SPUR AFRICAN GROWTH

The fintech market in Africa is growing rapidly, driven by a dynamic mix of large and small solution providers, with an increase in mobile payment solutions; new fintech applications and decentralized applications are supporting innovation in areas including agribusiness, financing, health care, energy, insurance, and many other sectors. Many of the solutions are leveraging functionalities of a mix of emerging technology solutions such as blockchain, AI, and IoT, bypassing traditional infrastructure and leapfrogging to mobile-enabled solutions. One area where we are witnessing an increase in the deployment and usage of emerging technology solutions is in e-commerce transactions, with a surge in payments infrastructure developed by fintechs to fill some of the gaps unmet by traditional banks. In 2019, African electronic payments accounted for about $19.3 billion in revenues, with $10 billion from domestic electronic payments.[14] Globally, e-commerce accounts for trillions of dollars, and this trend is likely to continue to rise as more complex digital tools emerge to enable greater efficiency and customer-centric products and services. Africa can boost its internet penetration rate, which was around 272 million internet users in 2019 (36 percent) and is predicted to reach 475 million users in 2025.[15]

Flexibility, harmonization around e-commerce rules, data access, and greater infrastructure investment, pulled together with a wider digitalization agenda across the value chain, will encourage greater accessibility, increased participation, and new entrants into the marketplace. In addition, this will enable greater access to more productive markets to foster growth. For example, it is predicted that more than half of global mobile money operators are in Africa, with the African mobile money economy predicted to grow rapidly. The world is expected to see a surge in mobile operators, predicted to reach 620 million new mobile subscribers by 2020, a global penetration rate of 75 percent.[16] E-commerce is still largely untapped across the continent, and many countries have limited participation owing to challenges around connectivity and other barriers in the e-commerce ecosystem. Underdeveloped digital infrastructures, fragmented financial and payment systems, affordability blocks, and the lack of education in digital skills contribute to some of the factors limiting countries' participation. E-commerce in Africa was predicted to be worth US$8 billion in 2014 and is estimated to grow to US$75 billion by 2025.[17] Indeed, Africa is well positioned to support this growth with major players such as Jumia expanding across the continent, including in key markets such as Nigeria. The most populated country in Africa, Nigeria is expecting a population growth of 200 million and is one of the leaders in fintech solutions provision and adoption. Many Nigerian innovations link to e-commerce activity, with groups such as Interswitch digitizing payments and processing up to 500 million transactions per month. Interswitch also runs Quickteller, which is a consumer-driven payments platform enabling financial inclusivity for a larger pool of customers to engage with financial and economic systems. Nigeria is a bustling country with a dynamic entrepreneurial ecosystem, and increasingly more digital firms and tech hubs are springing up, many of which are led by young entrepreneurs keen to transform the country.

Nigeria is not immune to the challenges faced by many of the African countries, as outlined in earlier sections. In Nigeria's case this includes the depreciating naira and monetary pressure from the drops in foreign reserves, but it also presents an opportunity to explore alternative currency solutions leveraging emerging technology such as blockchain. Regardless of the challenges, Nigeria has immense opportunity with rising incomes and a vibrant digital economy, and the internally driven investments in the start-up ecosystem have benefited the country, leading to expansions in Yabacon Valley and an increase in philanthropic support. This is growing across the continent, and it is inevitable that more players will enter the fintech ecosystem, especially if more investment is channeled toward better connectivity and a more decentralized and secure approach to data access with fewer of the tech giants monopolizing data ownership and access. Data ownership should be retained from sources that support innovation, local content development, and buildup of quality data pools in these countries, which is critical to support growth plans. If organizations are to grow and scale in these countries, data must become the core backbone, and it has to be clear when, how, and with whom data is being shared. More African countries need to establish clear data laws regarding how data is shared from one jurisdiction to the next. Data flowing securely across borders without compromise to data privacy can have powerful catalytic impacts, helping to spur seamless trade, higher levels of competitiveness, and greater transparency across value chains.

The digital revolution is really the data revolution building up interconnected platforms upon platforms and forming what many refer to as the digital economy. This digital economy will be driven by digital data. Blockchain technology can be an enabler to support much of this—the underlining technology supported by cryptography and encrypted data provides a secure platform by which data or other items of value can be exchanged, managed, shared, and monetized. This vehicle of trust leverages encrypted data and has helped bring efficiency gains and cost reductions to business value systems, allowing businesses to innovate through new business models in some countries. Because the technology is consensus driven and not reliant on a single entity or third party to verify or confirm transactions, the system enables greater trust, transparency, and transformation. This is not only critical for digital trade but key to drive sustainable development, building a thriving and more evenly spread people-centric Africa. Africa has not fully exploited blockchain's potential, but in time it will.

By acting as a trust engine and inclusivity vehicle, blockchain can help mitigate against perceived risk and allow multiple parties (regardless of jurisdiction) to interact, trade, and communicate, leveraging more productive and scalable value chains with minimal risk. This is key especially in the current global trading system, where diminishing trust has resulted in a loss of confidence and barriers for trade. Transactions in the trading system can easily be digitized, automating through instruments such as smart contracts[18] and even tapping some tokenized models to support the financing of trade. Blockchain is, however, still very poorly understood; the what, where, and how still puzzle many across the world, and the hype associated with its first application, bitcoin, has slowed the prospects for the technology to go mainstream. Blockchain is one of the distributed ledger technologies (DLTs)—technologies that have certain characteristics that make them special (e.g., their ability to help in verification and authentication processes).

Blockchain is an innovative technology built on DLT that allows for consensus-driven verification and sharing of information or value. Put simply, a blockchain is a "digital book of records" backed by cryptographically secure data. This digital book contains records of synchronized encrypted data that represents a chain of transactions or digital assets. This digital book of records or transactions or assets can be shared or distributed across a network of users or computers commonly known as nodes. The same copy of the digital book is accessible to multiple parties, and any changes made have to be agreed on or verified by the network of users rather than one entity. The records of transactions are time-stamped, making it difficult to manipulate them, and thus the transactions are very secure and easy to audit. The blockchain is unique in that it offers three core distinct characteristics: it is decentralized (not reliant on a central authority), immutable (tamper-proof), and consensus driven (must be agreed upon by the network). This mix brings greater levels of trust and transparency.

Despite widespread agreement that blockchain has massive potential to transform many sectors at scale, there remain technological, regulatory, governance, infrastructure, and structural challenges for countries that place specific limitations that will slow the pace for wide-scale adoption. Further work is needed with more investment in research and development in this area. It is not uncommon for a new technology to take time to come to fruition, nor is it necessarily a bad thing, but more research is necessary if we are to fully take advantage of the transformative opportunities that blockchain offers. Resolving some of the current barriers, including interoperability of blockchain systems, will not necessarily be as fast as the technology advances but will be critical for the wider, more scalable dissemination and adoption of the applications that are developed on the blockchain. A much earlier focus on research and development could have helped spur greater understanding around the technology, but this is now happening to a greater extent in some parts of the world, such as in China and much of Southeast Asia, and increasingly the appetite for cryptocurrency is growing in Africa. China is positioning itself to be the world leader in this space, evident from the public announcement by China's president Xi Jinping that China is focusing on the development of blockchain rather than cryptocurrency. In Africa there is a growing blockchain ecosystem, but this is mainly concentrated in a few of the dominant countries (South Africa, Kenya, Uganda, Nigeria, Rwanda, and Ethiopia). Nigeria has expanded its coverage of the cryptocurrency market with many engaging with bit-coin, which is the most popular cryptocurrency. With greater awareness of the underlying technology, blockchain is gaining more attention with major projects emerging from tech hubs as interest in digital assets continues to rise. Many institutions are looking beyond just cryptocurrency (by "cryptocurrency" I am referring to, for example, bitcoin, Ethereum, and Ripple) and are starting to tap offers from blockchain.[19] The combina-tion of blockchain and other emergent technologies within the fintech ecosystem can be the anchor needed for growth in many sectors of Africa. It is important that Africa nurture these next-generation technology hubs. But to do so, it has to strategically invest in conducting the research necessary to evaluate the opportunities that blockchain brings to national economies, noting that each of the African countries will be at varying stages in relation to digital skills and capacity, infra-structure, and economic development.

It is important to understand blockchain's relevance, if any, and clearly map out what this technology means for emerg-ing markets structures. Some of the blockchain opportunities available in Africa and to emerging markets are highlighted in the following section. In general, emerging technologies will be most prevalent and transformative in emerging markets, where developing nations face fewer barriers to adoption. For example, the opportunities that lie with leapfrogging onto mobile-based platforms, skipping interoperability challenges, can enable easier, faster addition of decentralized applications through the mobile. The mobile is an asset that will drive more opportunities, especially with millions of people expected to become mobile internet users by 2025. Africa's mobile indus-try is predicted to drive GDP contribution of $184 billion by 2024.[20] This also presents a strong foundation to boost the deployment of blockchain-based products and services that are supported not only by blockchain systems but a mix of emerg-ing technology solutions including AI, IoT, cybersystems, and big data. For example, the company Kuva has combined advances in three disruptive technologies—blockchain, peer-to-peer payments, and smartphones—to create a secure value store and payment system that works for everyone.

9.4   THE RELEVANCE OF BLOCKCHAIN IN THE CONTEXT OF AFRICA

One of the major problems facing many African countries is accessibility to sustainable liquidity and long-term financing. Many nations rely on development finance institutions to support financing, and many African countries have called for increased foreign direct investment, which is not always easy to attract. African markets are also generally perceived to be much riskier than other markets. But this is not always the case; at times the perceptions stem from a lack of understanding of local markets and how to do business in these markets, and at other times cultural barriers may get in the way. This is not to say that in some countries a combination of barriers exists (cultural, economic, political, and financial complexities). In addition, corruption in some nations makes it extremely difficult to do business in these countries. These issues are not unique to Africa, and the world has to recognize that Africa has massive business and trading opportunities. The other fundamental issue is the abundant lack of trust and transparency in African ecosystems, particularly with cross-border activities and foreign market engagements, which further hinders business opportunities and productive cross-border trade activity in these markets. Bringing in digitized trade and technologies like blockchain, which in effect is a mix of several preexisting technologies with unique characteristics, can help build trust between parties that might not otherwise interact with each other.

Tapping cryptographically secure data that is stored in the form of a shared ledger or as explained in the "digital book of records" (a.k.a. the blockchain) enables the visibility and sharing of information across networks. This means trust no longer resides with just one single entity; rather, the networks are empowered to come together, give consensus (through a consensus-enabled algorithm or code), and share the same source of real-time information with peer-to-peer networks to enable them to effectively govern, make decisions, and verify activity, thus building up the trust that is missing. It is through this process that trust is created among networks and systems. This concept of networks is an important element that must be well understood as it forms the basis of blockchain community networks. Networks and communities built on code form distinctive components of blockchain technology. The decentralization that comes with networks will be the game changer in the way society as a whole transitions and operates, giving more control, ownership, and democratized decision-making powers to the networks themselves. The composition of networks essentially means that anyone who is engaged as part of that community of networks (both open and private) will be the key driver of what happens in those networks. Layers of networks over networks will be created as technology advances. Governance is therefore key and becomes decentralized.

9.5   BLOCKCHAIN AS A CRITICAL FRIEND OF GOVERNMENT

It might come as a surprise to some, but blockchain is one of the most significant technologies of government. Skeptics argue that entities such as banks and governments will become irrelevant and obsolete when blockchain reaches mass adoption. This is not necessarily true, as governments will be some of the biggest winners should they choose to embrace blockchain, understanding clearly how to implement and leverage not just blockchain-based systems but a mix of different emerging technologies to reap economies of scale and even boost better governance structures. Governments are core to the overall success, development, and adoption of blockchain. To emphasize this even more, the efficiency gains and transparency boost that come from digitization and blockchain utilization are critical for governments, especially in emerging markets. Governments can capitalize on the economies of scale that emerging technologies and blockchain bring. A number of government functions can benefit: tax and revenue collection methods, record keeping and secure data management (on key things such as title deeds, health data, housing waiting lists, and land banks), automated documentation, auditable voting, provenance, and identity management.

A blockchain identity functionality entails a more secure manner of sharing "who is who," maintaining the privacy of individuals but helping to create a pool of reliable identities. This functionality is key for African economies because it enables better inclusion and better economic and financial integration. A robust digital identity system is paramount for Africa, given that many people today are unaccounted for or have lost their origins because of conflict and displacement. Governments are also key anchors mandated with improving the living standards of their citizens and supporting the sustainable development of their nations. In the context of Africa, the AfCFTA is a central element of this. Leveraging blockchain to ease the flow of trade is particularly key. Opening up borders and tapping blockchain to ensure more compliant, transparent, cost-effective, and sufficiently funded supply chains that open up new digital jobs and services are paramount. Blockchain transparency has enabled between 30 and 50 percent cost savings on compliance and up to 50 percent potential cost savings on key operations such as meeting "know your customer" (KYC) requirements.[21] In emerging countries, services are expanding and more digitization attached to these services will lead to more sustained growth, particularly for key demographics like women and young people who are creating the next generation of jobs. Some of these women and young people work in the informal sector, where they often do not have an identity or indeed their economic contribution is not captured properly. Africa benefits from a youthful human capital, which is expected to double to over 830 million by 2050, but youth unemployment is rising fast at an average of 6.2 percent in sub-Saharan Africa,[22] increasing the poverty gap between countries. By tapping the digital economy and valuable data from digital platforms (including mobile networks, which may or may not have blockchain-based applications embedded on them), government can begin to capture the data flowing from these to measure GDP contribution and tailor support services as well as formulate policies to support and introduce initiatives that help tackle unemployment and other challenges. In addition, governments can leverage digital financing as an alternative to traditional finance provision to service some of the lower ends of the markets, including many operators in the informal markets. As economies move toward cashless societies and access to money becomes more decentralized through innovations such as central bank digital currencies (CBDCs), there will be shifts toward better financial inclusion, particularly where economies are able to offer a hybrid of digital and cash systems to meet the needs in each economy. The African agriculture sector is already hugely benefiting from the use of technology. Supporting agrivalue chains in Africa will result in multiplier impacts, particularly if this includes deployment of blockchain, AI, and IoT systems and tapping smart contracts for agribusiness, insurance pooling, and financing.

Governments have an opportunity to use blockchain internally for better government public service provision, communications, and auditing and monitoring of government budget allocations that can be traced on the blockchain. Blockchain monitoring can also help automate government policies and align them with deliverables. The key question is to what degree governments are prepared for this level of transition, transparency, and traceability. It is encouraging to see that countries across the continent, including Nigeria,[23] are starting to develop their national blockchain strategies, aiming to use the blockchain to push adoption and pivot into the digital economy.

9.6 BLOCKCHAIN AND DERISKING MARKETS

With increased trust and transparency, networks can begin to operate more effectively, opening up new market access, derisking projects, and creating new avenues of financing. This is particularly important for Africa, which faces shortfalls in financing particularly at the lower end of the market spectrum, where MSMEs struggle to access the financing required for them to scale. For example, the continent's intraregional trade is currently getting only about 43 percent of trade financing, leaving a massive gap. Introducing blockchain-based trade financing platforms, building on novel approaches to providing financing, such as digital currencies, and implementing digital financing infrastructures can provide new avenues for income streams, helping to reduce the barriers and costs associated with trade financing. Furthermore, blockchain-based digital financing platforms can reinvent and unlock access to capital, widening the pool, type, and diversity of investors and projects that can utilize blockchain. This enables greater transparency and reduces the overall barriers associated with accessing financing. In addition, blockchain can be a good verification instrument for due diligence and cybersecurity. With greater transparency, Africa can begin to dismantle its negative "image problem" as a very "risky and corrupt region" and can open up opportunities for business and trade on a level playing field.

The emergence of the digital asset and token economy with a range of token offerings will rise, with marked impact in some communities. Putting it simply, tokenization is taking ordinary physical assets such as property, land, cars, and commodities and turning them into liquid digital assets that are placed on the blockchain and can be verified, transferred, traded, and audited. With value attached to these assets, new forms of liquidity can be created, and creative fund-raising models will appear. In addition, the decentralized nature of these models will lead to widening participation from various stakeholders, including the less wealthy members of society. This is key for inclusion and decentralization of wealth. These groups can choose to purchase decentralized tokens or shares in these asset classes at reduced costs, giving them access to wealth and valuable long-term assets. Many more investors and a bigger pool of MSMEs can benefit from tokenization, enabling speedier and more secure, transparent, and audible transactions. Derisking can also be achieved by embedding compliant algorithms, which helps alleviate concerns around anti–money laundering and KYC.

There will be a big shift toward platforms, the token economy, and deriving value from these digital assets. Africa has to have in place the foundation, including the connectivity and digital payments infrastructure, required to tap into these new models. It is also important that we don't get lost in the hype, as blockchain is still developing. Moving forward, we will begin to see some technology convergence, particularly as we tackle limitations of blockchain and other complementary technologies. These include issues around speed, regulation, governance, standardization, technical interoperability, and wide-scale adoption.

In the short to medium term, we will continue to witness the growth of digital assets and concentration from many of the world's central banks to explore the possibilities of CBDCs, for example. This does not mean that all future central banks will adopt digital currencies, as a country must consider many factors before introducing digital currencies. Additionally, digital currencies do not necessarily need to be designed with a layer of DLT/blockchain-based architecture, although DLT applications offer some significant benefits worth exploring. DLT-based design principles for digital currencies are being explored by several central banks around the world. In the context of Africa, CBDC could help support onboarding people unable to access traditional financing packages, including the unbanked, giving them access to a more secure, affordable digital payments infrastructure and access to affordable credit. Wholesale CBDC could support not only better cross-border and interbank transactions but also the flow of remittances, which are a key source of income for many people across Africa. Because existing payment systems and intra-African payments come with high costs and are fragmented, this presents a massive opportunity to provide alternatives that are cheaper, inclusive, and easy to use. The flow of money in Africa, as well as accessing it, remains challenging, but new models like CBDC and other decentralized offerings, including cryptocurrency, decentralized finance, and stable coins, could help rebalance and diversify the forms of money available in the market. A number of organizations in Africa are doing this.[24] The key to implementation of CBDC is its ease of use, security, accessibility, and adoption by the citizens of nations. Some caution should be exercised for digital currency implementation at this stage, especially for African economies that may not have the resources or capacity to fully deploy a CBDC in the immediate future but could at a later stage, after proper consultation and feasibility reviews to ascertain the implications of CBDC at the national level. Countries that decide to deploy these digital currencies should undertake feasibility studies on their impact.

9.7   BLOCKCHAIN AS A LEVER FOR THE SCALABILITY AND RESILIENCE OF MSMEs

MSMEs are a vital part of any economy, fueling economic growth and creating job opportunities for local communities. The African Union Commission clearly highlights the importance of supporting the development of MSMEs, as outlined in the African Union SME strategy.[25] MSMEs are key drivers of employment and contribute significantly to GDP growth; in Africa, approximately 70 percent of the total population is employed within the MSMEs' domain. MSMEs are dynamic in nature and spread across various sectors, making it harder to reach them to distribute tailored support. The setup of the MSMEs' ecosystem has layers of complexity, which makes it hard to do business with this network of operators. Many challenges exist to channel support that enables them to fully optimize value networks and build operational efficiency, so they scale and are competitively placed to grow. Leveraging digitization can be a means to support this competitiveness. The productivity of these MSMEs can be further improved through emerging technologies such as blockchain and AI, which can help support cheap, efficient, and transparent MSME value chains. Blockchain in particular can assist MSMEs operating within complex supply chains by unbundling the complexities, automating trade practices and processes, and making it easy to access financing, thus helping MSMEs grow.

In African countries, 70–80 percent of businesses can be grouped as MSMEs. The blockchain can help improve supply chain accessibility for these MSMEs to scale; the blockchain can also help the micro-entrepreneurial businesses, which often have no assets or collateral or credit history, to build creditworthiness and links to access liquidity and new markets. By facilitating seamless cross-border transactions through blockchain, MSMEs can be empowered to bring forward innovative business models and widen their access to markets and financing. Trade opportunities for MSMEs can be boosted through the full implementation of the AfCFTA, which is an important channel for MSMEs to utilize digital trade as a means for trade facilitation, growth, and diversification. African governments and policy makers must invest in creating the right enabling environment for digital trade, including tackling tariff and nontariff barriers, boosting manufacturing and industrialization capacity, developing accessibility to regional value chains, and utilizing digitization as a vehicle for development of Africa's MSMEs.

There is also a growing pool of MSMEs exporting and benefiting from trading expansion into other regional and international markets, an area where blockchain could have a significant impact. In sectors engaging in trade finance, pharmaceuticals, agribusiness, international exporting, manufacturing processing, and health care, blockchain could play a major role in improving efficiency, trust, and traceability to support more see-through supply chains and lucrative businesses operations. Exporters and importers can benefit from this technology and in turn improve innovation and productivity. In the following key points, we explore some of the benefits of the blockchain, particularly in relation to MSMEs.

- For MSMEs, **opportunities** presented using blockchain technology are numerous, but at the core of this technology is its ability to improve efficiency, build trust, and reduce costs. Blockchain can help improve access to global supply chains, trade finance, and more reliable data sets, which can help businesses design better models to sustain their operations. Because it operates in a more secure and transparent manner, blockchain reduces the complexities that come with opaque supply chains today. It can be costly for small businesses to go through the different stages within any given supply chain, at times dealing with a variety of players and their associated costs, resulting in additional issues around financing and the speed of transactions. Blockchain can help reduce these costs by streamlining supply chains, cutting out intermediaries and their transaction costs, and supporting more efficient processes and transactions.

- MSMEs engaged in **trading across borders** can be key beneficiaries of the use of cross-border blockchain and

AI-enabled systems that can capitalize on the ease of doing business because of more seamless digital platforms and e-commerce interventions. For example, businesses that trade across different jurisdictions deal with many different players, such as financing institutions, insurers, brokers, and trading partners, and many complex regulatory, compliance, and logistical pressures in these jurisdictions. These institutions all require various forms of documentation, but in some instances the same information is needed and the verification process is slowed down by having to repeatedly supply the same information to different parties. The reality in some markets is that some of these businesses do not have the documentation required. This occurs on both the import side and the export side at different stages of the trade supply chain. This repetition can be avoided, as the blockchain can hold the same information that can be shared with the relevant parties, where it is required in real time. The key is paperless trade and end-to-end digitization on secure interoperable platforms that enable these businesses to conduct valuable cross-border trade. A blockchain-based platform presents an opportunity for trading MSMEs to engage in more efficient cross-border trade—for example, by holding all necessary data for verification on the blockchain so that it is visible to all parties involved in a particular transaction, making it faster and less costly. This also leads to improvements in due diligence and better auditable financial information about the MSMEs.

- **Smart contracts for MSMEs**—The parties involved in business are able to view and amend records/transactions within the scope of agreed-upon rules through the use of smart contracts (or in simple terms, code with execution terms programmed into the blockchain system). The parties involved in the transaction must be able to trust the code. Blockchain platforms that use smart contracts allow for secure automated actions to be taken—for example, embedding instructions on future actions around identifying, moving, and tracking goods and settling payments quickly.

- **Building financial independence / creditworthiness**— End-to-end digitization with tools like blockchain will happen as businesses trade on platforms with better compliance, due diligence, and auditability embedded into processes and systems. Decentralized platforms supported by technologies such as blockchain and AI will help support financial freedom and inclusion. Furthermore, as outlined earlier, MSMEs are also struggling to access the necessary capital and seed funding, but the combination of blockchain and AI can help with this issue.[26] Through blockchain, better tracking of MSMEs' transactions will help create an auditable credit history that lenders can use to evaluate the suitability of MSMEs for additional financing. Data on the GDP that MSMEs generate can be tracked using secure nonbiased AI algorithms, particularly for those in the informal sectors for governments and others to provide more tailored policy and business support. The combination of a well-designed digital payments and mobile infrastructure in Africa (outlined earlier) and technologies like blockchain provides a recipe for increased trading opportunities and peer-to-peer transactions that are governed and secured by code, which could boost more trust and transparency across the network.

9.8 CONCLUSION AND RECOMMENDATIONS

Africa's opportunity to lead in the digital revolution is now. As outlined, the digital revolution is the data revolution driven by an expanding platform and token economy. Africa must and can capture these. Digital innovations are not new in the continent, as we have seen many new digital applications coming out of Kenya, Nigeria, and Rwanda. These innovative products are transforming many sectors and helping to build the next generation of creative fintechs and businesses that will contribute significantly to the economic growth of the continent. The world is witnessing the digital revolution, which is becoming an indispensable part of the wider economy. The digital economy in Africa needs to be strengthened with widening participation and collaboration from various actors, including innovators, policy makers, investors, fintechs, and many others. The continent's growth can be driven through the establishment of strong infrastructure systems, access to affordable financing and data, and investment in human capital, as well as by supporting a fully functioning single market through the AfCFTA that businesses can tap. Digital platforms will pave the way for more innovation, but it is critical that government, working with cross-sector stakeholders, tailor support by ensuring that policy frameworks, regulatory measures, and the general business climate are right, allowing innovation to thrive. Investing in systems and structural changes to stimulate internally driven solutions is paramount for the industrialization agenda that Africa needs to deliver through the AfCFTA and other supporting infrastructure. It is important that government, working collaboratively with other players, seize this moment to lead the data revolution and competitively place Africa on the global digital economy platform. Africa has to be strategic in approach and cautious about the impacts of potential threats outlined, including threats of high indebtedness and other unforeseen external impacts. The GCs are key for African growth. Leveraging digitization, data access, and ownership, the AfCFTA and youthful human capital will help lead Africa toward a transition that will support the long-term sustainability of inclusive and sustainable economies.

Further recommendations include the following:

- African economies are shifting toward industrialization within national economies as a push to enable growth and diversification. With this overarching objective, Africa must optimize mechanisms to support this, especially in key sectors including manufacturing, agriculture, health care, technology, and others.

- Many African countries face challenges around foreign exchange and high levels of debt, which is stopping these countries from growing. Key for governments will be to evaluate these challenges to minimize unnecessary debt accumulation and restructure debt where necessary to enable countries to grow and not hamper the prospects for industrialization. In addition, greater transparency on debt and the flow of financial instruments can be achieved even through the utilization of emergent technologies such as blockchain and AI.

- African economies can diversify the pool of financial instruments and bolster capital markets infrastructure to support the development of a strong liquidity market, which is a necessity for industrialization and growth.

- The GCs outlined in this chapter should be a focus for policy makers, governments, and other partners. The future will be built on strong partnerships and collaboration from a range of stakeholders working together to build the foundations of a strong Africa that strives for every country in the region to be a "production economy" and not just a consumer of finished goods that utilize many of Africa's raw materials. Africa must reap benefits from its own production capacity, which can be boosted with digitization.

- All African countries must prioritize investment in building the infrastructure and connectivity channels that are necessary to support the digital economy and its digital tools. The successful delivery of the AfCFTA will rely on a thriving digital economy that allows for connectivity, inclusivity, and transformation.

- Policy makers and decision makers must build a robust approach to data, explore data strategies, and utilize the digital tools available to manage data securely, ensuring a high level of consumer protection is embedded.

- Although some pockets of Africa have various digital innovations in place, these offerings need additional investments and additional tailored support so that they can be scaled and reach more markets.

- Investing in fintechs and digital financing products will hugely benefit African economies, particularly in regard to the rapidly expanding digitization and mobile penetration in many of the African economies. African leaders can work with innovators to develop more innovative funding platforms that provide accessibility to funding streams for fintechs and MSMEs.

- Policy makers and governments should invest in Africa-wide digital skills education and capacity-building programs that also cover emerging technologies (including blockchain, AI, cybersecurity, and data literacy), delivered at a Pan-African level, an area that the Global Policy House is covering in partnership with several global groups.

- Tackling challenges around access to affordable data, connectivity, and regulatory barriers will strengthen Africa's position to lead in digital innovations that can competitively place the continent on the global stage.

- Greater attention should be given to solutions that leverage blockchain, AI, and cybersecurity applications to build trust in trade and future-proof Africa, especially with growing challenges around cyberattacks, currency fluctuations, job losses, and opaque trading systems.

If Africa is to lead in the digital revolution, then ensuring no unintended consequences arise is important to safeguard African economies. It will be vital that the leadership in the various African countries be open to innovation and be key champions of digital solutions that will help tackle some of Africa's biggest challenges. As stated, now is the best time for Africa as the fintech/digital ecosystem matures and we see the implementation of the AfCFTA, which will be a major game changer for the continent by helping to open borders and facilitate a new wave of jobs (including digital jobs) that give many young Africans economic opportunity and wealth.

Blockchain technology, along with other key technologies, can play a pivotal and significant role in driving growth in the continent; it is an important catalyst that can support many sectors, including MSMEs. Blockchain technology, the trust and inclusivity vehicle for the African continent, is vital, but it should be noted that this technology is not a magic wand and cannot address everything. Instead, the power of the technology lies in its ability to connect, authenticate, verify, and be converged with other innovative technologies to support digital transformation and growth. The technology is not perfect or indeed fully developed and will see continuous improvements to support more advanced technical capability, scope, and interoperability. Africa can leverage existing success around mobile penetration and leapfrog to use technology to enable access to more liquid markets, build greater financial inclusion, and support more seamless, transparent trading supply chains. Technology is part of the solution and will be important to generate growth. But what is really key is what the technology and the data can do to enable inclusive growth and sustainable development so that many people benefit rather than just a few. Africa has access to the necessary tools, but more must be done to support upskilling, education, liquidity supply, and capacity building, ensuring strong governance as well as government policy alignment to facilitate success. Africa's time is now.

NOTES

1. E. Suzuki, "World's Population Will Continue to Grow and Will Reach Nearly 10 Billion by 2050," *World Bank Blogs*, July 8, 2019, http://blogs.worldbank.org/opendata/worlds-population-will-continue-grow-and-will-reach-nearly-10-billion-2050.

2. African Development Bank Group, "African Economic Outlook 2019: Africa Growth Prospects Remain Steady, Industry Should Lead Growth," January 17, 2019, https://www.afdb.org/en/news-and-events /african-economic-outlook-2019-africa-growth-prospects-remain -steady-industry-should-lead-growth-18925.

3. E. Smith, "The US-China Trade Rivalry Is Underway in Africa, and Washington Is Playing Catch-Up," CNBC, October 9, 2019, https:// www.cnbc.com/2019/10/09/the-us-china-trade-rivalry-is-underway -in-africa.html.

4. The AfCFTA is a trading agreement among fifty-four African Union member countries (at this writing). This agreement aims to create the largest single market set to help ease the free movement of goods and services across the countries' borders. Tralac Trade Law Centre, "African Continental Free Trade Area (AfCFTA) Legal Texts and Policy Documents," accessed December 31, 2019, https://www.tralac.org/re sources/by-region/cfta.html#legal-texts.

5. Cory N., Information Technology and Innovation Foundation, "Key Issues to Building an Open, Vibrant, and Integrated Digital Economy and Digital Trade Agenda for Sub-Saharan Africa," October 2019.

6. A. Haas, "The World's 10 Fastest Growing Cities Are Going to Be in Africa within 16 Years," World Economic Forum, October 21, 2019, https://www.weforum.org/agenda/2019/10/africa-cities-organisational -structure-cairo-institutions.

7. World Bank, "The African Continental Free Trade Area," July 27, 2020, https://www.worldbank.org/en/topic/trade/publication/the-african -continental-free-trade-area.

8. Disrupt Africa, "African Tech Startups Funding Report 2019," https://disruptafrica.gumroad.com/l/KAznE, accessed 12 July 2021.

9. World Economic Forum, "Shaping the Future of Digital Economy and New Value Creation," 2020, https://www.weforum.org/platforms /shaping-the-future-of-digital-economy-and-new-value-creation.

10. J. Manvika, A. Cabral, L. Moodley, S. Moraje, S. Yeboah-Amankwah, M. Chui, and J. Anthonyrajah, "Lions Go Digital: The Internet's Transformative Potential in Africa," McKinsey, November 1, 2013, https://www

.mckinsey.com/industries/technology-media-and-telecommunications /our-insights/lions-go-digital-the-internets-transformative-potential-in -africa#.

11. GSMA, "The Mobile Economy: Sub-Saharan Africa 2020," 2020, https://www.gsma.com/mobileeconomy/sub-saharan-africa/.

12. Manvika et al., "Lions Go Digital."

13. Senegal, in West Africa, is forging ahead with innovations and developing a nationwide e-commerce strategy to support the buildup of digital engagements.

14. McKinsey & Company, *McKinsey on Payments* 13, no. 31, March 2021, 47, https://www.mckinsey.com/~/media/mckinsey/industries /financial%20services/our%20insights/mckinsey%20on%20pay ments%2031/mckinsey-on-payments-issue-31.pdf.

15. GSMA, "The Mobile Economy."

16. GSMA Sub Saharan Africa, "The Mobile Economy 2017," April 3, 2016, https://www.gsma.com/subsaharanafrica/resources/the-mobile -economy-2017.

17. Manvika et al., "Lions Go Digital."

18. Smart contracts are self-executing codes that are written to allow for the execution of agreed terms or transactions at a future date when initial terms agreed are met. For example, smart contracts can be written to give automated instruction to execute a payment if goods are received from a cross-border transaction.

19. An example of an African company using blockchain is Binkabi, an e-bartering platform for SMEs that allows traders to settle transactions using blockchain and payments in local currency, using its own utility token. The focus will be on trade flows between Côte d'Ivoire and Vietnam. FurtherAfrica, "10 Companies Revolutionising Blockchain Technology in Africa," February 22, 2019, https://furtherafrica.com/2019/02 /22/10-companies-revolutionising-blockchain-technology-in-africa/.

20. GSMA, "The Mobile Economy."

21. Accenture Consulting, *Banking on Blockchain: A Value Analysis for Investment Banks* (Albany, NY: Accenture Consulting, 2017), https://

www.accenture.com/_acnmedia/accenture/conversion-assets/dotcom
/documents/global/pdf/consulting/accenture-banking-on-blockchain
.pdf.

22. African Development Bank, *Jobs for Youth in Africa*, March 2016, https://www.afdb.org/fileadmin/uploads/afdb/Images/high_5s/Job _youth_Africa_Job_youth_Africa.pdf; World Bank, "Unemployment, Total (% of Total Labor Force) (Modelled ILO Estimate)—Sub-Saharan Africa," World Bank, June 21, 2020, https://data.worldbank.org/indica tor/SL.UEM.TOTL.ZS?locations=ZG.

23. Government of Nigeria, "National Blockchain Adoption Strat- egy: Streamlining into a Digital Future" (proposed draft, 2020), https://bitcoinke.io/wp-content/uploads/2020/10/DRAFT-NATIONAL -BLOCKCHAIN-ADOPTION-STRATEGY.pdf?x46620.

24. Groups such as Binance, Paxful, Luno, and Bitpesa are utilizing blockchain, peer-to-peer networks, and cryptocurrency innovations to the African market to support the diversification and decentraliza- tion of access to money and technology innovations. As more of these players and institutional groups enter the market, we will begin to see more adoption.

25. The vision of the AU SME strategy is to "develop competitive, diversified and sustainable economies underpinned by dynamic, entre- preneurial and industrial sectors that generate employment, reduce poverty and foster social inclusion." African Union, *Annual Report on the African Union and Its Organs*, 65, https://docplayer.net/102527135 -Executive-council-thirty-second-ordinary-session-january-2018-addis -ababa-ethiopia.html.

26. Companies such as Twiga Foods have teamed up with IBM to use the supply chain finance platform to support local farmers and small businesses tapping blockchain and machine learning.

10 THE RISE OF REGTECH AND THE DIVERGENCE OF COMPLIANCE AND RISK

Amias Moore Gerety
and Lev Menand

The rise of regulatory technology (RegTech) promises to transform financial-sector risk management, dramatically improving compliance, lowering costs, and reducing counterparty risk. But in the financial sector, RegTech also threatens to increase frictions between banks and their government supervisors. This is because, as banks have become larger and more complex, supervisors have increasingly relied on compliance as a proxy for risk: assuming that a bank that cannot follow its own rules or comply with applicable regulations is engaged in the sort of operational and financial risk taking that might jeopardize the firm's financial health and financial stability more generally. Even when this assumption breaks down, supervisors often couch risk-related judgments in procedural terms to avoid charged disagreements about the likely outcomes of a bank's business decisions.

New automated audit processes will drive a wedge between compliance and risk: allowing financial institutions to engage in universe testing and to prove compliance—evaporating any relationship between the two. Accordingly, government supervisors may be forced to address issues of business risk directly. And internal risk managers and executives will also need to drill down on business-level decision-making as they too will be less able to rely on audit and compliance records to approximate business risk.

This chapter proceeds in three sections. Section 10.1 reviews the traditional approach to audit and compliance. Section 10.2 explores the promise of RegTech and how it is likely to transform audit and compliance over the next ten years. Section 10.3 considers some of the possible perils of "provable compliance" and how the ability of regulated institutions to demonstrate compliance with bright-line rules will increase pressure on supervisors assessing bank safety and soundness.

10.1 TRADITIONAL AUDIT AND COMPLIANCE

Most audit and internal compliance today uses a sampling methodology. Auditors ask for 7 percent or so of the files from a business process. Then people review those files and write a report about any errors they find—covering both deviations from stated policies and procedures and systematic problems that may have contributed to the pattern of errors they see in the sample.

The atomic unit of analysis in any audit is the work of creating a detailed sequence of what happens in a business process: the audit log. With the rise of automation, the work of auditors has become more difficult, not less. Anyone who has created a computer program is familiar with the challenge of re-creating and understanding a precise sequence within an automated process. An unexpected result in the final output will force the programmer to go back and check each input and each intermediate step until she has identified where the program took an unexpected turn.

In systems that are combinations of manual steps and automated steps, often with millions of lines of code, auditors must master the step-through process of what the computer program has done in the business process and try to re-create the mind-set and decision framework of the people who took the manual steps.

This system is inefficient, error prone, and subject to bias in sampling error. Business processes in a modern financial institution can be thought of as decision trees with thousands of branches. Auditors often cannot hope to sample records that reflect all those branches. This system is also subject to error because the auditors' work is itself manual and completed by humans. Human auditors cannot be expected to diagnose mistakes or errors that exist in the branches of those decision trees with 100 percent accuracy. This is one of the reasons redundancy is built in—internal audit, external audit, and supervisory examination.

10.2 THE PROMISE OF REGULATORY TECHNOLOGY

Despite the attention paid to technological innovations such as machine learning and blockchain technologies, many of the advances in regulatory compliance technology are driven simply by the plummeting price of data storage. As data storage has become cheaper over the past decade, systems are now designed to record and store data about all inputs into a system and all outputs (both intermediate and final), as well as to record metadata about human interventions into the business process. In practical terms, this means that auditors have access to such items as the identity of any employee who took an action, the exact time of day the action was taken, and even how long the employee looked at a screen before taking action. In compliance terms, this means that modern workflow systems can be, and now often are, built with detailed audit logs created automatically. The hardest part of any audit—simply understanding what happened when—is now recorded in real time and has become machine readable. Moreover, the drastic reduction in the cost of storage means that financial institutions not only can build, but should be building, these automatic audit logs into all-new enterprise systems.[1] As the science fiction writer William Gibson said, the future is here, it's just unevenly distributed.

Already today, systems that are built with these automatic audit logs enable compliance professionals to move beyond sampling methodologies to *universe testing*. They can build systems that represent their policies and procedures and analyze and compare every audit log that a system produces against those policies and procedures. Where policies and procedures are deterministic, universe testing can be similarly deterministic. For example, an auditor can in minutes see every file in which an employee issued a mortgage that deviated from the firm's mortgage origination policy in the second quarter of 2017 in the state of California.

But even where policies are not deterministic, universe testing is already taking place. For example, broker-dealers are required to record all communication between their employees and their clients.[2] For many years, auditors have reviewed these communications using sampling, but technology has made these communications alternately easier and harder to track. For example, phone conversations used to be practically impossible to record at scale; but now, broker-dealers have the technological capability to capture and store those communications. And although chat-based platforms make communications capture easier in theory, the proliferation of encrypted personal chat services has made it harder to track and capture this next wave of communications technology. Many start-ups and internal teams are using voice-to-text and natural language processing technology to run 100 percent of these recorded conversations through a set of compliance rules and flags to identify potential risks. Some companies are even experimenting with pushing these compliance flags out to end users, such as software that monitors text as it is being typed and, in effect, asks users, "Are you sure you want to say that?" While these rules are not foolproof—there are, no doubt, both false positives and negatives—they demonstrate that the possibilities for universe testing are not limited to fully automated or deterministic systems.

From a business manager's perspective, audit and compliance boils down to two hard tasks. The first is to create systems, whether through training, checks and balances, or automation, that seek to ensure the company will do the right thing in the moment of any transaction or business process. The second, historically much harder than the first, is to prove to a regulator or an external auditor at some given point in the future that the company *did* the right thing at any given point in the past.

Even the first is much harder than it appears: modern financial institutions, including ones that we think of as small, will complete thousands of customer transactions each day, and each transaction will have dozens of steps. We're all familiar with the paperwork that accompanies a mortgage, but the business manager must also codify the steps necessary to have his employees reliably and accurately produce that paperwork in a way that follows both the law and the business imperative of good customer service. The second task of proving compliance is where the difficulty and discipline of audit and compliance have developed. It is this second mission that has governed the practices described above of sampling, audit log, and business process re-creation. And it is in this second task that the power of automation begins to transform the discipline of compliance.

Once a company is capable of universe testing against a business process, that company can not only create and analyze the audit log of that process but also reliably represent to any outsider whether the process was compliant. Universe testing enables the digital equivalent of signed checklists with both granularity (any transaction) and scale (all transactions). The state of the art: provable compliance.

Provable compliance is not the end of the story, however. In fact, as we map out the future of risk and compliance, it is just the beginning. When it is possible to automatically tell an auditor or an internal control system, "Yes, I know what actions were taken by which people, at what time, according to what policies," this introduces the potential for a drastic change in the compliance mind-set. If it is possible to monitor systems in real time, then applying rules in real time can become possible as well—imposing business logic inside of enterprise systems. For example, today many banks approach anti–money laundering (AML) by training staff during onboarding and through written policies and procedures. Training is then combined with traditional sampling-based audits. But these policies do not typically constrain the actions of a bank's AML personnel, who generally conduct free-form manual investigations across a variety of internal and external data systems, documenting their actions in checklists and a written risk report. Today's RegTech solutions allow a bank to directly enforce its policies inside the workstations of its employees—giving them guideposts on expected or required next steps, automating the data sources from which research must be conducted, and storing reports in an audit log of actual actions taken and a structured data format that can be repurposed or analyzed for a variety of purposes inside a bank.

The difference between these two approaches is like the difference between driving while reading a map and driving with the aid of Google Maps. If you take a wrong turn while navigating according to an analog map, no one in the car can be exactly sure where you went wrong or what to do next. But if you use Google Maps, the GPS not only can alert you at the point of each turn to help avoid incorrect navigation but also can automatically reroute you back to your destination. Moreover, the data collection from these systems is now being used to power the possibility of self-driving cars, just as RegTech systems are helping financial institutions collect the data necessary to automate more and more complex decisions about AML risk.

This extension of rules and policies into real-time feedback or constraints can be termed "programmatic compliance." In its strong form, programmatic compliance describes a state where it is not possible for a business system to take a noncompliant action. To date, the complexities of business processes and required decision-making have made programmatic compliance impossible for all but the simplest systems, but the frontiers of programmatic compliance are moving closer all the time. Soon we will be able to use machine learning and other advanced analytics to embed nuance and judgment by capturing human decisions over time and replicating them in more and more cases.

To understand the potential implications of these advances, consider how provable programmatic compliance would affect counterparty risk. For example, in a derivatives trade between two broker-dealers, both dealers would be able to attach an audit log showing how the trade proceeds will be directed and the status of any collateral. The ability to accept risk from a counterparty starts to change drastically if systems can immediately measure that party's compliance, reducing the uncertainty premium embedded in risk calculations. Consider another example: money laundering compliance. If a counterparty can use an audit log to prove that they did not take significant risk originating a transaction or if the data history is strong enough that a bank can trace the history of any transaction in an automated way, both parties' AML burden drops because they are no longer facing these unknowns. This is not something that is possible today, nor is it something that will happen tomorrow. But it is something that is fast approaching as IT departments get better and better at testing and proving compliance in high-volume, scalable ways.

10.3   THE PERILS OF PROVABLE COMPLIANCE

Like any technological transformation, provable and programmatic compliance will bring its own challenges and create new risks. One of these challenges is likely to involve the way universe testing will alter the relationship between heads of business lines and risk managers (on the level of the firm) and between financial institutions and their regulators (on the level of the system overall).

Risk managers, boards of directors, and government regulators are all charged with monitoring and managing risk taking at and across financial institutions. Risk management involves the identification and evaluation of risks—measurable probabilities that certain negative outcomes will occur in the future—and the application of resources to minimize and control the likelihood of these negative outcomes. Some risks are easy to measure and address: interest-rate risk, for example, can be managed using simple derivatives. Other risks are amorphous and difficult to control—for example, counterparty risk, the likelihood that one of the parties fails or is otherwise unable to perform its contractual obligations as promised. Counterparty risk today necessarily involves an estimation of other firms' solvency risk management capabilities, as well as systems to monitor and aggregate those estimates over time. It is particularly difficult for third-party monitors, such as board committees and outside examiners, to assess these sorts of risks and determine whether the business is managing them appropriately. It is well known in banking that managers have incentives to take more risk than would be preferred by society at large.[3] Risk management and oversight requires a firm and its overseers to mediate between optimistic and pessimistic views of an uncertain future state. It is also true that regulators, board members, and risk managers will have less detailed and less direct knowledge about the risks embedded in any business transaction.

Compliance, by contrast, is the practice of monitoring business actions for consistency with rules—including laws and regulations, and policies and procedures. Unlike risk, which involves judgments about the future (based on understandings gleaned from the past), compliance involves judgments about the past (based on information gathered about the past). While assessing compliance can be difficult, it is more susceptible to objective evaluation than risk management. Perhaps as a result, supervisors and other officials charged with managing risk taking across the firm tend to focus on a business's compliance with bright-line rules. Examiners often assume, either implicitly or explicitly, that poor compliance means inappropriate levels of business risk. Indeed, for the past two decades, bank supervisors in particular have focused on compliance. Bank supervisors likely rely on compliance checks because they are easier to conduct and more difficult for banks to dispute. They are also more objective: supervisors can point to definitive evidence that a bank did not follow the rules. There is never definitive evidence—until it is too late—that a bank has taken on too much risk.

Take the "London Whale" scandal, for example, which involved a $6 billion loss in a single quarter on a twelve-figure bet on exotic derivatives at J.P. Morgan's commercial bank.[4] These losses precipitated the largest safety and soundness penalty ever levied. Yet, despite the fact that the traders involved had been empowered to make a levered bet about the direction of the global economy and had increased the bank's balance sheet exposure to the risk as the bet began to move against them,[5] the rationale provided by supervisors was procedural: the consent orders faulted the bank merely for failing to adequately supervise its traders, properly value its investments, "implement adequate controls," and "ensure significant information . . . was provided in a timely and appropriate manner to examiners."[6]

By couching supervision in such technical, procedural terms, the banking agencies rendered their orders easily defensible, especially to constituencies with different perspectives on risk and regulation. No one could argue with the Fed that J.P. Morgan was noncompliant. But, had the Fed faulted the bank for its risk taking and not for its compliance violations, commentators and bank executives might have argued that the bank was justified in taking such large risks.

This technocratic approach is also borne out in recent research that exposes new data about the supervisory process and the pressures that have come to bear on both risk managers at banks and regulators. For example, data released by the Federal Reserve Bank of New York shows the different topics supervisors focus on, called "Matters Requiring Attention" (MRAs), in their confidential letters to banks.[7] Figure 10.1 breaks out MRAs by issue type, with the most procedural matters in dark gray at the bottom of the stack and the most substantive ones lightly shaded at the top. Procedural supervision is more common for the larger banks than for the smaller ones. Only 8 percent of MRAs at large banks were related to their loan portfolios, compared with 27 percent of MRAs at state member banks. Nearly 80 percent of supervisory activity at the larger banks fell into the first three, largely procedural, categories, whereas 55 percent and 56 percent fell into these categories for state member banks and smaller bank holding companies, respectively.

Part of the significant focus on risk modeling among the large banks is that this data covers the period when the largest banks became subject to the Comprehensive Capital Assessment and Review, the Fed's supervisory stress tests. The data suggests that despite the popular conception of the stress test as a quantitative assessment of bank balance sheets, it was the qualitative component with a focus on risk modeling that drove the MRAs. The Fed assumed that if a bank was not good at managing its capital planning process, it probably should not be allowed to pay out capital even if the Fed's quantitative analysis suggested that the bank's balance sheet was strong. Whether a bank has enough capital to sustain its business through a sharp macroeconomic contraction is difficult to determine because it involves projections about the future. It

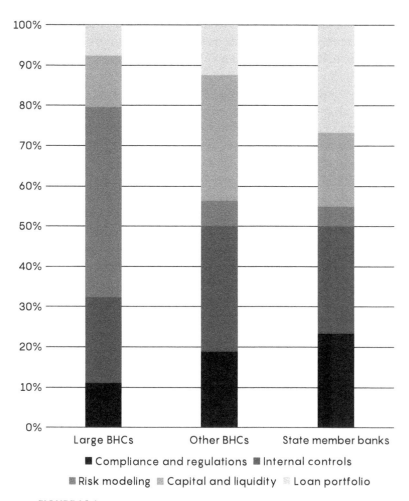

FIGURE 10.1

MRAs by issue type.

Source: Paul Goldsmith-Pinkham, Beverly Hirtle, and David Lucca, *Parsing the Content of Bank Supervision*, Federal Reserve Bank of New York Staff Reports 770 (March 2016), https://www.newyorkfed .org/medialibrary/media/research/staff_reports/sr770.pdf?la=en.

is far easier to assess whether a bank followed a careful capital planning process to decide how much capital to pay out to its shareholders because this involves merely collecting information about the past.

This sort of *proceduralism*—the focus on compliance instead of risk and couching judgments about excessive business risk in terms of compliance—reduces conflict: conflict between supervisors and bank executives, conflict between supervisors and senior officials in Washington (who are often lobbied by large financial institutions to rein in overeager junior examiners), conflict between supervisors and Congress (which is populated by many legislators who are uncomfortable with broad supervisory discretion), and conflict between supervisors and lawyers, who, themselves, prefer the legal certainty of bright-line rules. As one might expect, the greater the imbalance of power between supervisors and the firms they oversee, the more supervisors will fear conflict and seek refuge in the neutral discourse of process and the bright-line clarity of regulations.[8]

Even if this supervisory emphasis on compliance as a risk indicator has been helpful, the rise of automated compliance and programmatic compliance will decouple the relationship. Both compliance and risk have traditionally been disciplines that marry process discipline with human expertise and experience, and therefore weaknesses in one were presumed to indicate weaknesses in the other. The ability to impose compliance discipline through implementation of automated systems means that this may soon cease to be the case. If so, supervisors will no longer be able to predict who is going to be well positioned for macroeconomic shocks or operational risks tomorrow, based on who was following the rules yesterday. This decoupling is likely to place new pressures on supervisors and disrupt an equilibrium where supervisors can use the neutral language of compliance failures to support judgments about excessive risk taking. The judgments that banks make about risk are much closer to business judgments, such as about the future performance of the financial system and whether it is appropriate to undertake a business transaction. These judgments will force regulators directly into the zone of conflicts, where they have to second-guess business executives without being able to claim superior expertise or concrete evidence of mistakes.

As we look forward, we should think not only about the benefits of RegTech but also about the pressure it will place on the policy apparatus and the existing political equilibrium between the regulator and the regulated.

10.4 CONCLUSION

The rise of RegTech offers enormous benefits. RegTech will help banks improve compliance with their own policies and outside rules and regulations. This adherence should lower the cost of capital, reduce counterparty risk, and further public policy aims. But it may also begin to change, at least in the banking sector, the relationship between the regulators and the regulated. As the compliance gap shrinks, it will become harder for bank supervisors to use compliance as a proxy for business risk. Bank risk managers and regulators will have to move their dialog into the zone of uncertainty about future financial and economic performance. Regulators represent the public's interest in restricting financial firms' risk taking. But doing so without the comforting language of procedural weakness will require more trust and more explicit conversations about society's appetite for risk in the banking system.

Both financial firms and regulators will need to take steps to prepare for the reality of compliance automation and to benefit from its potential. Financial firms should take the following steps:

- *Focus on high-value experiments.* Take advantage of technology and data improvements by choosing focused experiments in areas where compliance is more data driven and, in particular, where it includes high volumes of third-party data sources. The difficulty of working with third-party data will be lower, and the value of processing it well will still be material. Focus on scaling the learnings from each experiment, not just the specific programs that succeed.

- *Map business processes from end to end.* Track the full journey of a business process from the provenance of each data point through to the transactional record, controls, compliance, and audit. Firms do not need to rebuild their processes all at once, but they need to be aware of their needs at each step to make sure that the control functions get the right data inputs and can attach early enough to benefit from the potential advances in automation.

- *Focus on the frontier of the easy.* Many of the possibilities discussed above do not require technological breakthroughs; they require only careful application of existing, often open-source, technology. Too often, innovation groups focus on breakthrough tech like quantum computing, which is usable only in a lab, and lose sight of the very real gains that could come from building cloud native applications or automating routine steps. Especially for innovation in compliance, financial firms don't have to chase the frontier of what's possible.

Financial regulators should take the following steps:

- *Practice jujitsu, not tug-of-war.* Given how quickly technology is spreading, regulators (mainly lawyers and economists) may worry that they don't have the technological expertise to keep up. As described above, technology should make it easier to create high-quality audit logs and manage large volumes of data. Regulators don't have to compete with financial firms in a tug-of-war over who has better tech capabilities; they can act more like a jujitsu master: using the greater power of technology to ask for and receive better, cleaner data from financial institutions.

- *Don't lose focus on risk.* The end goal for financial regulation is the creation and maintenance of a stable financial system that provides services to the economy in ways that are consistent with a society's values. Regulators and, in particular, policy makers should resist the temptation to accept the equilibrium where rote compliance is the focus of policy, supervision, and enforcement. Automation will make it easier to achieve rote compliance and will increasingly reveal that compliance systems cannot substitute for business judgments about risk.

NOTES

1. Fifteen years ago, no IT department could have created an automatic audit log of every action that was taken in every system in a bank. The technical challenge of recording every action was too hard (most computer programs stored intermediate steps only long enough to calculate the next action) and data storage was far too expensive.

2. FINRA Rule 3110, https://www.finra.org/rules-guidance/rulebooks/finra-rules/3110, accessed July 2021.

3. See, for example, L. Bebchuk and H. Spamann, "Regulating Bankers' Pay," *Georgetown Law Journal* 98, no. 2 (2010): 247–287, also Harvard Law and Economics Discussion Paper No. 641. See also A. Admati and M. Hellwig, *The Banker's New Clothes* (Princeton, NJ: Princeton University Press, 2013).

4. To put the loss in perspective, J.P. Morgan at the time typically made a profit of approximately $5 billion per quarter across its entire business. It is also worth noting that the Whale losses happened in a benign credit market when interest rates were stable and interbank lending conditions were normal. See *JP Morgan Annual Report*, 2014, https://www.jpmorganchase.com/content/dam/jpmc/jpmorgan-chase-and-co/investor-relations/documents/JPMC-2014-AnnualReport.pdf.

5. "Those holdings were created, in part, by an enormous series of trades in March, in which the CIO bought $40 billion in notional long positions which the OCC later characterized as 'doubling down'

on a failed trading strategy." US Senate, Permanent Subcommittee on Investigations, *JPMorgan Chase Whale Trades: A Case History of Derivatives Risks & Abuses*, 2013, 4, https://www.hsgac.senate.gov/imo/media/doc/REPORT%20-%20JPMorgan%20Chase%20Whale%20Trades%20(4-12-13).pdf.

6. JP Morgan Chase Bank, N.A., Order No. AA-EC-2013-75, O.C.C. (September 2013), at 3 ("the Bank's oversight and governance . . . were inadequate"); JP Morgan Chase & Co., Docket No. 13-031-CMP-HC, F. RES. (September 2013), at 4 ("JPMC exercised inadequate oversight"); OCC Order, supra note XX at 3 ("the Bank's valuation control processes and procedures . . . were insufficient to provide rigorous and effective assessment of valuation").

7. P. Goldsmith-Pinkham, B. Hirtle, and D. Lucca, *Parsing the Content of Bank Supervision*, Federal Reserve Bank of New York Staff Reports 770 (March 2016), 44, https://www.newyorkfed.org/medialibrary/media/research/staff_reports/sr770.pdf?la=en.

8. L. Menand, "Too Big to Supervise: The Rise of Financial Conglomerates and the Decline of Discretionary Oversight in Banking," *Cornell Law Review* 103 (2018): 1527.

11 ON GOVERNANCE AND (TECHNICAL) COMPLEXITY

John D'Agostino
with contributions from Sharmila Kassam

Governance is becoming more of an issue as technology, and technology companies, become more intimate parts of our personal and social fabric. By examining a unique data set in the field of finance, we hope, through the lens of finance and asset management, to provide insight into some of the modern challenges created when technology integrates with legacy systems and propose some methods for improving governance and avoiding failure.

Governance and complexity have a somewhat strained relationship. Intuitively, they are proportionally related. The more esoteric the business strategy, the more complex the organizational structure or processes are, the more intertwined management is with assets (i.e., conflicts), the greater the need for rigorous independent oversight and financial stewardship. Yet time and again, when things fall apart, the postmortem shows a dramatic variance between the complexity of the underlying instrument and the robustness of the oversight. Often, this variance is shocking in its starkness and simplicity.

Recent history contains several illustrative examples. Bernard Madoff's multibillion-dollar fund utilized a strip-mall audit and accounting firm and issued trade statements listing purchase and sale prices of stocks well outside the entire daily trading range. Theranos's board consisted of wealthy and elite members without even the most basic understanding or curiosity of the underlying science—leading them to believe claims of innovation dramatically outside the reach of what was achievable by the largest public competitors. WeWork's CEO took more than *$2 billion* out of the company before any substantive investor liquidity event occurred—including a $1.7 billion exit package simultaneous to a revaluation down to $8 billion, extracting ~21.5 percent of all shareholder value while being removed from the company by said dissatisfied shareholders. By the time this volume is published, there will likely be other examples.

Not everyone in charge of governance is at fault. While transparency, or specifically the mechanisms to facilitate transparency, has arguably never been more accessible, the notional values of losses wholly or partly attributable to governance and control failures continue to increase, whether due to fraud, irrational exuberance, or collective delusion.

As more public money flows into investment strategies historically limited to sophisticated investors, newer, more sophisticated models of governance are necessary to ensure that the control systems overseeing these increasingly complex and sophisticated investments are up to the challenge. In the absence of effective governance, the increasing complexity of these investments is likely to compound larger errors, much like the 2008 financial crisis, leading to larger and more frequent *black swan*–like failures, which will exacerbate retail investor losses.

Excellent academic research is available on public company corporate governance, owing to the availability of large data sets. Private company governance is far more difficult to analyze because board participation is noninstitutionalized and widely spread out, resulting in relatively few data/decision points. Consolidation has occurred to some degree in one specific niche: the boards of asset management/fund entities. Therefore, we have access to a relatively large (more than 1,500) data set around board composition, powers, and functions.

Asset management has undergone a technical evolution similar to that of most industries over the past ten years. By assigning an admittedly subjective, but consistent, determination of complexity, we can draw some observations along with a framework for how governance should respond to increasingly technical or structural complexity.

We start with the basic methodology. Fortunately, asset managers are required to lay out the specific nature and drivers of their strategy in an offering memorandum or prospectus. In this document, they also need to describe the risks associated with their approach, both external and internal. It is *generally* considered reasonable that first-order liquid assets are less complex (large-cap US equities, for example, are less complex than options or other derivatives). The first step, then, is to score firms by the complexity of the markets they engage in. Next, we can scan these descriptions for examples where a quantitative approach is identified as a primary strategy driver and/or where data, engineering, or software is identified as a key performance risk (as opposed to human capital). Finally, as asset management firms' corporate structures tend to be fairly consistent, we can identify those firms with additional corporate structure complexity beyond the norm. By weighting these three characteristics (performance drivers, risk, and corporate structure complexity), we identify a data set of ~35 percent of the total available universe as complex.

Once we have identified these categorizations, we can compare boards across complex versus less complex firms and see how this function has adapted over time. From this, we can draw a framework—one that hopefully is useful across a variety of industries—for how governance should adapt to complexity.

Finally, astute readers will undoubtedly notice that a major (arguably the primary) variable of proper governance (namely, economic incentives) is not covered in detail. There is sufficient academic literature covering alignment of interests, and it is unlikely we will be able to solve the conundrum of how to balance too little alignment / "skin in the game" (in which indifference toward negative results leads to recklessness) with too much skin in the game (in which the desire for positive results leads to recklessness). We should assume that a reasonable level of aligned economic incentives is maintained in accordance with current best practices and compensation levels.

11.1 DATA FRAMEWORK

We gained access to a sample set of about seven hundred boards of directors of asset management entities. These records included access to all formation documents, board activities, functions, and decisions over the life of the entity (mean life of five years).

The first step was to group the entities into "simple" versus "complex" categories. For this we took information from the entity offering documents. Asset management firms are generally required to list their strategies and risk details. By scraping these documents for keywords around asset classes, strategies, and identified risk, we were able to divide these entities into three categories:

A (simplest): Liquid asset classes with all publicly available pricing (i.e., Level I assets), fundamentally driven strategies with low turnover. The risks highlighted in these types of entities—that is, interest rates, equity fund flows, and market beta along with human error as they are discretionary driven—tend to be macro oriented.

B (moderate): Liquid to illiquid asset classes with mostly publicly available pricing (Level II assets), fundamental or systematic strategies with low to medium turnover. Risks for moderate complexity investment strategies tend to involve both macro factors and trade/strategy execution. While discretion may still be utilized, trading signals are mostly systematically generated, so success/failure is less dependent on external market forces.

C (complex): Liquid to illiquid assets with public or model-driven pricing (Level III assets), systematic or quant-driven strategies with medium to high turnover. Highly complex strategy risk is based mostly on internal execution, data quality/availability, technical failure or failure to maintain technical (i.e., programming development) edge relative to competitors.

We then looked at the following board activities and their characteristics:

- Meeting frequency
- Management communication frequency
- Number of board committees
- Size of the board
- Average years' experience per board member

We also manually looked at a subset of twenty-five complex managers and compared them with a sample set of twenty-five simple managers and looked more deeply into the following:

- Director specialty experience, specifically STEM (science, technology, engineering, and mathematics) experience
- Diversity

Finally, we engaged in survey conversations with several dozen directors and governance professionals (such as compliance officers and general counsels) of firms engaged in a relatively complex approach to asset management. This allowed us to see whether data patterns for addressing complexity were empirically present.

From this data set, a few observations became immediately apparent.

11.1.1 Complexity and Frequency of Board Activity Appear to Be Directly Related

More complex strategies generated 20 percent more board interactions than simpler strategies, adjusting for size (i.e., on a per-$50-million-assets basis). This relationship begins to break down at the $3-billion-assets mark / thirty employees, indicating that the operational, financial, and human resources complexity of larger firms begins to narrow the natural spread that technical complexity creates with regard to governance activity. Notably, the percentage of email traffic between board members and management increases by almost 55 percent, with phone calls and board meeting frequency going up a smaller percentage. This could indicate the volume of data being transmitted or, since most data transmissions are done over a secure portal, the clarification or discussion of that data. From our secondary data set, complex strategies are two times more likely than simpler strategies to utilize encryption or secure (FTP, or File Transfer Protocol) channels to communicate data.

Data-driven firms tend to approach all aspects of the business in a data-driven manner. Therefore, we see more extensive codification of processes and procedures, greater use of comparative tools for decision-making, a greater number of meetings before decisions are finalized, and codification of the decision-making process, which is then subject to an internal or external peer review to ensure it is in line with industry standards and conforms to stated internal policies.

It seems reasonable, therefore, that directors should engage with management in both formal communications (minuted meetings) and informal communications (periodic reporting and email, phone, and face-to-face contacts/updates) at a frequency proportionate to the degree of complexity. Since no standard benchmark for engagement frequency exists, directors should seek to emulate the internal pace—that is, if product design intervals increase during a growth period, director interaction should proportionally increase. This is sometimes counterintuitive, as during times of increased pressure, outside governance and compliance functions tend to recede in efforts not to impede growth; but the opposite should be true. Governance should integrate into the pace of growth without causing or being seen to cause an impediment.

11.1.2 Complexity Affects Board Composition and Skill Sets

A January 2019 study from Columbia / Harvard University[1] showed that despite the Financial Stability Board (FSB) clearly taking issue with pre-crisis financial bank boards, stating that they "had directors with little financial industry experience and limited understanding of the rapidly increasing complexity of the institutions they were leading" and consequently "were too deferential to senior management," the percentage of bank boards with prior banking experience *decreased* from 15.69 percent in 2007 to 15.38 percent in 2011. In fact, virtually all of the FSB recommendations were largely ignored.

In our data set, we find that complex strategies have, on average, 15 percent larger boards on a per asset basis. These boards have 25 percent more committees, indicating a desire to compartmentalize board functions and apply specific domain expertise to relevant decisions. Again, at a larger asset size, the variance between simple and complex strategies begins to break down, perhaps because of efficiencies of scale or diminishing returns on governance investment. Asset management firms tend to reach critical mass at around the $4 billion range.

Complex firms' governance professionals have, on average, three and a half years or 30 percent more experience cited in their résumés than the governance professionals in simple firms and are more than two times more likely to have advanced science degrees. If we consider only the nonmanagement board members, we still see similar variance to simple strategies.

In some ways these data observations match with intuitive predictions. We would expect that firms deploying more complex technical strategies would require more governance involvement, and that those in positions of responsibility would possess more, and more specific, experience or education.

Yet, interestingly, the proportional increase in sophistication does not appear to have any effect on firm performance. Complex firms are as likely to fail in the first five years of operation as simple firms. And while it makes sense that the largest failures would, owing to their size, likely showcase high levels of pedigree and sophistication, the point remains that governance sophistication does not appear to have a mitigating effect on large-scale failure.

To help explain this, we conducted about fifty survey conversations with governance professionals in complex firms, with a focus on understanding the perceived weaknesses of their governance practices. The patterns that emerged in these conversations formed a framework that appears to be directly proportional to the degree of technical complexity of the underlying company and appears as a set of recurring problems.

The most jarring data point from the interviews is the degree to which board sophistication/experience resulted in less governance engagement than the mean complex entity in the larger data set—almost 50 percent less (estimated) engagement. There appears to be an optimal point where experience and sophistication versus capacity and availability of directors crosses over. Firms that choose board members below this point run the risk of building incompetent boards or ones intimidated by management; those who cross over it are at risk of having a board with neither the time nor the motivation to be actively engaged.

11.1.3   Complexity Intimidates

Sociologists and public planners are often tasked to address *wicked problems*—problems whose social complexity means that it has no determinable stopping point. Moreover, because of complex interdependencies, the effort to solve one aspect of a wicked problem may reveal or create other problems.

Directors need to maintain the balance between respect for the technical complexity underpinning the company strategy and the skepticism necessary to ensure they are not blinded to embedded faults. Continuing education and maintaining an external, impartial, and perhaps even competitive/skeptical expert resource is the foundation of building a *cynically enthusiastic approach* toward complexity. This should include the following:

- Respect for complexity, requirement for clarity
- Continual learning

In complex scenarios, those in charge of governance are less likely to voice concerns out of fear their contributions will be deemed uninformed or they themselves will be seen as nonqualified. There is no better empirical example of this than the years leading up to the global financial crisis, where an unwillingness to challenge overly complex financial structuring led to a cascade of risk that reverberated through the global financial system.

With the benefit of hindsight, many professionals who were in a governance position at that time express regret at not speaking out more strongly regarding obvious, simple problems with the complex mathematics that turned bad credit into good credit. Yet the culture of complexity that led to an element of hero worship of those who could create these highly complex structured products was not a one-time phenomenon. New York University professor Scott Galloway has made a career of studying the way investors and boards lose their direction because of hero worship. This behavior can mask outright fraud, but perhaps even more problematically, it can prevent directors from acting as necessary checks and balances of misguided CEOs.

In our discussions with directors who had been on boards where substantive (nonfraudulent or without accusation of fraud) failure occurred, all referenced one of two problems with their approach toward senior management, with about 70 percent referencing some form of manipulation (short of outright fraud) and the other 30 percent referencing some form of "hero worship," where they felt intimidated by superior technical knowledge and were unable or unwilling to ask for clarifying information.

Directors have to walk a fine line between cynicism and enthusiasm. In order to build an appropriately cynical yet enthusiastic approach, directors require confidence in the form of direct or indirect technical expertise.

11.2   SOLUTION: BOLSTER CONFIDENCE WITH INTERNAL *AND* EXTERNAL SKILL SETS

Continuing education exists for many professions where an expectation of accountability exists alongside an understanding of the skills and knowledge needed to be refreshed or supplemented to an evolving complexity—such as in the fields of law and medicine. But these requirements also apply to accounting and certain forms of finance. The theory is that these professions demand increased responsibility for laypeople, and this responsibility demands periodic skill review to maintain certain licenses.

Governance responsibilities may not dictate life or death, and while the absence of good governance may lead to incarceration, legal assistance is likely more important in that respect. However, it is certainly reasonable to assume that good governance standards carry as much responsibility as a quality accountant or financial adviser. And just as we expect an attorney representing a technology company to understand the basic elements of that technology, or an accounting firm to understand the nature of the assets (digital or physical) in order to value them or determine their tax status, we should expect directors to either enter into their positions with a reasonable technical underpinning or take the time and attention to procure one in their role.

Yet it is almost unheard of to demand continuing education or even basic competency standards from directors. A continuing education program for directors would place an increased onus on the role, but ultimately derisk the individual and company. There may be a legal argument for increased accountability if a presumption of knowledge is made, but the basic tenets of fiduciary responsibility generally do not allow ignorance as a defense. However, evidence of continuing education may make it more difficult to say that, at worst, a good-faith effort was made to retain relevant core knowledge required to protect investors.

In addition to, versus as a replacement for, governance, professionals need to develop a locus of independent resources for sanity checking advanced technical assumptions/claims. Just as the media has bifurcated to the point where it is useful to gather a range of sources to approximate accuracy and lower the probability of bad information, governance professionals need a range of knowledge resources, from within and, perhaps most importantly, outside the industry within which they serve. Gathering these resources will help reduce the probability they are being fed bad or biased information owing to fraud, irrational exuberance, or simply the existence of a self-perpetuating echo chamber.

These external resources do not need to be superior or competitive. Obviously, directors carry significant material, nonpublic information and have a responsibility to management and shareholders to maintain strict confidentiality. However, this doesn't mean they can't integrate themselves into the technical community and develop a sounding board to understand where the mean consensus is on research and functional capabilities, and then use their judgment to determine whether their company's progress is within a normal range of operations—and if not, determine whether their competitive edge can reasonably explain the variance.

Finally, a brief word on compensation and conflicts. Much has already been written on the topic, and compensation benchmarks are readily available. However, our interviews reveal that notional compensation value may not be the only benchmark to consider when evaluating the effect compensation has on governance.

In retrospect, board members whose personal income derives from the same underlying technology utilized by the company highlight their bias from that shared interest as a factor in their inability to acknowledge problems or challenges. In other words, it appears that the more knowledgeable a board member is regarding the underlying complexity, the greater their financial separation should be from the outcome. This may appear counterintuitive, as having skin in the game (in the form of stock-based compensation, for example) is generally considered to be a good thing. However, we know that linking compliance or risk-control functions to trading performance in asset management can lead to a misalignment of interests and direct or subconscious pressure to allow excessively risky behavior. It seems reasonable, therefore, that directors who are subconsciously biased toward an outcome for a certain type of technology will be resistant to its faults.

11.3 INVESTORS DRIVE NEXT-GENERATION GOVERNANCE BOTH EXTERNALLY AND INTERNALLY

Shareholders—that is, investors—seek investment opportunities with the highest levels of governance yet, ironically, often do not scrutinize their own governance with the same rigor. Investors can vary from those less institutionalized (with less organizational structure and formal governance) to institutional investors from both the private and the public sectors, which typically have an established governance structure.

As discussed, that corporate entities or asset managers need governance to scale, investors' governance structures need to adapt as the complexity of investment strategies increases.

Over the past fifteen years, more institutional investors have adopted significant asset allocations that have moved from public stocks and bonds to private investment strategies with a variety of underlying assets, less transparency, and longer durations needing more rigorous oversight.[2] Investors have sought these strategies for their illiquidity premium, and for various reasons these investments target returns exceeding the investors' necessary return hurdles. Anecdotally among public pension investors, the rate of changes in allocation to these alternative investments has far exceeded the rate of evolution of the investors' governance framework.[3] This complexity premium often sought from asset managers is not always recognized internally by investors as needing more resources to maintain the investors' fiduciary oversight.

A reality is that the investors often have limited resources and skill sets, so the need for seeking human capital that is either hired or "trained up" for this type of investing is critical not just at the staff level but also at the governing body level. Budgets are also often limited for resources, so the future should maximize technology to more effectively and efficiently create oversight functions of managers. Like other industries—retail, financial services, energy, or agriculture—technology is making functions easier and more precise; however, the complexity involved in institutional investors' adoption of those technologies requires a level of skill that is itself a hurdle.

An example of a future use of technology by investors is IBM and Northern Trust partnering to apply blockchain (its security-rich distributed ledger system) to a private equity fund administered by Unigestion, a Switzerland-based private equity manager with $20 billion under management.[4] The solution is based on open-source Linux Foundation Hyperledger Fabric. The general partner board of Unigestion noted that the technology "provided us with an infrastructure that will enable the fund to be serviced in a digital environment, introducing a new collaborative ecosystem to the private equity market where all actions are undertaken on a common, open and transparent platform."

11.4   REGTECH

RegTech, short for regulation technology, is seen as a massive potential market. The global accounting firm KPMG estimated in 2019 that spending on RegTech will soon equal about 40 percent of the ~$270 billion of total US financial service compliance spending. Unsurprisingly, investment flows continue to grow, and an expanding suite of RegTech start-ups has emerged. Most of these solutions address the need for governance to be informed and the capabilities to monitor, using artificial intelligence and similar tools to (1) source, screen, organize, and present the vast amount of legacy and new data, rules, and decisions; and (2) review, in real time or with low latency, transactions, messages, and actions of employees and stakeholders. Technology that can deploy sentiment analysis to understand qualitative rule changes across multiple countries, for example, will certainly reduce the risk of governance failure due to ignorance. Software that can screen millions of stock trades in real time and search for patterns that indicate compliance breaches will lessen the chance of governance failure due to oversight limitations. Both play a vital role in empowering governance through brute-force application of computational power that allows those in chance of governance to scale their observation capabilities alongside the businesses under their charge. It remains to be seen how adaptable these systems will be when challenged by complex purposeful, or even subconscious, attempts by market participants to breach rules, or how the technology will respond to pervasive ethical breaches—as opposed to strict rule breaches. In all likelihood, compliance RegTech will get smarter over time and begin to mimic the basic tenets of legal and moral oversight. The question of how long, and whether, it can keep up with the equally rapid evolution of its market adversaries remains to be seen.

However, informational and observational capacity are just two elements charged to governance. Fiduciary responsibility—founded on the notion that individuals should place the interests of others before their own—is more difficult to solve through computational power. This is because the advantages one party has over another are complex, nuanced, subject to interpretation, and multifactored—all characteristics that stymie code-based compliance systems. Attempts are being made in the digital assets space, with decentralized autonomous organizations looking to automate complex social, commercial, and financial functions through code. While these measures appear promising, and likely impactful around simple transactions (e.g., conclusively determining titles for home or auto insurance purposes), governance failures, outside of straight fraud, also occur when participants, completely aware of the rule set governing behavior, nonetheless convince themselves a course of action is allowed. This generally comes from their interpretation of the rules or their determination that the particular facts and circumstances allow for an exemption. Both scenarios are very difficult to reduce to a decision tree that can be monitored by computer code. To put it differently, RegTech is (currently) excellent at catching indication of fraud, very good at monitoring binary decisions, good at helping to monitor first-order complexity decisions, but may struggle against the complex, perhaps even well-intentioned, delusion that has caused some of the most significant governance failures.

11.5 LANGUAGE AND COMPETENCIES SHIFTING TO REFLECT THE FUTURE STATE

Over time, we may see that fintech as a specific focus or practice area within governance will disappear, as technology in all forms saturates financial services to the point where it is simply an essential part of how capital flows through economic systems. This day does not appear to be far off,[5] with digital currencies poised to replace cash in the near future.

Just as a corporate director of a Japanese company invariably speaks Japanese, it will not be long before directors and governance professionals will invariably be fluent in the language of technology.

Ultimately, good governance comes down to taking the robustness that management uses to build high-performing teams and applying it to the construction and maintenance of high-performing boards. As technology evolves, boards must also evolve, and principles of continual learning, dynamic restructuring, and conflict mitigation can assist in maintaining parity.

NOTES

The author would like to thank the significant contributions to this chapter by Sharmila Kassam, former deputy CIO of Texas Employees Retirement System.

1. S. Rajgopal, S. Srinivasan, and Y. T. F. Wong, "Bank Boards: What Has Changed since the Financial Crisis?," SSRN, January 1, 2019, https://papers.ssrn.com/sol3/papers.cfm?abstract_id=2722175.

2. A. Whyte, "Public Pensions Pour More Money into Private Equity," *Institutional Investor*, January 31, 2019, https://www.institutionalinvestor.com/article/b1cy61jsl24097/Public-Pensions-Pour-More-Money-Into-Private-Equity.

3. L. Farmer, "Politicizing the Portfolio," Governing.com, December 2018, https://archives.erepublic.com/GOV/GOV_Mag_Dec2018.pdf.

4. Y. Bobeldijk, "Northern Trust, Unigestion and IBM Team Up for Private Equity Blockchain," *FN London*, February 22, 2017, https://www.fnlondon.com/articles/northern-trust-unigestion-and-ibm-team-up-for-private-equity-blockchain-20170222.

5. D. Michaels and P. Vigna, "The Coming Currency War: Digital Money vs. the Dollar," *Wall Street Journal*, September 22, 2019.

12 RESPONSIBLE TECHNOLOGY: ADVANCING TRUST AND SECURING THE ECOSYSTEM

Ajay Bhalla

Responsible technology—new and emerging technologies like AI, biometrics, and cyber—stand to perform an unprecedented and positive role for society. But for them to be successful, public, government, and industry trust is essential.

How, then, can an environment be created and sustained that strikes the right balance between enabling technology development to continue to keep pace with user demand, while ensuring the right guardrails are in place so that we can all build and maintain trust in them?

12.1 WHERE WE ARE

12.1.1 It's about Trust

My friend was talking about driverless cars recently. "If my car crashed as often as my computer does—I'd be worried," she said. "And if my computer was *driving* my car, I'd be terrified."

Of course, those who design driverless cars are only too aware of the leap of faith required for people to trust their lives to a machine. That's why they invest so much in research, testing, and security. The technology needs to be infallible. It needs to be *trusted*. The only way my friend and millions of others will get into a car that drives itself is when they trust the technology behind the wheel.

Trust can be defined as "a confident relationship with the unknown."[1] Engendering that confidence is the big challenge facing innovators today. Your new technology may be great, but will it be *trusted*? Gaining this trust is becoming more important because people are being asked to entrust much more of their lives to technology. My friend will tolerate her computer crashing every now and then if she only uses it for Netflix, Twitter, and her daily news feed. She won't tolerate a computer crashing her car, messing up her home security, and sharing details of her private life with the rest of the world.

12.1.2   Challenges

When we look around, there are plenty of examples to undermine our confidence in new technology. We're familiar with the little horror stories: the talking toy doll that can be hacked by anyone with a smartphone,[2] the fish tank connected to Wi-Fi that lets fraudsters access a Las Vegas casino database,[3] and the virtual voice assistant that emailed an individual's private conversation to a work colleague.[4]

And there are the big horror stories: the Equifax hack in which the personal data of half the population of the United States was stolen;[5] the Cambridge Analytica scandal, which still reverberates around Facebook; and the cyberattacks on power stations in Ukraine and against oil pipelines in Turkey.

12.1.3   Digital Convergence and the Internet of Things

There are a number of reasons for this insecurity, not least the fact that the internet evolved to connect people, not to make them feel secure. This connection didn't matter so much when our online lives were separate from our offline lives. It *does* matter now that they are intertwined. Whether it's your phone connected to your watch, home, or car, everybody has multiple interconnected devices—we're never really offline. It is anticipated that by 2025, 50 billion devices will be connected to the internet,[6] each of them a link in an enormous chain. Some strong, some weak, some smart, some dumb. The casino was hacked through a thermometer, the pipeline was hacked through a video camera, and the doll was hacked through a $2 microphone. Cheap, insecure, and often peripheral devices can become ticking time bombs on the internet of things.

12.1.4 Exponential Growth in Data

These connected devices are creating an exponential growth in data; 90 percent of it has occurred in the past few years alone.[7] New technologies like 5G will further accelerate this growth. But while we may *create* the data, we often don't own it, control it, know who has it, or who will use it. In theory we should know, but when was the last time you actually read a clickwrap agreement? A group of university professors once calculated that it would take seventy-six working days to read all the privacy documents one agrees to in a single year.[8] Even if our data starts off in a secure environment, there's no guarantee it will stay there.

12.1.5 Age of Artificial Intelligence

There's an important reason that data is so sought after—it is the fuel for artificial intelligence (AI). AI is wonderful. It is being used to improve crop yields, tackle world hunger, predict earthquakes, and transform health care. But we need to ensure that the insatiable demand for data doesn't undermine our digital ecosystem in the way that the race for oil and gas has created problems for our natural ecosystem.

These are *the principal challenges that face innovators today. It's no longer acceptable to just "move fast and break things," to place innovation and product development above all else, not least security and well-being.*

12.2   A GUIDE TO RESPONSIBLE INNOVATION

So what should we be doing instead to foster responsible innovation? It starts with security by design. In the following pages I will outline a high-level guide to responsible innovation.

12.2.1 Security by Design

First, recognize that every connected entity needs to be a secure entity, no matter how small or apparently insignificant. If it can't be secured, it shouldn't be connected.

Second, responsibility for security lies with the producer, not the end user. Millions of connected devices haven't had a security update in years, because the owner hasn't done so. If it can't be patched remotely, it shouldn't be connected.

Third, secure the network. Even a safe car becomes unsafe on dangerous roads. In the real world, this safety is a collective endeavor: dedicated planners design and build the highway network, automobile manufacturers make sure their vehicles are safe, police ensure that users abide by the rules, and governments and industry bodies regulate all of the above. It's time we gave our superhighways the same consideration.

At Mastercard we know something about security by design. We are custodians of a network that processes 75 billion transactions per year. That means securing not just every card, payment device, and terminal on the network, but also the payment rails that connect them. There's good reason for putting security at the heart of this. Financial institutions are three hundred times more likely than businesses in other industries to suffer an attack.[9] For banks, cybersecurity is now their top board-level priority;[10] they're investing heavily to stay ahead of the criminals. Industry bodies like our own—EMVCo—have for many years set standards and specifications in payment security globally.

12.2.2 Privacy by Design

The second tenet of responsible innovation is privacy by design.

For too long, personal data has been considered a commodity rather than a possession. Privacy by design challenges this notion. It means minimal data collection—only what is needed, not what is wanted. It means giving individuals control of their data and how it is used, rather than having them sign it away in clickwrap contracts. And it means handling their data with the highest standards of security and integrity.

Privacy by design is at the heart of Mastercard's new ID service. The company is creating a user-centric digital identity that is owned, managed, and controlled by the individual and requires neither further aggregation of identity data nor the creation of centralized data structures.[11]

This doesn't stop Mastercard from innovating to harness the societal value of data. Anonymized consumer transaction data has limitless applications for development research, for example. By allowing researchers to use data-driven insights, the Mastercard Center for Inclusive Growth is assisting in new programs to improve the economic growth and financial inclusion of the world's vulnerable communities.

12.2.3   Use Security to Drive the Consumer Experience

Third, align security with the consumer experience. This is crucial. Do not trade security for convenience.

Take the example of biometric authentication, where the password is replaced with the person. Techniques like fingerprint and facial recognition are far more secure than knowledge-based solutions, such as passwords, PINs, and logins. Think of the hundreds of accounts, passwords, PINs, and memorable data you've accumulated. It's no surprise that most people choose passwords that are easy to remember and then use them across multiple accounts. This practice makes individuals vulnerable to fraudsters. Biometrics provides a solution by enabling the automated recognition of individuals according to physiological traits—fingerprint, face, or voice, for example. Explicit biometrics such as fingerprint, face, or palm can be combined with passive biometrics (behavior) and device ownership to enable multifactor authentication and frictionless transactions.

The main driver for biometric adoption is not security but the fact that 90 percent of users prefer the experience.[12] It's why Mastercard put usability at the heart of its Five Factor Framework to help financial institutions adopt biometrics.

12.2.4 Ethics and Governance

Finally, a word on the role of ethics and governance in technology innovation.

Technology can be used for good or bad. AI, for example, has implications for security and privacy. It can be deliberately misused by bad actors. Unwittingly, it can also introduce bias and discrimination in decision-making and propagate or amplify biases inherent in the data. In commerce, the self-reinforcing nature of AI products can create monopolies and encourage herd behavior. Machines may be capable of complex calculation, but so far they have been unable to make qualitative or moral judgments. So the next time a company tells you it's using AI to take care of business, ask who's taking care of the AI. And if the whole thing sounds like a black box, walk away, for the sake of all of us.

Mastercard has committed to an AI governance framework around the core values of trust, integrity, and respect. It follows a process that begins with an evaluation of the intended purpose for which we want to use AI, then moves through data and model evaluation, design and risk scoring, and continued monitoring for bias and unintended consequences. The organization has established similar principles for the use of privacy and data too.

This isn't just about obeying the law. For one thing, legislators can't keep pace with technological innovation. The General Data Protection Regulation (GDPR), for example, is a success story that took years to debate and implement. For all its strengths around the protection of consumer data, it now finds itself at loggerheads with one of the most transformative technologies of the modern era—blockchain. GDPR mandates the "right to be forgotten," but distributed ledgers are designed to last forever. They are decentralized and immutable—a tamper-proof record that sits outside the control of any one body. GDPR isn't disappearing, and neither is blockchain. But the industry, both businesses and regulators alike, needs to work closer together to build an environment where new technologies like blockchain can thrive and evolve, while still ensuring that the right accountability safeguards are built into the way they are developed. There are other challenges with open banking, where new players are entering a sector whose security is challenged more than any other. Open banking rules force financial institutions to share data, whereas GDPR rules restrict them from doing so.[13] One regulation rubbing up against another.

There is no simple answer to this, except to say that doing things right requires thought, cooperation, collaboration, and mutual support. In our digital ecosystem we are codependent as never before. It is possible to succeed responsibly; Mastercard created a seamless and secure payment network that operates across hundreds of countries, thousands of stakeholders, and billions of transactions. We have long understood that securing our network means securing our customers, merchants, cardholders, and the wider ecosystem too.

12.3 RESPONSIBLE INNOVATION AND TRUST

Responsible innovation creates trust, and trust keeps the world turning.

I do believe that one day my friend will allow herself to be driven by an autonomous vehicle. The time will come when she takes a leap of faith and steps inside, but not before she's confident she'll be safe. People are often being asked to take a leap of faith these days—trusting technology they don't understand, giving data to people they can't see, forming relationships with businesses they don't know.

And no matter how impressive the innovation or how daz-
zling the technology behind it, the decision of whether to
trust it will be made by the smartest machine that exists—the
human being.

NOTES

1. R. Botsman, *Who Can You Trust?* (London: Portfolio Penguin, 2017).

2. "#Toyfail: An Analysis of Consumer and Privacy Issues in Three
Internet-Connected Toys," Forbrukerrådet, December 2016, https://
www.forbrukerradet.no/wp-content/uploads/2016/12/toyfail-report
-desember2016.pdf.

3. A. Schiffer, "How a Fish Tank Helped Hack a Casino," *Washington
Post*, July 21, 2017.

4. S. Wolfson, "Amazon's Alexa Recorded Private Conversation and
Sent It to Random Contact," *The Guardian*, May 24, 2018.

5. T. S. Bernard, T. Hsu, N. Perlroth, and R. Lieber, "Equifax Says
Cyberattack May Have Affected 143 Million in the U.S.," *New York
Times*, September 7, 2017; S. Cowley, "2.5 Million More People Poten-
tially Exposed in Equifax Breach," *New York Times*, October 2, 2017.

6. Some forecasts, such as from International Data Corporation, show
up to 75 billion devices by 2025, but we say over 50 billion to be conser-
vative (e.g., "Connected Devices Will Generate 79 Zettabytes of Data by
2025," *IoT Business News*, August 10, 2020, https://iotbusinessnews.com
/2020/08/10/08984-connected-devices-will-generate-79-zettabytes-of
-data-by-2025/).

7. M. Belfiore, "How 10 Industries Are Using Big Data to Win Big,"
Watson Blog, July 28, 2016, https://www.ibm.com/blogs/watson/2016
/07/10-industries-using-big-data-win-big/.

8. A. M. McDonald and L. F. Cranor, "The Cost of Reading Privacy
Policies," *I/S: A Journal of Law and Policy for the Information Society* 4,
no. 3 (2008): 543–568.

9. R. Ungario, "Cyberattacks Are 300 Times as Likely to Hit Financial Firms Than Other Companies: A Sweeping New Report Finds

They're Not Prepared," *Business Insider*, June 20, 2019, https://markets .businessinsider.com/news/stocks/cyberattacks-impact-major-threats -to-financial-firms-not-prepared-2019-6.

10. J. Boehm, P. Merrath, T. Poppensieker, R. Riemenschnitter, and T. Stahl, "Cyber Risk Measurement and the Holistic Cybersecurity Approach," McKinsey & Company, November 18, 2018, https://www .mckinsey.com/business-functions/risk/our-insights/cyber-risk-measure ment-and-the-holistic-cybersecurity-approach.

11. Mastercard, https://www.mastercard.us/en-us/issuers/products-and -solutions/mastercard-digital-identity-service.html, accessed July 12, 2021.

12. G. Lovisotto, R. Malik, I. Sluganovic, M. Roeschlin, P. Trueman, and I. Martinovic, "Mobile Biometrics in Financial Services: A Five Factor Framework," conference proceedings, July 11, 2017, https:// newsroom.mastercard.com/eu/files/2017/06/Mobile-Biometrics-in -Financial-Services_A-Five-Factor-Framework-compressed3.pdf.

13. D. Bonderud, "Open Banking and the Closed Ecosystem: The Tech Banks Need to Navigate GDPR," *BizTech*, September 23, 2019, https://biztechmagazine.com/article/2019/09/open-banking-and -closed-ecosystem-tech-banks-need-navigate-gdpr#:~:text=Security -,Open%20Banking%20and%20the%20Closed%20Ecosystem%3A%20 The,Banks%20Need%20to%20Navigate%20GDPR&text=To%20 meet%20the%20growing%20demands,application%20program%20 interfaces%2C%20or%20APIs.

CONCLUSION

The dawn of the new decade brings numerous innovations to bear on the world's biggest problems. It also brings new intensity to the externalities that impact fintech and financial services, from government instability to global health crises.

While we were working on this book, the SARS-CoV-2 / COVID-19 ("novel coronavirus") pandemic was sweeping the world. Many countries simply shut down in a matter of weeks, sequestering citizens in their homes. Researchers frantically raced to understand how the virus is transmitted, which interventions are best at containing it, and what the effects are of eliminating most in-person aspects of an economy for an extended period of time.

And many of the ideas we discussed in *Global Fintech* suddenly became urgent and immediate. Physical money? That's a transmission vector. Time to go digital. In-person bank branches? Not relevant, since everything is digital. The limits of the old system went from inconvenient to pressing: How can you put a wet signature to paper if you don't own a printer and can't go to a printing store? How does an open-outcry trading pit work when individuals have to stay six feet from others? (Hint: it doesn't.) Markets gyrated wildly. Cryptocurrencies, curiously, appeared to be largely uncorrelated to general equities, and indeed went on a historic bull run, rising more than 300 percent between August 2020 and July 2021.

As educators, the authors in this volume have been tinkering with online learning for years, so perhaps we have been less affected than some of our colleagues as we were already equipped to pivot to a fully virtual instructional model. Yet MBA students pursuing fintech studies reasonably ask their institutions why they are paying such a high sum of money for what often amounted to a series of webinars. Demand began to rise for better education solutions, and competition intensified. Following online platform provider Coursera's IPO, MIT and Harvard, notably, sold the commercial assets of their competing effort edX to course purveyor 2U, Inc. for more than $800 million. 2U's relationship with MIT began in 2015 when a subsidiary, GetSmarter, first put our MIT fintech class and then our Oxford fintech class online into over 150 countries. We arguably provided foundational knowledge for many of the innovators now shaping the fintech future. And so we come full circle.

Digitization and distance collaboration, along with digital money and fully electronic identity, suddenly become the norm rather than the experiment. Will this continue once the worst of the pandemic has passed? Even as vaccine trials were bridging to initial deployments into global populations, the acceleration of fintech appears to show staying power. Fintech company valuations reached new heights, suggesting that public markets investors believe the digital transformation of financial services has durability in the coming years.

Despite the overcast skies, the innovators described in this book are all working to create a brighter tomorrow that encompasses improved access for the poor, greater stability and more choice for more economies, and enhanced capacities for all. During uncertain times, these digital pioneers are working to shape a new, more positive future.

David L. Shrier and Alex Pentland
Cambridge, MA, and London, UK, July 2021

CONTRIBUTORS

David L. Shrier is a futurist and innovation catalyst with expertise in artificial intelligence (AI), data/analytics, fintech, digital identity, cybersecurity, and collaborative innovation. He is the CEO of Esme Learning Solutions, an AI-enabled edtech platform that works with top universities such as the Massachusetts Institute of Technology, the University of Cambridge, and the University of Oxford, and the CEO of Adit EdTech (NYSE: ADEX), a special-purpose acquisition company (SPAC). David is on the board of Copper Technologies (UK) Ltd, a markets infrastructure provider for institutional crypto trading. His innovation consultancy, Visionary Future, works with corporations and governments to advance next-horizon growth initiatives, such as the Commonwealth Fintech Toolkit he developed for the Commonwealth of Nations. He holds an appointment as Professor of Practice, Imperial College Business School, Imperial College London. Previously he was an associate fellow with Said Business School, University of Oxford, and a lecturer and futurist at MIT, where he also held positions as managing director of Connection Science and new ventures officer at MIT Sloan. David specializes in helping established organizations build new revenue and new markets. Notable engagements include Kyriba, Dun & Bradstreet, Wolters Kluwer, Ernst & Young, MIT, GE/NBC, the Walt Disney Company, AOL Verizon, and Starwood, as well as private equity funds.

He has led a number of private equity and venture-capital-backed companies as CEO, CFO, or COO, either in interim or full-time capacities, and has cofounded four AI-enabled MIT spinouts. His books include *Augmenting Your Career*, *Basic Blockchain*, and, together with Professor Alex Penland, *Trusted Data*, *New Solutions for Cyber Security*, and *Frontiers of Financial Technology*.

Alex "Sandy" Pentland holds triple professorial appointments at the Massachusetts Institute of Technology in the Media Lab (SA+P), the School of Engineering, and the School of Management. He also directs MIT's Connection Science initiative, the Human Dynamics Laboratory, and the MIT Media Lab Entrepreneurship Program, and has been a member of the advisory boards for the United Nations, the American Bar Association, Google, Nissan, Telefonica, and a variety of start-up firms. For several years he co-led the World Economic Forum Big Data and Personal Data initiatives. He has pioneered the fields of computational social science and wearable computing, generating several successful start-ups and technology spin-offs. He previously helped create and direct MIT's Media Laboratory, the Media Lab Asia laboratories at the Indian Institutes of Technology, and Strong Hospital's Center for Future Health. In 2012, *Forbes* named Sandy one of the "seven most powerful data scientists in the world," along with the founders of Google and the chief technology officer of the United States, and in 2013 he won the McKinsey Award from *Harvard Business Review*. His books include *Honest Signals*, *Social Physics*, *Trusted Data*, and *Frontiers of Financial Technology*. He was named to the National Academy of Engineering in 2014. Sandy holds a BGS from the University of Michigan and a PhD from MIT.

Ajay Bhalla is president of cyber and intelligence solutions for Mastercard. He also serves as a CEME Senior Fellow at the Fletcher School, Tufts University, and as MIT Connection Science Fellow at the Massachusetts Institute of Technology.

Michelle Chivunga is founder and CEO of the Global Policy House and senior adviser to the Government of Bermuda, the African Union, WUSME, and Fintech4Good. She was recently appointed as the Africa lead for the International Chambers of Commerce UK.

John D'Agostino is an American business executive and entrepreneur. Currently he leads strategic advisory firm Dagger Consulting and also serves on the boards of hedge funds providing independent oversight and governance.

Mark Flood is a senior research scholar at the Center for Financial Policy, a visiting research scientist at the University of Maryland Institute for Advanced Computer Studies, and program manager at the Defense Advanced Research Projects Agency.

Amias Moore Gerety is a partner at QED Investors, a leading venture capital firm focused on financial services. Formerly he served for eight years in the Obama administration, including as the president's nominee and as acting assistant secretary for financial institutions at the US Department of the Treasury.

Oliver R. Goodenough is a research professor at Vermont Law School, an affiliated faculty member at Stanford's CodeX Center for Legal Informatics, a research fellow at the Gruter Institute for Law and Behavioral Research, a lecturer at the University of Vermont's School of Business Administration, and an adjunct professor at Dartmouth's Thayer School of Engineering. He is also special counsel at Gravel & Shea PC and a member of the board of Skopos Labs.

Thomas Hardjono is currently the CTO of Connection Science and technical director of the MIT Trust-Data Consortium, located at the Massachusetts Institute of Technology. Over the past two decades he has held various industry technical leadership roles, including distinguished engineer at Bay Networks, principal scientist at VeriSign PKI, and CTO roles at several start-ups.

Sharmila Kassam serves as executive director of the AIF Institute. She is former deputy chief investment officer of the

Texas Employees Retirement System. She is also an ILPA policy adviser and instructor, and a faculty member for the National Institute for Public Finance Certificate in Public Treasury Management (CPTM) program.

Boris Khentov is senior vice president of operations and legal counsel at Betterment. Before joining Betterment, Boris practiced tax and capital markets law at Cleary Gottlieb Steen & Hamilton LLP. He has a JD from Northwestern Law.

Alex Lipton is cofounder and chief information officer at Sila, visiting professor and dean's fellow at the Hebrew University of Jerusalem, and Connection Science fellow at the Massachusetts Institute of Technology. He is an advisory board member at numerous fintech companies worldwide.

Lev Menand is an academic fellow, lecturer in law, and postdoctoral research scholar at Columbia Law School. He previously served as senior adviser to the deputy secretary of the Treasury from 2015 to 2016 and as senior adviser to the assistant secretary for financial institutions from 2014 to 2015.

Pinar Ozcan is professor of entrepreneurship and innovation at Saïd Business School, Oxford University. She is also the academic director of the Oxford Future of Finance and Technology (Fintech) Initiative at Oxford.

Matthew Reed is former chief counsel at the Office of Financial Research and former chairman of the global LEI system's regulatory oversight committee.

Markos Zachariadis holds the Greensill Chair of Financial Technology (FinTech) and is full professor of information systems at Alliance Manchester Business School at the University of Manchester. He is a member of the World Economic Forum's Global Future Council on Financial and Monetary Systems and a FinTech Research Fellow at the Cambridge Centre for Digital Innovation, University of Cambridge.

INDEX

Adams, Douglas, 15
ADB (Asian Development Bank),
 112
African Continental Free Trade
 Area (AfCFTA), 221, 222–226,
 234, 239, 243, 245–246, 247n4
African Development Bank, 219
African fintech advances,
 219–249
 AfCFTA relevance to, 221,
 222–226, 234, 239, 243,
 245–246, 247n4
 African context for, 219–222,
 232–233
 African Trade Observatory, 225
 artificial intelligence, 223–224,
 226, 231, 235, 239, 241,
 244–245
 big data analytics, 232, 235, 244
 Bitpesa, 17, 76, 249n24
 blockchain, 223–224, 226,
 228–242, 244–246, 248n19,
 249n24, 249n26
 conclusions and recommendations, 242–246
 Continental Online Mechanism, 225

credit system access, 236, 238,
 239, 242, 245
cybersecurity, 85, 236, 245
data protection regulations, 228
derisking markets, 236–238
digital and cryptocurrencies,
 230–231, 235, 237–238,
 249n24
digital financial services, 76,
 80–81, 83, 85
digitization efforts, 222–232
e-commerce, 225, 226–227, 241
financial inclusion via, 8, 21,
 227, 235, 237–238, 242, 246,
 249n25
government relations and,
 233–236, 243
growth spurred by, 226–232
identity systems, 234–235,
 237
industrialization and, 243–244
infrastructure to support, 224–
 225, 243, 244–245
internet of things, 224, 226,
 231, 235
key growth components,
 221–222, 243, 244

African fintech advances (cont.)
  leapfrogging technology, 8, 21, 223, 226, 231, 246
  mobile money, 80, 223, 227
  mobile technologies, 8, 21, 80–81, 83, 223, 224–227, 231–232, 235, 242, 245–246
  M-Pesa, 8, 76, 80, 223, 224
  MSMEs and, 220–222, 223, 236–237, 238–242, 245–246, 249n25
  Pan-African Payments and Settlements System, 225
  regulations and laws, 224, 228, 239–240
  tokenization, 236–237
African Union, 221, 222, 225–226, 238–239, 249n25
AI. *See* Artificial intelligence
Airbnb, 64
Airfox/AirTokens, 123–124
Alibaba, 10, 187, 195, 198
Alipay, 20
Amazon
  Amazon Pay, 20
  big data analytics, 187
  digital financial services, 10, 68, 195, 198
  as platform firm, 62
Anti-money laundering (AML) policies. *See* Money laundering prevention
Apple
  Apple Card, 26
  Apple Pay, 20
  digital banking, 198
  Net Promoter Score, 11

  as platform firm, 62, 64
  Siri, 9
Application programming interfaces (APIs)
  as boundary resources, 61
  as contracts, 61–62
  defined, 60
  digital banking, 177–178, 196
  external, 60
  as integration technology, 61
  internal or closed, 60
  open, 58, 59, 60–62, 178
  as products, 62
Arizona
  fintech regulations, 100, 102
  regulatory sandboxes, 207, 208–209
Artificial general intelligence, 19
Artificial intelligence (AI), 19–26
  African fintech advances, 223–224, 226, 231, 235, 239, 241, 244–245
  artificial general intelligence, 19
  data quality, 22
  digital banking, 182, 185, 187–188, 193, 195–196, 198
  as disruptive technology, 8–9
  edge effects, 36, 46, 47–48, 55
  ethical and moral issues, 23–25
  expert systems, 19–20
  financial services and, 21
  fundamentals of, 19–20
  machine learning, 9, 19, 20, 46, 47–48, 55, 249n26
  regulation, 25–26
  as responsible technology, 283, 285, 288

robo-advisory services, 36, 182, 185

workforce changes with, 11–12

Asian Development Bank (ADB), 112

ATMs (automated teller machines), 20–21, 77, 79, 178–179

Atom Bank, 65, 173, 180, 184, 185

Audit processes
automated, 251, 255
automatic audit logs, 253–254, 265n1
programmatic compliance, 257, 262
provable compliance, 255–263
RegTech effects, 251–252, 253–263
sampling-based, 252–256
traditional, 252–253
universe testing, 254–255

Australia
blockchain, 105
open banking, 58, 61
regulatory sandboxes, 210

Automation
audit processes, 251, 255
digital banking, 195–196
workforce effects, 44–45

Bahamas, digital financial services, 81–82

Bahrain, regulatory sandboxes, 210

Bain & Company, 11

Bancorp, 180

Banerjee, Banny, 92

Bangladesh
cybersecurity issues, 149
digital financial services, 85

Banking. See Digital banking; Open banking

Bank of America, 38–39

Barbados, jurisdictional competition, 102

Basic Blockchain (Shrier), 14

Berlind, David, 60

Bermuda, jurisdictional competition, 102

Betterment, 3, 36–37, 39–55

Bhalla, Ajay, 3, 283

BIC (Business Identifier Code), 144, 145

Big data analytics, 19–27
African fintech advances, 232, 235, 244
data abstraction, evaluation, and analysis, 156, 159–165
data quality, 21–22, 26
digital banking, 20–21, 26–27, 185, 187, 195–196
as disruptive technology, 9–10
ethical and moral issues, 23–25
financial services and, 20–21, 26–27
fundamentals of, 19
identity, 27
mobile technologies, 20, 21, 22, 23–24
potential advancements, 22–24
regulations and laws, 25–26
social physics, 22–24
unsolved problems, 26–27

Big data analytics (cont.)
  variety, 19, 159
  velocity, 19, 159
  volume, 19, 159
Big tech platforms, 68–69, 109–
    110, 196–198. *See also* Plat-
    form firms
Binance, 249n24
Binkabi, 248n19
Biometric identification, 76, 81,
    83–84, 180, 183, 283, 287–288
Bitcoin. *See also*
    Cryptocurrencies
  blockchain, 13, 107, 113–114,
    138–142, 150–151, 160–163,
    231
  cybersecurity, 113–114
  digital banking and, 174, 196
  digital financial services with,
    76
  mining operations, 104, 114,
    141, 161
  regulations and laws, 104, 106,
    113–114
  risks to banking system, 86
Bitpesa, 17, 76, 249n24
Blockchain, 12–18
  African fintech advances, 223–
    224, 226, 228–242, 244–246,
    248n19, 249n24, 249n26
  basics of, 12–13
  bitcoin, 13, 107, 113–114, 138–
    142, 150–151, 160–163, 231
  consensus mechanism, 13, 15,
    17, 137, 139, 141, 142–143,
    160–162, 229–230, 233
  cyber resilience, 15–16,
    149–150, 238–242

cybersecurity, 14, 16, 18,
    113–114, 139–140, 148–150,
    163, 236
data abstraction, evaluation,
    and analysis, 156, 159–165
data protection conflicts,
    288–289
decentralized, 96, 117, 160,
    162, 165, 230, 233, 289
defined and described, 14–16,
    229–230
derisking markets, 236–238
digital and cryptocurrencies,
    13, 17, 100–101, 107, 109,
    113–114, 120–126, 138–142,
    150–151, 157–163, 230–231,
    237–238
digital banking, 187, 188, 193,
    195
digital financial services, 17,
    77
as disruptive technology, 10
distributed nature, 13, 14, 18
error remedies and dispute res-
    olution, 139–140, 142, 158
financial system stability and
    systemic oversight with,
    107–109, 143, 155–165
future applications and devel-
    opments, 18, 151–153
generativity, 107
governance applications,
    279–280
government relationship with,
    233–236
identity and, 138–139, 141,
    143–148, 150–155, 160–161,
    163–165, 234–235

immutability, 13, 18, 159, 230, 289

jurisdictional issues, 96, 100–103, 240–241

latency mechanisms, 161–163

Merkle trees, 16

MSME advances, 238–242, 246

networks and communities, 233

on-chain vs. off-chain assets, 118

permissioned, 138–139, 149

public, 150–151, 161

regulations and laws, 92, 96, 99, 100–102, 104–109, 113–128, 150, 163, 166–168

regulatory sandboxes, 206–207

scalability, 141, 150–151, 153–155, 230, 238–242

securities trading, 137–143, 156, 158, 162–165

terminology, 129n2

tokens, 118–119, 121, 123–124

trust and confidence building via, 13–15, 17, 99, 116, 120–127, 138, 143–155, 228–230, 232–233

use cases, 16–18, 137–155

Blockstack, 122

Blomfield, Tom, 82

Bonsen, Joost, 1

Brainard, Lael, 109

Brazil, open banking, 58

Bridgewater, 21

Britcoin, 196

Brynjolfsson, Erik, 12

BurstIQ, 18

Business Identifier Code (BIC), 144, 145

California
  California Consumer Privacy Act, 25, 204
  fintech regulations, 116

Cambridge Analytica scandal, 284

Canada
  open banking, 58
  regulatory sandboxes, 210

Carney, John, 101

Carney, Mark, 86

Case studies. See Use cases

Cayman Islands, jurisdictional competition, 102

Central banks
  as buyer-of-last-resort, 174
  digital currency interests, 104, 157, 190, 191, 235, 237–238
  digital financial service role, 79, 80–81
  governance role, 104
  as lender-of-last-resort, 174, 176
  limits on parties able to access, 192
  liquidity interventions, 157–158
  narrow vs. fractional, 192–193
  systemic oversight, 108, 156–157

CFPB (Consumer Financial Protection Bureau), 207, 210

CGAP (Consultative Group to Assist the Poor), 78, 207, 210

Challenger banks, 59

Chaum, David, 190

Checks
  as negotiable instruments, 118–119
  processing, 38–53

Chemical Bank, 179
China
  African trading with, 220
  banking system, 174
  big data analytics, 23–24
  bitcoin mining, 114
  blockchain development, 230
  digital banking, 190, 197
  digital currency, 17, 86–87,
    190
  digital financial services, 8
  regulations and laws, 197
  regulatory sandboxes, 210
  social credit score, 23–24
Chivunga, Michelle, 219
Citi, 11, 20–21, 178–179
Citibank, 179
Clinton-Magaziner e-Commerce
    Principles, 97, 98
Cointelegraph, 121
Collateral, 140–142
Colombia, digital financial ser-
    vices, 85
Columbia University, 273
Committee on Uniform Securi-
    ties Identification Procedures
    (CUSIP) number, 144
Commonwealth Fintech Tool-
    kit, 77
Commonwealth of Nations
  digital financial services, 80–82
  regulations and jurisdictional
    competition, 93–94, 102, 112
  regulatory sandboxes, 216
Consultative Group to Assist the
    Poor (CGAP), 78, 207, 210
Consumer Financial Protection
    Bureau (CFPB), 207, 210

Consumer protection
  digital financial services, 78,
    85, 86
  regulatory sandboxes for, 203,
    207, 210
Contracts
  APIs as, 61–62
  regulations and laws, 98–99,
    115, 116–117, 126–128
  severability clauses, 126
  smart (*see* Smart contracts)
Convergence, 7, 10–12,
    284–285
Corporate governance. *See*
    Governance
Coursera, 294
COVID-19 pandemic
  cryptocurrency resilience in,
    13, 293
  digital banking effects, 173,
    192–193
  digital financial services
    advances in, 7, 293–294
  educational changes in, 294
Cowls, Joshua, 24–25
Credence goods, 120. *See also*
    Harm prevention; Trust and
    confidence
Credit cards. *See also specific firms*
  big data analytics, 20
  cybersecurity, 286
  digital financial services and,
    80, 87
  e-credit cards, 183
  network effects, 65
  open APIs, 60
  privacy protection, 287
  theft of data, 87

Credit system. *See also* Credit
  cards
  African access, 236, 238, 239,
    242, 245
  banking industry role,
    174–176
  big data analytics, 20, 22–24,
    26
  digital banking and, 181–183,
    185, 193–194, 196–197
  digital financial services
    extending, 74, 77, 80, 83,
    85, 86
  financial inclusion, 23, 177,
    238, 242
  identity tied to credit profile,
    77
  interest rates or usury, 83
  lines of credit, 176
  regulations and laws, 92
  risks to stability of, 86
Cryptocurrencies. *See also* Bitcoin; Digital currencies
  African interests, 230–231, 235,
    237–238, 249n24
  blockchain, 13, 100–101, 107,
    109, 113–114, 120–126,
    138–142, 150–151, 157–163,
    230–231, 237–238
  COVID-era resilience, 13, 293
  cybersecurity, 113–114
  digital banking and, 174, 196
  market capitalization, 13
  regulations and jurisdiction,
    92, 100–104, 106, 109–110,
    113–114, 120–126
  risks to banking system, 86,
    109–110, 157–159

  taxation of, 103
  tokens, 121, 123–124
CUSIP (Committee on Uniform
  Securities Identification Procedures) number, 144
Cybersecurity
  African fintech, 85, 236, 245
  APIs, 59, 60
  artificial intelligence for, 36
  big data analytics, 23, 26
  blockchain, 14, 16, 18, 113–
    114, 139–140, 148–150, 163,
    236
  consumer experience driven
    by, 287–288
  digital banking, 180, 188, 196
  digital financial services, 77,
    84–85, 87
  disclosure of risks, 150
  platform business models, 66,
    67
  responsible technology, 284–
    285, 286, 287–289
  securities trading, 139–140

D'Agostino, John, 267
DAO (decentralized autonomous
  organization), 117, 120–121,
  139–140, 281
Dark pools, 146, 164
Data analysis. *See* Big data
  analytics
Data privacy. *See* Privacy issues
Data security. *See* Cybersecurity
Davis Wright Tremaine, 207
DBS Digibank, 180
Debit cards, 20. *See also* Credit
  cards

Decentralized autonomous orga-
    nization (DAO), 117, 120–
    121, 139–140, 281
Decentralized finance (DeFi),
    198, 238
Deep learning, 9, 195
Delaware, fintech regulations,
    100–101, 115, 116
Derisking, 26, 147, 236–238
Developing economies. *See also*
    African fintech advances
  blockchain, 231, 235
  derisking harm, 26
  digital banking, 177, 189
  digital financial services, 74,
      77, 83, 85
  mobile technologies, 8
  regulatory sandboxes, 207
DFS. *See* Digital financial services
Diem. *See* Libra (now Diem)
Digital banking, 173–200. *See
    also* Open banking
  APIs, 177–178, 196
  artificial intelligence, 182, 185,
      187–188, 193, 195–196, 198
  banking industry status quo
      and, 173–177
  bank perspective, 185–188, 189
  big data analytics, 20–21,
      26–27, 185, 187, 195–196
  biometric identification, 180,
      183
  blockchain, 187, 188, 193, 195
  building and designing,
      195–198
  capital assets and, 175–176,
      191–194
  convergence revolution, 10–12

credit services, 181–183, 185,
    193–194, 196–197
current fintech trends, 177–178
customer constituencies,
    188–189
customer perspective, 181–183
cybersecurity, 180, 188, 196
depositors and, 176, 177
derisking, 26
digital and cryptocurrencies,
    174, 190–191, 195, 196
digital asset management, 183
digital natives, 180–181, 189
document digitization, 2
e-credit cards, 183
edge effects in transition,
    35–56
financial ecosystem shaped by,
    194–195
financial inclusion via, 177,
    180, 184, 189
first-wave companies, 178–179
foreign exchange services, 183
fractional-reserve banks, 174,
    175, 181, 192–194
full-stack business model, 188
hybrid approaches, 179–180
incrementalists, 178–179
integrated services, 196–198
internet banks, 179
investor perspective, 183–185,
    186
invisible banking, 197
IT infrastructure, 180, 186–187
key requirements, 181–188
legacy systems and culture
    inhibiting adoption, 176–
    177, 179, 185, 196

mobile technologies, 1, 8, 178,
    180, 182–183, 184
money creation and, 197
narrow banks, 174, 175–176,
    191–194
online banking, 179
open banking effects, 178
overview of, 173–177
peer-to-peer services, 182, 183,
    184, 190, 195, 197
platform envelopment, 11
privacy issues, 187, 195
reform needed, 173–174
regulations and laws, 188,
    197
second-wave companies,
    179–180
smart banks, 188
stock market pressures, 197
third-wave companies,
    180–181
too-big-to-fail banks and,
    173–174
Digital cash, 174, 181, 190, 195,
    203
Digital currencies. *See also* Cryp-
    tocurrencies; Virtual curren-
    cies; *specific currencies*
  African interests, 230–231, 235,
      237–238, 249n24
  blockchain, 13, 17, 100–101,
      107, 109, 113–114, 120–126,
      138–142, 150–151, 157–163,
      230–231, 237–238
  central bank, 104, 157, 190,
      191, 235, 237–238
  digital banking, 174, 190–191,
      195, 196

initial coin offerings, 97, 99,
    121–125
nonbank, 190 (*see also* Bitcoin;
    Digital cash)
private bank, 190–191
regulations and jurisdiction,
    92, 93, 97–104, 106, 109–110,
    113–114, 120–126
risks to banking system, 86–87,
    109–110, 157–159
stable coins, 191, 238
taxation of, 103
trade coins, 191
Digital financial services (DFS),
    73–90
  artificial intelligence, 21
  big data analytics, 20–21,
      26–27
  blockchain use, 17, 77
  building blocks for effective,
      78, 79
  central banks' role, 79, 80–81
  consumer protection, 78, 85,
      86
  context for, 73–75
  convergence revolution, 10–12
  COVID-era advances, 7,
      293–294
  cybersecurity, 77, 84–85, 87
  derisking, 26
  description of, 75–82
  digital currencies and (*see* Digi-
      tal currencies)
  digital inclusion/exclusion,
      82–83
  edge effects in transition,
      35–56
  e-money issuance, 78, 79

Digital financial services (DFS)
    (cont.)
  enabling environment for, 79
  examples of deployments,
    80–82
  financial inclusion via, 73–87
  financial literacy, 85, 86
  future development consider-
    ations, 82–87
  hybrid models, 76
  identity, 76, 77, 81, 82, 83–84
  interest rates or usury, 83
  mobile technologies, 8, 73, 76,
    79, 80–81, 83
  nonmobile technologies, 73,
    76, 77–78
  opportunities, 85–87
  overview of, 73
  privacy issues, 84, 86
  regulatory environment, 73,
    78, 79, 80–82, 83–84, 85–86
  retail agents, 78
  risk-based customer due dili-
    gence, 78
  risks to banking system,
    86–87
  systems and infrastructure, 76,
    77, 79, 84–85
  three dimensions model,
    75–78
  transactions, 75–76, 84–85
Digital inclusion/exclusion,
    82–83. See also Financial
    inclusion
Disruptive technologies, 8–10.
    See also specific technologies
  artificial intelligence, 8–9
  big data analytics, 9–10

distributed ledger technology,
    10 (see also Blockchain)
  mobile technologies, 8
Distributed ledger technology
    (DLT), 10. See also Blockchain
Dodd-Frank Act, 164
Dun and Bradstreet DUNS num-
    ber, 76, 144

eBay, 64
e-commerce
  African fintech advances, 225,
    226–227, 241
  regulations and laws, 97, 98,
    116–117
Ecosystems
  APIs as contracts between
    agents in, 61
  blockchain, 142, 230
  digital banking shaping finan-
    cial, 194–195
  digital financial services, 79
  digital or cryptocurrency use,
    124
  edge effects in, 35
  MSME, 239
  open banking collaboration
    in, 59
  platform firm role in interac-
    tive, 63, 66
  stability of financial (see Finan-
    cial system stability)
Edge effects, 35–56
  automation impacts, 44–45
  Betterment example, 36–37,
    39–55
  build vs. buy analysis, 40–41
  check processing, 38–53

common identifiers of multiple data sets, 46, 51–52
consequences of errors, 43–44
defined, 35
digital disconnects, 37–38
fragmentation, 42–43
friction, 37–38
holistic customer-centric experience, 54
human-labeled data, 46–47
machine learning, 46, 47–48, 55
morale effects, 44–45
overview of, 35–36
problem vs. solution focus, 52–53
record linkage problem, 45–46, 51–54
retirement savings management, 37–51
simplification effects, 49–51
stability goals, 38
technology as means not end, 54–55
workforce effects, 44–45
wounded workflows, 36–37
ELIZA digital therapist, 9
Email identity, 154
Emerging economies. *See* Developing economies
E-money, 78, 79
Employees. *See* Workforce
EMVCo, 286
Enigma MPC, 124
Equifax, 284
Estonia, digital banking, 180
Ethereum, 113, 139–140, 231

Ethical and moral issues
artificial intelligence, 23–25
big data analytics, 23–25
governance and, 288–289
responsible technology, 283–291
Ethiopia, fintech advances, 230
European Union
African trading with, 220
blockchain policies, 167
data protection regulation, 25, 84, 114, 204, 288–289
digital banking, 185, 191
digital currencies, 191
open banking, 58, 59, 61, 62, 178
platform firms, 65, 69

Facebook
big data analytics, 187
Cambridge Analytica scandal, 284
digital financial services, 68–69, 195, 196
generativity, 107
Libra (now Diem), 1, 17, 86–87, 102–103, 106, 109–110, 125–126, 191
as platform firm, 62, 64
tag recommendations, 47
Federal Deposit Insurance Corporation, 165
Federal Identity, Credential, and Access Management program, 153
Federal Reserve
capital assets, 192
check processing, 39

Federal Reserve (cont.)
  Comprehensive Capital Assess-
    ment and Review, 260, 262
  creation of, 175
  cybersecurity, 149
  financial stability and regula-
    tions, 108, 110, 114, 164–165
  Matters Requiring Attention,
    260, 261
  provable compliance to,
    259–262
  settlement system, 162
Federal Reserve Bank of New
    York, 149, 162, 260, 261
Fidor Bank, 180
Financial inclusion
  African fintech advances for, 8,
    21, 227, 235, 237–238, 242,
    246, 249n25
  big data analytics aiding, 23
  credit system, 23, 177, 238,
    242
  derisking by withdrawal from,
    26
  digital banking for, 177, 180,
    184, 189
  digital financial services for,
    73–87
  digital inclusion and, 82–83
  financial literacy and, 85, 86
  leapfrogging technology for, 8,
    21, 246
  regulatory sandboxes aiding,
    206
Financial Industry Regulatory
    Authority, 125
Financial literacy, 85, 86
Financial marketplaces, 62

Financial services system frame-
    work, 74
Financial Stability Board, 108,
    109, 273
Financial Stability Oversight
    Council, 108
Financial system stability
  blockchain and, 107–109, 143,
    155–165
  cybersecurity threats to, 149
  data abstraction, evalua-
    tion, and analysis for, 156,
    159–165
  digital and cryptocurrency risks
    to, 86–87, 109–110, 157–159
  edge effects and, 38
  governance mechanisms for,
    104, 106, 157, 161, 164–165
  interventions mechanisms,
    156, 157–159
  networks of connection and,
    148
  regulations and laws for, 107–
    110, 113
  regulatory sandboxes for, 203
  systemic oversight, 155–165
FinHub initiative, 121–122
Fintech
  African advances (see African
    fintech advances)
  defined, 92
  digital services (see Digital
    banking; Digital financial
    services)
  edge effects, 35–56
  foundations of, 7–31
  governance and complexity of
    (see Governance)

open banking (*see* Open
  banking)
overview of, 1–3, 293–294
regulation of (*see* Regulations and laws; Regulatory
  sandboxes)
regulatory technology,
  251–266, 280–281
responsible technology,
  283–291
use cases, 16–18, 137–171
Fintech foundations, 7–31
  artificial intelligence, 8–9,
    11–12, 19–26
  big data analytics, 9–10,
    19–27
  blockchain, 10, 12–18
  convergence, 7, 10–12
  disruptive technologies, 8–10
  regulation, 25–26
  unsolved problems, 26–27
Flood, Mark, 91, 137
Floridi, Luciano, 24–25
Foreign exchange services,
  183
Fractional-reserve banks, 174,
  175, 181, 192–194
France, digital banking, 179
Fraud
  artificial intelligence to detect,
    36
  blockchain deterrence of, 16
  blockchain use in, 113, 123,
    139–140
  cybersecurity against (*see*
    Cybersecurity)
  defined, 120
  digital banking, 188

digital financial services,
  84–85, 86, 87
governance for protection
  from, 268, 281
identity authentication and,
  84, 147, 149, 287
machine learning to prevent,
  20
RegTech identifying, 281
regulations and laws, 95, 97,
  99, 112–113, 120, 123
securities trading, 139–140
Frontiers of Financial Technology
  (Shrier and Pentland), 2, 10
Fuzzy matching, 46, 53

Galloway, Scott, 275
Gates, Bill, 203
General Data Protection Regu-
  lation (GDPR), 25, 84, 114,
  204, 288–289
General Motors (GM), 203
Gerety, Amias Moore, 251
Germany
  big data analytics, 24
  digital banking, 180
GetSmarter, 294
Gibraltar, jurisdictional competi-
  tion, 102
Gibson, William, 254
Global Financial Innovation
  Network (GFIN), 210, 216
Goldman Sachs, 11, 26
Goodenough, Oliver R., 91, 137,
  203
Google
  artificial intelligence, 20
  big data analytics, 187

Google (cont.)
  digital financial services, 10,
    68, 195, 196
  Maps, 256
  as platform firm, 62, 64
  search engine, 20
  TensorFlow, 9
Governance, 267–282
  board activities, 271, 272–273
  board composition and skills,
    271, 273–274
  categorization of firms,
    270–271
  central banks' role, 104
  compensation and, 278
  complexity and, 267–282
  continuing education require-
    ments, 276–277
  data framework, 270–276
  digital and cryptocurrencies,
    104, 106, 157, 161
  economic incentives and,
    269–270
  ethics and, 288–289
  ex ante, 110–111
  external resources supporting,
    277–278
  failures of, 267–268, 281
  fiduciary responsibility and,
    281
  future developments, 281–282
  internal risk management sys-
    tems, 164–165
  intimidating nature of com-
    plexity, 274–276
  investors driving, 278–280
  overview of, 267–270
  public vs. private company, 268

RegTech role, 280–281
  responsible technology and,
    288–289
  self-regulation and, 125
Guernsey, regulatory sandboxes,
  210

Hadoop, 16
Hardjono, Thomas, 77, 91, 137
Harm prevention
  regulations and laws for, 96,
    97–98, 120–127
  regulatory sandboxes for,
    207
Harvard University, 273, 294
Health care and medicine
  African fintech advances, 226
  blockchain use, 17–18
  digital banking integration
    with, 182, 196
High-frequency trading (HFT)
  algorithms, 156, 162
Hong Kong, regulatory sand-
  boxes, 210
HSBC, 2
Hyperledger, 143

IBM, 249n26, 279
ICObench, 121
ICOs (initial coin offerings), 97,
  99, 121–125
IdeMix, 152
Identity
  addressability of, 153–154
  African identity systems, 234–
    235, 237
  attribute authority, 154–155
  big data analytics, 27

biometric identification, 76, 81, 83–84, 180, 183, 283, 287–288

blockchain and, 138–139, 141, 143–148, 150–155, 160–161, 163–165, 234–235

common identifiers of multiple data sets, 46, 51–52

current infrastructure for authenticating, 144–148

data-driven distributed computation, 152–153

digital financial services, 76, 77, 81, 82, 83–84

future developments, 151–153

identity theft, 84

interoperability of systems managing, 145

"know your customer" regulations, 26, 79, 83, 145, 154, 177, 192, 197, 234, 237

legal trust frameworks authenticating, 153, 154

networks of connections and, 147–148

privacy issues and, 150–151, 153, 155, 160–161, 234, 287

public key pairs, 150–151, 154

revelation of, authority for, 147, 155, 160–161

scalability of system authenticating, 141, 150–151, 153–155

securities trading records, 138–139, 141, 163–164

self-asserted, 150–151, 155

self-identification, 145–146, 147

smart contracts for binding and revealing, 148, 152, 153

trusted source verification, 146, 154

ultimate beneficial owner, 27

verifiable attributes, 154–155

verifiable pseudonyms, 152

Illinois
  fintech regulations, 117
  regulatory sandboxes, 207

India, digital financial services, 73, 81. *See also* Paytm

Initial coin offerings (ICOs), 97, 99, 121–125

Interest rates, 83

Interledger, 143

Internal Revenue Service, 103

International Monetary Fund, 106

International Organization for Standardization (ISO), 127

International Swaps and Derivatives Association, 159

Internet banks, 179

Internet of things (IoT), 195, 224, 226, 231, 235, 284–285

Interswitch, 227

Investments. *See also* Securities trading
  African, 220, 223, 224–225, 244–245
  big data analytics, 21
  digital banking and, 182, 183–185, 186
  digital financial services for access to, 74
  in fintech, 2, 7, 245

Investments (cont.)
  governance protecting,
    268, 278–280 (*see also*
    Governance)
  investment management edge
    effects, 35–56
  regulations and laws, 97, 99,
    105, 116, 120–126
  retirement savings, 37–51,
    182
  rollovers, 37, 39, 42–44, 46,
    48–51
iTunes, 67

Jackson, Josh, 168
J.P. Morgan, 173–174, 191,
    259–260, 265n4, 265–266n5,
    266n6
Jumia, 227
Jurisdiction
  blockchain crossing, 96,
    100–103, 240–241
  competition for, 100–103
  extraterritorial, 95
  regulations and laws, 95–96,
    100–103, 114–115
  regulatory sandboxes and, 100,
    102, 206
Justice Department, regulatory
    enforcement, 115

Kassam, Sharmila, 267, 282
Kenya, fintech advances, 80,
    223, 230, 242
Khentov, Boris, 3, 35
Klapper, Leora, 83
Knight Capital, 139

"Know your customer" (KYC)
    regulations
  African fintech advances, 234,
    237
  big data analytics, 26
  digital banking and, 177, 192,
    197
  digital financial services, 79, 83
  identification systems, 145, 154,
    234
KPMG, 280
Kramer, AJ, 49, 51, 53
Kuva, 232

Labor. *See* Workforce
Laws. *See* Regulations and laws
Legal Entity Identifier (LEI) Sys-
    tem, 76, 126, 127, 145, 159
Legal trust frameworks, 153, 154
Lehman, 141
Lessig, Lawrence, 112
LHV Pank, 180
Libra (now Diem)
  backlash against, 1, 17
  regulations and jurisdiction,
    102–103, 106, 109–110,
    125–126
  risks to banking system, 86–87,
    109–110
  trade coin foundations, 191
Linux, 64, 279
Lipton, Alex, 173
Liquidity interventions, 157–158
"London Whale" scandal,
    259–260, 265n4, 265–266n5,
    266n6
Luno, 249n24

Machine learning, 9, 19, 20, 46, 47–48, 55, 249n26

Madoff, Bernie, 97, 267

Malawi, digital financial services, 80–81

Malta, jurisdictional competition, 102

Marconi, Guglielmo, 8

Markit Red Code, 144

Massachusetts, fintech regulations, 116

Massachusetts Institute of Technology (MIT), 1, 9, 12, 17, 45, 73, 138, 178, 191, 294

Mastercard, 60, 64, 286–289

Mauritius, jurisdictional competition, 102

McKinsey, 225

Menand, Lev, 251

Merkle trees, 16

Merton, Robert, 73

Metro bank, 184

Mexico, digital financial services, 85

Micro, small, and medium-sized enterprises (MSMEs), 220–222, 223, 236–237, 238–242, 245–246, 249n25. *See also* Small and medium-sized enterprises

Microsoft, 64, 203

Minitel, 179

MIT. *See* Massachusetts Institute of Technology

Mitch, Eleanor, 17

Mitsubishi UFJ (MUFJ)/MUFG coin, 190–191

Mobile technologies
African fintech advances, 8, 21, 80–81, 83, 223, 224–227, 231–232, 235, 242, 245–246
big data analytics, 20, 21, 22, 23–24
digital banking, 1, 8, 178, 180, 182–183, 184
digital financial services, 8, 73, 76, 79, 80–81, 83
digital inclusion/exclusion, 83
as disruptive technology, 8
interoperability, 81
mobile money, 80, 223, 227
mobile payment platforms, 20
open banking, 62

Money laundering prevention
African fintech, 237
digital banking, 188, 190, 192, 196–197
digital financial services, 78, 79
RegTech use, 256–257
regulations and laws, 78, 112

Monzo, 65, 82

M-Pesa, 8, 76, 80, 223, 224

MSMEs. *See* Micro, small, and medium-sized enterprises

Muchanga, H. E. Albert, 225

MUFJ (Mitsubishi UFJ)/MUFG coin, 190–191

Mullen, Mark, 173

N26, 65

Nakamoto, Satoshi, 13, 16

Narrow banks, 174, 175–176, 191–194

NASA, 15

Nasdaq, 17, 108
National Association of Secu-
    rities Dealers, 125. *See also*
    Nasdaq
National Futures Association,
    111
National Institute for Science
    and Technology, 127
NetBank, 179
Net Promoter Score (NPS), 11, 74
Network externalities or effects,
    64–65, 66, 72n21
New York, fintech regulations,
    101, 116, 117
New York Federal Reserve, 149,
    162, 260, 261
New York Stock Exchange, 125
New York University, 160, 275
Nigeria, fintech advances, 81,
    223, 227–228, 230–231, 236,
    242
Nonbank financial institutions
    convergence, 10
    credit services, 193
    cybersecurity risks, 87
    digital currencies, 190 (*see also*
        Bitcoin; Digital cash)
    digital financial services, 74,
        78, 79, 80, 87
    e-money issuance, 78
Northern Trust, 279
NPS (Net Promoter Score), 11, 74
NZIA, 81

OakNorth, 82
Off-chain assets, 118
Office of Financial Research
    (OFR), 108, 127, 156, 160, 165

On-chain assets, 118
OPAL Project, 23
Open banking, 57–72
    big tech disruptions, 68–69
    competition and new entrants
        to market, 59, 62, 65–69
    customer education on, 70
    customer loyalty and, 67
    digital banking effects, 178
    embracing vs. resisting, 59
    goals of, 58
    legacy structural and cultural
        changes for, 66
    open APIs, 58, 59, 60–62, 178
    overview of, 57–59, 69–70
    platform business models,
        62–69
    regulations, 57–58, 60–61, 62,
        69, 178, 204, 289
    re-intermediation role with,
        65–66, 67
    third-party payer access, 58, 60
OpenID Exchange, 153
Oracle, 16
Organisation for Economic Co-
    operation and Development,
    167, 216
Ozcan, Pinar, 57

Palmer, Benjamin, 11
Paragon/ParagonCoins, 124
Paxful, 249n24
Paystack, 224
Paytm, 73, 76, 77–78, 81
Peer-to-peer (P2P) payment
    systems
    African fintech advances, 233,
        242, 249n24

big tech platforms, 68–69
digital banking, 182, 183, 184, 190, 195, 197
digital financial services, 76
identity authentication, 147, 152–153
Pentland, Alex, 1, 2, 3, 7, 10, 77, 91, 137, 173, 294
PGP (Pretty Good Privacy) system, 150–151, 155
Philippines, cybersecurity issues, 149
Platform firms. *See also specific firms*
big tech, 68–69, 109–110, 196–198
competition in banking, 65–68
core competencies, 63, 66, 68
data feedback loops, 65, 66
digital banking, 11, 177
digital platforms, 63
economics and strategy of, 62–65
key functions and principles, 63, 64
multisided market creation, 63
network externalities or effects, 64–65, 66, 72n21
open banking business models, 62–69
open vs. closed platforms, 67–68
platform curation, 65
platform envelopment, 11, 68
transaction cost reductions, 64, 66
Prestel, 179

Pretty Good Privacy (PGP) system, 150–151, 155
Privacy issues
data privacy, 25, 84, 86, 150, 204, 228
design to address, 286–287
digital banking, 187, 195
digital financial services, 84, 86
identity and, 150–151, 153, 155, 160–161, 234, 287
Probabilistic record linkage, 46, 53
Pseudonyms, 152
Public key pairs, 150–151, 154

Quickteller, 227

R3 Corda, 14, 108, 129n2
Real bills doctrine, 175
Record linkage problem, 45–46, 51–54
Reed, Matthew, 91, 137
Registration and licensing systems, 111, 112, 121–124, 146
RegTech. *See* Regulatory technology
Regulations and laws, 25–26, 91–135. *See also* Governance; Regulatory sandboxes; Regulatory technology
adding laws applicable to fintech, 126–127
adding provisions applicable to fintech, 118–119
African fintech, 224, 228, 239–240
artificial intelligence, 25–26
ban on activities, 110

Regulations and laws (cont.)
  blockchain, 92, 96, 99, 100–
    102, 104–109, 113–128, 150,
    163, 166–168
  code as internal regulation,
    112–114
  cognitive acceptability of, 107
  conflicts between multiple,
    288–289
  contract, 98–99, 115, 116–117,
    126–128
  coordination and standard set-
    ting, 127–128
  cybersecurity, 150
  data protection, 25–26, 84,
    204, 228, 288–289
  digital and cryptocurrencies,
    92, 93, 97–104, 106, 109–110,
    113–114, 120–126
  digital banking, 188, 197
  digital financial services, 73,
    78, 79, 80–82, 83–84, 85–86
  e-commerce, 97, 98, 116–117
  enabling rules, 79, 100–103,
    116–119, 239–240
  ex ante approaches, 110–111,
    120
  existing interest protection via,
    103–105
  existing law applicability to
    fintech, 120–126
  existing provision applicability
    to fintech, 116–117
  ex post approaches, 111–112,
    120, 122–124
  financial innovation and,
    91–94
  future developments, 166–168

  general applicability, 115–128
  generativity of, 107
  goals of, 96–110
  harm prevention via, 96,
    97–98, 120–127
  as institutional framework for
    private exchanges, 96–97,
    98–99
  jurisdiction, 95–96, 100–103,
    114–115
  legal specification language,
    127–128
  mitigating wider and second-
    ary effects via, 105–110
  multinational efforts, 112,
    126
  negotiable instruments,
    118–119
  open banking, 57–58, 60–61,
    62, 69, 178, 204, 289
  quality and conduct standards,
    111, 127–128
  reasons for, 94–95
  registration and licensing sys-
    tems, 111, 112, 121–124, 146
  regulators and regulatory agen-
    cies, 114–115
  regulatory capture, 97
  regulatory framework, 92
  regulatory toolkit, 110–112
  self-regulation, 111, 125
  smart contract, 117, 119,
    127–128
  social acceptability of,
    106–107
  stock exchange, securities, and
    investments, 97, 99, 100,
    105, 116, 120–126

systemic stability via, 107–110, 113

taxation and public revenue, 99, 103, 106

terminology, 92, 129n3

trust and confidence building via, 99, 104–105, 110, 116, 120–127, 146

Regulatory sandboxes, 203–218
application process, 213–214
authorization requirements, 214–215
benefits and opportunities, 205–206, 214
collaboration, 204, 205, 214, 215–216
concerns and responses, 206–207
defined, 204
existing initiatives and models, 207–211
government considerations, 211–214
jurisdiction, 100, 102, 206
market segment targets, 211–212
overview of, 203–204, 216
participating departments/ leadership, 211
program design, implementation, and evaluation, 215–216
project elements/criteria, 212–213
rationale and goals, 205–206
stakeholder input, 215
steps to developing, 214–216

Regulatory technology (Reg-Tech), 251–266
automated audit processes, 251, 255
automatic audit logs, 253–254, 265n1
benefits of, 263
data storage costs and, 253, 265n1
future steps, 263–265
governance role, 280–281
overview of, 251–252
programmatic compliance, 257, 262
promise of, 253–257
provable compliance, 255–263
risks and perils of, 257–263
traditional audit and compliance vs., 252–253
universe testing, 254–255

Renaissance Technologies, 21

Responsible technology, 283–291
artificial intelligence, 283, 285, 288
challenges, 284–285
consumer experience, 287–288
convergence and IoT, 284–285
current status, 283–285
cybersecurity, 284–285, 286, 287–289
design of, 286–287
ethics and governance, 288–289
exponential growth in data, 285
overview of, 283
privacy protection, 286–287

Responsible technology (cont.)
  responsible innovation,
    285–290
  trust and, 283–284, 289–290
Retirement savings
  digital banking, 182
  edge effects of managing, 37–51
  rollovers, 37, 39, 42–44, 46,
    48–51
  taxation issues, 43–44
Ripple, 17, 231
RMB Coin, 17, 86–87
Robo-advice, 36, 182, 185
Rollovers, 37, 39, 42–44, 46,
  48–51
Romer, Paul, 94
Russia, digital currencies, 190
Rwanda, fintech advances, 230,
  242

Safe-Bio Pharma, 153
Sand Dollar, 82
Sarbanes-Oxley Act of 2002, 164
Satmetrix, 11
Securities and Exchange Commission (SEC), 97, 100, 108,
  112, 114, 120–125, 150
Securities Exchange Act of 1934,
  99, 122–125
Securities trading. See also
  Investments
  blockchain, 137–143, 156, 158,
    162–165
  chain of custody, 141
  cybersecurity, 139–140
  error remedies and dispute res-
    olution, 139–140, 142–143,
    158

high-frequency trading algo-
    rithms, 156, 162
  identity authentication vs.
    anonymity, 138–139, 141,
    163–164
  latency reductions, 156
  RegTech use, 257
  regulations and laws, 97, 99,
    100, 105, 116, 120–126
  regulatory sandboxes to pro-
    tect, 203
  secondary markets, 138
  settlement and hypothecation,
    140–142, 162, 165, 203
  smart securities, 127
  transaction cancellations, coor-
    dination of, 158
  transaction monitoring,
    142–143
  transaction records and trading
    markets use case, 137–143
Selfkey, 114
Senegal, e-commerce strategy,
  225
Sesame, 196–197
Shrier, David L., 2, 3, 7, 10, 48,
  73, 77, 91, 137, 173, 203, 294
Simple Bank, 180
Singapore
  digital banking, 180
  jurisdictional competition, 102
  open banking, 58
  regulatory sandboxes, 209–210
Siri, 9
Small and medium-sized enterprises (SMEs)
  African, 220–222, 223, 236–237,
    238–242, 245–246, 249n25

digital banking, 177, 180, 185, 189, 196, 197

open banking, 57, 68

Smart banks, 188

Smart contracts

African fintech advances, 229, 235, 241–242

blockchain and, 117, 119, 127–128, 148, 152, 153, 229, 235, 241–242

defined, 128, 248n18

identify authentication, 148, 152, 153

regulations and laws, 117, 119, 127–128

techno-legal aspects of, 128

Smart securities, 127

Social physics, 22–24

South Africa, fintech advances, 230

SRI International, 15

Sri Lanka, cybersecurity issues, 149

SRISK indexes, 160

Stable coins, 191, 238

Stanford University, 39

Starling, 65

Stein, Jon, 36

Suriname, blockchain use, 17

SWIFT (Society for Worldwide Interbank Financial Transfers), 17, 65, 91, 144, 146, 149

Swift, Sam, 46–47

Switzerland

Financial Stability Board, 108, 109, 273

jurisdictional competition, 102

Symbiont, 101

Systemic stability. *See* Financial system stability

Taxation

blockchain use, 18, 234

regulations and laws, 99, 103, 106

retirement rollovers, 43–44

Tax Equity and Fiscal Responsibility Act of 1982 (TEFRA), 137, 138

TechFin, 109–110. *See also* Platform firms

Telegram Group Inc., 124

Tencent, 10

TensorFlow, 9

Tesla, Nikola, 8

Theranos, 267–268

Thomson, Anthony, 185

Tokens

asset-backed, 192, 236–237

digital banking managing, 183, 190, 192

fiat-backed, 192

as on-chain vs. off-chain assets, 118

regulations and laws, 118–119, 121, 123–124

tokenization, defined, 236–237

utility, 121, 123

TON Issuer Inc., 124

Trade coins, 191

Transactions

cancellations, coordination of, 158

cost of, 61–62, 64, 66, 67, 188

Transactions (cont.)
  digital financial services,
    75–76, 84–85
  e-commerce (*see* e-commerce)
  monitoring, 142–143
  transaction records and trading
    markets use case, 137–143
    (*see also* Securities trading)
Transferwise, 11
Transparency
  African ecosystem lacking,
    232
  blockchain, 14, 18, 149, 160,
    229, 234, 236
  financial system stability with,
    109
  governance facilitating, 268
Trust and confidence
  African ecosystem, 232–233,
    245–246
  blockchain creating, 13–15, 17,
    99, 116, 120–127, 138, 143–
    155, 228–230, 232–233
  defined, 284
  in digital financial services,
    78, 87
  legal trust frameworks, 153,
    154
  regulations and laws encourag-
    ing, 99, 104–105, 110, 116,
    120–127, 146
  responsible technology engen-
    dering, 283–284, 289–290
  trusted source verifying iden-
    tity, 146, 154
Trusted Data (Hardjono, Shrier,
  and Pentland), 77
Tufano, Peter, 73

Turkey, cyberattacks in, 284
Twiga Foods, 249n26
Two Sigma, 21
2U, Inc., 294

Uber, 64, 67, 107, 205
Uganda, fintech advances, 230
Ukraine, cyberattacks in, 284
Ultimate beneficial owner, 27
Underserved/unserved financial
  needs, addressing. *See* Finan-
    cial inclusion
Uniform Commercial Code
  (UCC), 118–119
Uniform Electronic Transactions
  Act (UETA), 116–117
Unigestion, 279–280
United Arab Emirates, regulatory
  sandboxes, 210
United Kingdom
  African trading with, 220
  banking system, 175
  big data analytics, 24
  blockchain policies, 167
  digital banking, 173, 179, 180,
    184, 185, 190, 196
  digital currencies, 86, 190, 196
  digital financial services, 82
  Financial Conduct Authority,
    57, 204, 208, 210
  open banking, 57–58, 59, 61,
    62, 204
  platform firms, 65
  regulations and jurisdiction,
    102, 167
  regulatory sandboxes, 204,
    207, 208, 210
  surveillance, 24

United Nations Sustainable Development Goals, 82, 221
United States
  African trading with, 220
  check use, 38–39
  peer-to-peer payment systems, 68
  regulations and laws (*see* Regulations and laws)
  regulatory sandboxes, 207, 208–209, 210
University of California, Berkeley, 8
U-Prove, 152
Use cases, 137–171
  blockchain, generally, 16–18
  blockchain for identity, trust, and data security, 143–155
  blockchain for stability and systemic oversight, 155–165
  blockchain in securities trading, 137–143
  conclusions and future developments, 166–168
  transaction records and trading markets, 137–143

Venmo, 20
Vermont, fintech regulations, 100, 102, 115, 117, 143
Virtual currencies, 98, 101, 103.
  See also Digital currencies
VISA, 60, 64, 65, 80
Visionary Future, 93
Voice-enabled software, 9, 20

WeChat, 1, 8, 196–197
Weizenbaum, Joseph, 9

Western Union, 17, 76
WeWork, 268
Wicked problems, 274–275
Workforce
  African labor market, 223, 234–235, 239, 246
  artificial intelligence effects, 11–12
  automation effects, 44–45
  innovation effects, 96
  morale of, 44–45
World Bank, 8, 80, 81, 83, 85, 222
World Development Report (World Bank), 81, 85
World Economic Forum, 224
Wounded workflows, 36–37
Wyoming, fintech regulations, 100, 102, 115, 117

Xapit, 80
Xi Jinping, 230

YouTube, 64

Zachariadis, Markos, 57
Zambia, digital financial services, 80
Zynesis, 82